D0200215

Conversations on Religion

Conversations on Religion

Edited by

*Mick Gordon and
Chris Wilkinson*

continuum

Continuum
The Tower Building, 11 York Road, London SE1 7NX
80 Maiden Lane, Suite 704, New York, NY 10038

www.continuumbooks.com

Editorial and this collection copyright © Mick Gordon and Chris Wilkinson, 2008.

All rights reserved. No part of this publication may be reproduced or
transmitted in any form or by any means, electronic or mechanical, including
photocopying, recording, or any information storage or retrieval system,
without prior permission in writing from the publishers.

First published 2008.

British Library Cataloguing-in-Publication Data
A catalogue record for this book is available from the British Library.

ISBN 978-0-8264-9909-7 (paperback)

Designed and typeset by Kenneth Burnley, Wirral, Cheshire
Printed and bound in Great Britain by The Cromwell Press, Wiltshire

Contents

CONCORDIA UNIVERSITY LIBRARY
PORTLAND. OR 97211

Notes on Contributors

Mick Gordon is a theatre director and dramatist. He is the founding Artistic Director of On Theatre and was Associate Director of London's National Theatre and Artistic Director of London's Gate Theatre. His plays include *Grace, On Love, On Death, On Ego* and *On Religion*.

Chris Wilkinson is an award-winning theatre director and journalist. He has written for the *Scotsman, The Financial Times, Prospect Magazine* and the *Guardian* (online).

Muhammad Yusuf Al Hussaini is an Imam and a research fellow of the Interfaith Alliance.

Karen Armstrong's first book *Through the Narrow Gate* (1981) described her seven years as a nun in a Roman Catholic order. It became a bestseller. Since 1982 she has been a freelance writer and broadcaster.

Don Cupitt is an ordained priest and a fellow of Emmanuel College Cambridge. He lectured on the philosophy of religion for over 30 years between 1965 and 1996 and has written over 40 books on the subject.

Professor Richard Dawkins is an evolutionary biologist and holds the Charles Simonyi Chair for the Public Understanding of Science at the University of Oxford. His books include *The Selfish Gene* and *The God Delusion*. He recently founded The Richard Dawkins Foundation for Reason and Science.

Dr Abdelwahab El Affendi is a senior research fellow at the Centre for the Study of Democracy, University of Westminster and a co-ordinator of the Centre's Democracy and Islam programme. he was a member of the core team of authors for the UN's *Arab Human Development Report 2004*.

Giles Fraser is the Vicar of Putney and formerly lecturer in philosophy at Wadham College, Oxford. He writes for the *Guardian* and the *Church Times* and is a regular contributor to Radio 4's *Thought for the Day*.

Professor John Gray is Emeritus Professor at the University of London. His books include *Straw Dogs*, *Al Qaeda and What it Means to be Modern*, *Heresies* and *Black Mass – Apocalyptic Religion and the Death of Utopia*.

Professor A. C. Grayling is Professor of Philosophy at Birkbeck College, University of London, and a Supernumerary Fellow of St Anne's College, Oxford. He is the author of numerous philosophical books, and is also a distinguished literary journalist and broadcaster. His most recent books are *Towards the Light*, published by Bloomsbury, and *The Choice of Hercules*, published by Weidenfeld & Nicolson. He is a Contributing Editor of *Prospect* magazine, and a Fellow of the Royal Society of Literature.

Shelina Zahra Janmohamed is a writer and commentator on British Islam. She was born and brought up in London and studied at New College, Oxford. She writes her own blog at www.spirit21.co.uk. She has also been published in the mainstream press and appears regularly on TV and radio to comment on Islam, Muslim and Muslim women's issues. She writes regularly for *The Muslim News*, the UK's most widely circulated Muslim newspaper. She is also involved in developing social and cultural events for young British Muslims, as part of creating a new British Muslim culture and identity. Shelina works in the technology industry, and is married and lives in London.

Professor Alister McGrath is Professor of Historical Theology at Oxford University. His recent books include: *The Twilight of Atheism* and *Dawkins' God: Genes, Memes, and the Meaning of Life*.

Baroness Julia Neuberger was one of Britain's first female rabbis and is a Liberal Democrat member of the House of Lords. Her most recent book is *The Moral State We're In*.

Professor Tariq Ramadan is a fellow of St Anthony's College, Oxford, Doshisha University (Kyoto, Japan) and at the Lokahi Foundation (London). He is a Visiting Professor (in charge of the chair: Identity and Citizenship) at Erasmus University (Holland). He is the author of several books including *Western Muslims and the Future of Islam* and *In The Footsteps of the Prophet*.

Sir Jonathan Sacks is the Chief Rabbi of the United Hebrew Congregations of the Commonwealth. His books include *The Politics of Hope* and
The Dignity of Difference.

Dr Azzam Tamimi is the Director of the London-based Institute of
Islamic Political Thought (IIPT). His most recent book, *Hamas: Unwrit-
ten Chapters*, was published by C. Hurst & Co. in November 2006. He is a
regular commentator on a number of Arabic satellite channels including
Aljazeera and Alhiwar and frequently makes appearances on a number of
English channels.

Rev. Dr Fraser Watts is Reader in Theology and Science at the University
of Cambridge, Director of the Psychology and Religion Research Group,
and a Fellow of Queen's College. He is a former President of the British
Psychological Society, and is Vicar-Chaplain of St Edward's Church in
Cambridge.

Ann Widdecombe has been a Conservative MP for Maidstone since 1987.
She has held various ministerial positions including Minister of State for
Prisons and Immigration and Under Secretary of State in the Department
of Employment. She has written four novels.

Rowan Williams is a distinguished theologian and as Archbishop of
Canterbury is head of the worldwide Anglican communion.

Professor Lewis Wolpert is a distinguished developmental biologist, and
is an emeritus professor at University College. He is the author of *Six
Impossible Things Before Breakfast*. His son Matthew is a writer and
comedian.

Introduction

Mick Gordon

The conversations presented in this book began as the research for a piece of theatre. I am the Artistic Director of On Theatre, a theatre company I founded to dissect and explore the experience of being human. The company is called On Theatre, as each piece of its work is *on* a given subject, and because the pieces it produces are more like theatrical essays than conventional plays. On Theatre researches, develops and presents one theatre essay a year and to date has produced pieces *On Love, On Death, On Emotions, On Ego*. And these conversations allowed On Theatre to create its most challenging work to date: *On Religion*.

I am fascinated by religions and the questions that surround them. How do we define religion? Can we define faith? Why in our twenty-first-century's post-Enlightenment world are so many people religious? Why do, and how can people believe in a supernatural god or gods? Is religion dangerous? Does it have a value? What should our ambition for religion be? I wanted to work out what I think about religion by asking a wide variety of religious thinkers and commentators what they believed.

I grew up in the Northern Ireland of the 1970s. A child of the troubles and the peace movement, my first word was 'splosion, my first grown-up argument was with a Religious Education teacher and my first political act was a boycott of a Scripture Union kids' club. As a teenager I experienced Ireland's Protestant and Catholic religions as exclusive, divisive and potentially violent brands, and the ideas of god on which they were variously based, as alienating and judgemental. Later, and because of my work in the theatre, I began to understand what seems to be one attraction of religion – the goal that great theatre shares with religion: the attempt to codify and deliver an experience of the transcendental.

I use the theatre to explore the experience of being human because theatre is the art form of the human scale. The theatre is a place, or an event, where a group of people come to witness their representatives, the actors, move and reveal and unpack themselves. And my theatre essays are carefully designed to explore people and their relationships to themselves, to others and to their particular social surroundings. So when I make a theatre essay I try to begin the creative process in a very direct, human way: by meeting people, asking simple questions and then listening carefully to the responses.

My first conversation on religion was with the acclaimed English philosopher and anti-religionist, A. C. Grayling. Given my upbringing, it is probably not surprising that I had been drawn to Grayling's critique of what he terms, the religions of the book; Islam, Judaism and Christianity. And because I was going to limit the scope of my enquiry to these three religions he seemed an interesting starting point. I had long admired the clarity of his writing and when I met him I liked him, and the positive and humane way he talked about the potentials of life. As it turned out, he would become the co-writer of the theatre essay *On Religion*. This was to do with his anti-religionist views and more because I was genuinely intrigued to see if a collaboration between a theatre-maker interested in exploring life in all its grubby contradictions, and a philosopher whose fundamental commitment is to clear, rational argument, could actually work.

My second conversation was with Chris Wilkinson, who became the co-editor of this book. He had followed On Theatre's work and felt he had much to contribute to any conversation on religion. He was right. Chris is a theology graduate from Cambridge and a talented young journalist. And perhaps more importantly, his interest in the subject of religion wasn't simply intellectual but really very personal because Chris is a serious atheist and his mother is an Anglican priest. Chris suggested many of the conversations presented in this volume.

The theatre demands argument and balance. It's no good at didacticism. In my experience an audience will just not accept it. In our different ways, A. C. Grayling and I had spent most of our adult lives criticizing organized religion. So how could we begin to imagine that we could put an authentic religious voice on stage let alone understand one? Did we even have to? Instinct said we did, conversation would tell.

I had seen the priest, Giles Fraser, the spoon in the pot of British Anglicanism, in action. He had officiated at the wedding of a friend and had given a beautiful address advocating contemplation on, what he called, the dance of truth and love. We met again at his church in Putney where he spoke with passion about his quest for 'better religion'. He sees himself as a religious moderate, a failed atheist who has found a great beauty in the otherness of the Christian conception of God. He criticizes Grayling and Dawkins as radical empiricists and advocates a space for religion which is about not knowing.

Listening to Archbishop Rowan Williams was a pleasure. An intricate and incisive theologian, he explained what religion meant to him sitting in a large armchair in Lambeth Palace, two wooden shepherds' crooks leaning casually against the wall behind him. His notion of an open religion seemed generous and compassionate and utterly at odds with the vehement African and American wings of the Anglican Church which he currently leads. In his explanation of the Holy Trinity it is clear how he finds reassurance and strength in its complexity.

The developmental biologist, Lewis Wolpert, has argued that science is the best way to understand the world, and that for any set of observations, there is only one correct explanation. In conversation he introduced us to his son, Matthew, a devout and one-time evangelistic Christian. It was fascinating to watch their two distinct worldviews interact as they discussed what religion meant to them. And they allowed each other their clear differences of opinion with smiles of bemusement and love.

At over 70 years of age, Don Cupitt, author of *The Sea of Faith* and self-styled atheist priest, is still exploring and re-evaluating what religion means to him. Wearing huge dark glasses to protect his failing eyes he advocated a religion of life, a religion without God, a religion celebrating the force of the human spirit.

Muhammad Al Hussaini is a gentle and learned Imam and a research fellow for the Interfaith Alliance. His hope is that the Muslim world takes ownership of the violent passages in the Qur'an. He quoted Jonathan Sacks, agreeing that 'scripture without tradition and commentary to provide a context for it is like nuclear fuel without protection'. And he argues that what we find in the Muslim world today is an entire generation who have no access to necessary, contextualizing, Islamic scholarship.

Tariq Ramadan explains religion as a continual search for meaning and Islam as the latest revelation confirming all the others. For him, religion is the structured way to keep us connected and 'Why?' is the question that helps human beings to remain humble. He wants to see a radical shift in the nature of Islamic authority which challenges the traditional hegemony of the Muslim scholars.

For John Gray religion's all about myth. He talked in an expansive and generous manner, pointing to what he sees as underlying connections between the great religions and the secular movements of the twentieth century. He argues that the fundamental connection between religion and secularism is human beings' need for meaningful myths. So for him, modernists who believe in a guiding principle of progress are caught in as much of a fiction as those who believe in Judeo-Christian or Islamic myths.

Alister McGrath has moved from being an aggressive atheist to being a proselytizing Christian. He too sees life as a quest for meaning and the framework of meaning he now finds most satisfying and hopeful is Christianity. The word he uses most often to describe his relationship with his religion is transformative and he sums up his moral confidence by explaining that in any difficult situation he tries to ask himself Gilbert Sheldon's famous question: What would Jesus do?

Abdelwahab El Affendi, like Tariq Ramadan, wants to reinterpret Islam. He works from within the tradition, attempting to reformulate it in a way which conforms to his liberal tendencies. He argued quietly and with a smile that Islamic fundamentalists want to drag people kicking and screaming into paradise. He firmly believes that there is a problem with countries, groups and movements that want to impose *Shariah*.

Richard Dawkins trusts science because it is a belief-system which allows itself to be proven wrong. He spoke passionately about the scientific project as an attempt to discover the truth about the world on the basis of specifically evaluated evidence. Religions are dangerous, he argues, because they claim knowledge about what is true in the world on the basis that it was written in a holy book, handed down by a tradition or revealed by some kind of inner communication with God. In this way he sees religion as being actively hostile to the scientific project because it teaches people to be content with a lack of rigorously tested evidence.

Julia Neuberger doesn't think Richard Dawkins will ever understand what she means by religion let alone appreciate the value of religious practice to individuals and communities. As she talked about Reformed Judaism she explained how many Jews, for quite a lot of the time, are not sure whether they believe in God or not. But they continue to practise as if they believed. She calls this giving God the benefit of the doubt.

Fraser Watts is a psychologist and priest and sees no contradiction in his dual professions. He uses two languages to talk about God; an impersonal language that talks about God as a kind of totality of all things but also a language which expresses the idea of God in personal terms. And he explains why he was drawn to Christianity and how he believes that there is something psychologically reassuring about building a responsible partnership with God.

Azzam Tamimi is probably the most controversial figure in this book as he is seen by some as an apologist for Palestinian violence in Israel. He spoke about the tensions between Palestine and Israel and was very careful to argue that the root of the problem was political, not religious. Most fascinating is his explanation as to why criticism of the Prophet can be so painful for Muslims and his exposition of what he sees as the Qur'an's two concepts of *jihad*.

Ann Widdecombe is certain: the Catholic Creed is a statement of fact, Genesis explains the order of creation, and society should go back to basics. We wouldn't have AIDS, she argues, if the whole world had stuck to the Church's teaching of faithfulness within marriage and chastity before it.

Karen Armstrong and Shelina Janmohamed both identify first principles that clarify and inspire their separate faiths. Karen Armstrong, a one-time Catholic nun, talks of The Golden Rule present in all great religions: Look into your heart, discover what it is that gives you pain, and then refuse, under any circumstance whatsoever, to inflict that pain on anybody else. Shelina Janmohamed, a young British Muslim, begins her definition of religion with the idea of universal first principles which all religious specifics need to be measured against.

Chief Rabbi Jonathan Sacks thinks that religion is answerable to the world – scientifically, aesthetically and morally. And he argues that Muslims, Christians and Jews must recognize that they are all part of Abraham's family. It is a richly diverse family, he says, and, of course, all of the best arguments take place within the family.

We met 18 people altogether and began each conversation in the same way, by asking for a definition of religion. As you might imagine, no two definitions completely accord and their differences are fascinating. What I find most striking re-reading the interviews is that each person met has something very much in common: a passionate commitment to his or her own beliefs and ways of seeing the world. We human beings are strange in our attachments to our beliefs, whether inherited, imbibed or chosen. And we find them difficult to let go of, or even to change. For better and for worse, this is our commonality. And when I read this book I am left wondering how we can further understand, and attempt to take responsibility for, these different beliefs and positions that seem to mean so much to us.

1

A. C. Grayling

Do you have a working definition of the term religion?

I do. The essence of religion is commitment to belief in something super-natural, something outside the natural order. And in fact it's more complex than simply that, because the supernatural thing (or things) also has to be an intelligence of some kind, with aims, purposes and intentions, and it has to be interested in us for some reason. If revealed religion is anything to go by, this supernatural agency has to be interested in us enough to want us to wear certain things, to shave or not to shave, to eat or not eat certain things on certain days; to do this and not that. It is absurd once you think about it: this supernatural agency is said to punish us in ways, or reward us in ways, that no human father or mother would ever dream of punishing or rewarding their own children. Like forcing people to sing hymns for eternity, or throwing them into hellfire: human parents obviously would not do such things. Some illegitimately try to extend the use of the term, calling Marxism a religion, or they say, 'Well you're an atheist and that's a religion as well.' This is a misuse of the term. So it's of the essence of religion that there is this commitment to the existence of something supernatural which has an interest in us and makes a demand upon the world that we occupy. That is religion.

In general terms, there are three aspects to debate about religion. The first is a metaphysical one. This concerns whether or not there exist in the universe any supernatural entities: this takes the standard form of arguments for the existence of God. The second main area is the question of morality: whether the idea of ethics makes any sense at all unless there is some kind of final sanction. It happens, of course, that in almost all the large religions the ultimate sanction is that if you don't obey its dictates, you will fry. The ultimate sanction is an appeal to force, the threat of punishment. Although nowadays, Christianity has reinvented itself and says:

'we should be nice to one another because God loves us, and wants us to love one another', all in soft focus. But you only have to look at the murals and altar pieces in the *Altepinakothek* in Munich to see how coercive Christianity has been for most of its existence, threatening miscreants with hellfire. For anyone who does not accept the simple-minded idea that doing good is a response to threats of punishment and promises of reward by a supernatural being in an afterlife, the question is how to treat others humanely and with respect, and recognize principles that are worth observing in the conduct of life, independently of the ancient threat-reward myths. In part the issue between religious and humanist ethics turns on a logical point, which is that being threatened with punishment for not doing something is not a *logical* reason to do it. It may be a pru-dential reason to do it: if some much bigger fellow comes along and says, 'I'm going to punch you unless you do this or that', and there is no other recourse, it might be sensible to comply, but that's a matter of pragmatics, not logical entailment. So that's the second issue, the moral issue. And the third is the spiritual issue. Human beings are complex and have very deep and sensitive emotional responses – to beauty, friends, the need for love and human companionship. We are capable of thrilling in response to nature and to art and music. And a lot of lazy thinking has it that we would not be like that unless 'the spiritual' is somehow vaguely connected to the supernatural – as when people stand on a hilltop and look at a beautiful sunset across the sea, and want to do something to express the depth of their response. So they say, 'Oh thank you God for a beautiful world!' whereas what they ought to be saying is: 'Isn't it wonderful that we human beings can experience so wonderfully this sense of connection with nature, that we have this feeling for the numinous, and for the value of things'. I mean by this to articulate an idea of a secular spirituality, an ability to have a rich, emotional, response to life, to others, and to the world, which does not trade on simplistic and antiquated supernatural beliefs.

Religion was mankind's very earliest science and technology. Human beings once thought that thunder was caused by big, powerful, invisible versions of themselves walking on the clouds. When the wind blew they thought it was some big agent puffing out its cheeks and blowing. So then they thought they could propitiate these powerful agents and persuade them to be on their side, by sacrificing virgins or bulls, and that this would bring rain when the crops needed it, and keep the rain away when the crops didn't need it – and so on. That was their science and technology in the exact sense that it was their explanation of how things work (science), plus a method of controlling those forces (technology). But the human tragedy is that most things humans have ever believed have remained as part of the layer cake, the geology, of our minds – or more accurately, of our cultures. And the less people know about the world, the easier it is to reach back to these very simple answers. 'Why is there a universe?' 'Because God created it.' Yet the idea of a god is a much murkier idea than the idea of the universe. If you say, 'Why is there a universe?' and someone answers, 'Because God created it', it's a bit like saying: 'Why is there a universe?'; 'Because Fred sucked a lollipop'. In short, it's no explanation at all. It's just reaching for a sound. And yet people are anxious to have closure: they want everything neatly explained; they want an answer to every question. So they reach for these simplistic, ancient, stone-age superstitions in order to do it, instead of being prepared for open-textured enquiry and uncertainty. We should be prepared to not have answers to everything, and to be part of the process of finding out. This is the mature, scientific way of looking at the world.

How do you define faith?

Faith is a stance or an attitude of belief independent of, and characteristically in the countervailing face of, evidence. It is non-rational at best, and is probably irrational given that it involves deliberate ignoring of evidence, or commitment despite lack of evidence. But it's at least non-rational in the sense that the wellsprings of faith are emotional or traditional, or because of what is effectively brainwashing in childhood. It involves basing a commitment on grounds other than rational or conscious choice. Consider: if there were such a thing as an intelligent and otherwise educated adult who had never been exposed to religious views before, and if you offered this individual an account of any one of the major religions, or major religious traditions, and asked him to accept it, he would undoubtedly just laugh.

And belief?

Belief is the attitude of mind of taking something to be true. It is the state of regarding some proposition or set of propositions as true. The difference between belief and knowledge is this: belief is a state of mind in which you take some proposition or theory to be true on evidence that underdetermines it, or even if there is no evidence for it, or countervailing evidence against it. Knowledge, by contrast, requires the truth of what is believed, and sound justification for believing it. So you can believe a proposition which is false, but you can't *know* a proposition when it is false. Knowing is not just a state of mind, but a relationship between a given state of mind – believing with suitable justification – and fact. And so that relationship cannot exist if the other side of the equation, the truth part of it, is not there.

How do you describe yourself in relation to religion? Are you an atheist?

In terms of the traditional but misleading terminology used in these debates, yes I am an atheist. But I do not like the word 'atheist' for the following reason. There are two ways of approaching a debate about religion. One way involves giving your religious opponent half the territory and having a debate about theism and atheism. What I mean by this is that if I say to somebody: 'I am an atheist', I then have a discussion about whether there is such a thing as a God, but in doing so I have already got on to terrain which is a waste of time. Compare this: if I said to somebody that I don't believe in fairies and that we should now have a debate about the existence of fairies, or gnomes or goblins, and that I'm an afairiest, or an agoblinest, then I've already made a concession to debating something irrational and misconceived. So I do not call myself an atheist, I call myself a naturalist. I give a positive cast to this, and I say: 'The universe is a natural realm, governed by natural laws.' So the question of whether there are supernatural agencies, or fairies, or angels or devils, becomes an irrelevance. We are not even contemplating that. Whereas, if you talk about atheism, you are already talking about something on the theist's territory, because you are already taking seriously whether or not we should be discussing it.

So that's one way of approaching it. The other more fruitful and accurate way of approaching matters is to see religion as a man-made historical phenomenon, and moreover one which has imposed on humankind an assortment of terrible burdens: falsehoods, priesthoods and a distortion of human nature – for example by distortion of human sexuality. It has been a powerful instrument of social and political control, imposing hegemony over thought and conduct wherever and whenever it can.

If you think about it in those terms, you get a different perspective on matters and you suddenly notice things about religion. One thing you notice is that the religions of the book, Judaism, Christianity and Islam, are, all three of them, young religions. So indeed is Hinduism (which doesn't exist as such, incidentally; 'Hinduism' is a name given by the British in India to the assorted traditions and polytheisms they encountered in the subcontinent). But all of these religions are very recent in historical terms. Humankind in the form of *Homo sapiens sapiens*, modern man, is anything up to 100,000 years old in evolutionary terms. But we are talking about religions that have existed only for the last 2,000 to 3,000 years. For thousands of years before them there were other religions, probably polytheisms which were animistic and which were really those early attempts to try and explain how the world works – early science and technology. But at some point in the evolution of human thinking, people came to feel, either consciously or unconsciously, that unless you avoided the cracks in the pavement, unless you touched every bar in the railings, terrible things would happen. And there arose this idea that you have to control and organize behaviour to stay on the right side of the supposed conscious forces governing nature, and do what your predecessors did; and thus beliefs became institutionalized. So then you had an institution in human societies which, until very recent times, was total. It governed everything, every aspect of your life, all the taboos and the observances and the rituals which were believed to be vital to your life, to the growth of the crops and the rainfall and everything else. You are looking at a man-made institution, and with it a history of oppression and distortion and bad thinking as one of its most salient effects.

Would you say something about the role of myth in religion?
In one good sense, religion just is myth. Consider the fact that there is nothing particularly original about the core Christian stories. Think about the many other versions of what appears in the Christian story, versions long antedating it in Middle Eastern mythology or in Greek mythology, not least the idea that a god makes a mortal woman pregnant and she gives birth to a heroic, extraordinary figure. I mean this is Zeus and Io and Leda and Alcmene and many others; and frequently elsewhere in mythologies.

There is a real disconnect between the traditional, biblical New Testament legend – the version of Christianity which most people in their C of E ('Christmas and Easter') practice believe, and what theologians themselves believe. So when Jenkins, the Bishop of Durham, said, 'Of course the resurrection and the virgin birth are just myths, but important ones for Christianity', it caused a tremendous uproar among the parishioners, but no theologian would have been at all surprised. I can remember when I was a student at Oxford talking to a theologian and he said what would seem obvious to any sophisticate of the Church or a theological college, 'Of course we don't believe in a little old man with a white beard; I mean there's nothing out there: God is an idea/a construct/an ideal/a mystery/take your pick.' I wonder: if you scratched Rowan Williams deeply and asked 'Just how close is your conception of the Godhead to this simple picture that you teach children in Sunday school?' what would would his answer be? Well, I think you'd find it pretty different.

But more generally on the subject of myth, there is the fact that anybody who was egregious, in the literal sense of that term, in legend or in history or in the folk memory of the tribe, was regarded in ancient times as divine in some way. The analogy is with Homer. If you see Homer (if he actually existed) down the road digging his vegetable garden, you might think 'How did he manage to write the *Iliad*? He's just an ordinary chap!' And then you might conclude that obviously it could not have been him who did it really, but something – a muse, a genius – who sat on his shoulder and 'inspired' (breathed into) him, so that in effect he was taking dictation; this is an instance of the idea that great things must come from outside. And in the same way, it was believed that spectacular individuals have to have come from outside – have to have been sons of God; this is very common in history.

You have criticized institutionalized religion. The philosopher Don Cupitt offers a religious perspective which seeks to abolish any idea of traditional religious identity. He is also radically opposed to any kind of religious authority, religious hierarchy or religious structure.

Well also he has the view that the God of the residual religion he is thinking of is an internal one; it's a postulated one, the real existence of which you don't actually commit yourself to.

So there is this idea of God as the embodiment of our ideals.

Apparently. But of course in this respect Cupitt is reprising something which has been tried often enough before. For example the religion of humanity that Auguste Comte and the positivists of the nineteenth century tried. They wanted to have Sunday services which were not about a god, but were all about praising the human ideal. There have been repeated attempts at trying to find substitutes for the things that religion gives people, and it is an interesting point. Religion can give some people a sense of certainty, or a sense of security in a world which is otherwise very uncertain; it can help you face the fear of death and what supposedly lies after death; it gives you the comfort of having a hand to hold in the dark; it can provide explanations and make things neat; these are all things that people want from religion. And people have tried to find substitutes for it when they have got to the point where they can no longer believe in the metaphysical content of religion. But why search for substitutes, why go in for prevarications? Science and humanism are far richer alternatives.

But going back to the question of religious authority for a moment, do you know the Grand Inquisitor scene in *The Brothers Karamazov*? There the idea is that if Jesus really was the son of God and came back today, the authorities would not let him resume his ministry because he would upset everything. Instead they would have to lock him up and keep him out of the way in order to preserve the fabric of the status quo. The analogue of this is the idea that the Pope knows that it's all a load of rubbish, but goes on with it because it keeps the lid on everything.

Cupitt is interested in the distinction between what people think they believe and what they actually believe.

That is a vital point. If you stop people coming out of church and ask them what they believe, or rather what they think they believe, and what the doctrines of their church teach, they may well not know what to say about either. In fact I challenge you to do this: wait outside a parish church on any Sunday morning, and as people come out say to them: 'Can I just ask you, since you're a practising Christian, what happens to you when you die? Do you sleep in the earth in your grave until the last trump, when there's a general resurrection, or does your soul go immediately to heaven?' Now Catholics will say that their souls go to purgatory to be purged of their sins. What about the souls of un-baptized babies whose only sin is the inherited one of their parents' sexual act, which conceived them? Hard to say: the Roman Catholic Church is thinking of getting rid of the doctrine of limbo, which surely shows you how seriously to take all this stuff. But a person in the Church of England would be very much in two minds. There would be a similar question if you stopped outside different synagogues and asked the question: 'Is there life after death?' Some Jews say there is, some do not know, and others say not; yet these latter still believe there is a God. So it's often pretty ambiguous, and many people don't really know what they believe. And of course, in 'traditional societies' as they are now called, people often don't distinguish between the natural and the supernatural. The world is all one thing and the gods and spirits are simply part of the natural order, so that is different again.

It's rather like the old Irish lady who's asked if she believes in leprechauns, and replies, 'I do not, but they're there anyway!' But fundamentally, the idea is that the religious beliefs of most people are inchoate in a literal sense. They don't actually have a definite, determinate form. When most people really sit down to think about what it is that they believe, they realize that the unformed, nebulous impression or sense they have does not readily match any orthodoxy. Which is why a lot of people today, if you say to them 'What do you believe?' say 'Well, I don't believe in the God of the Church but there is Something – you know, a higher power, or something.' And they are happy to leave it as unformed or as ill-formed as possible. They often do not challenge themselves.

You referred earlier to religion as offering 'a hand to hold in the dark' and there is a body of evidence that suggests that religious people cope with stress a lot better than non-religious people.

It is no doubt right to say that religious people suffer less stress than unreligious people. But one response to that is to say: 'Well, it's obviously a bad thing, then, to suffer less stress – because you have paid too high a price. What you've done is to shuffle off responsibility for yourself. You've taken a pre-packaged solution to all of life's problems off the supermarket shelf of ideas, and think it gives you an answer for everything, so that life is all very simple and somebody else is going to take care of things.' And that is typical of anyone who's signed up to any ideology completely, whether Marxists or Catholics or whatever else. People who submit themselves to a totalizing ideology *ipso facto* think it provides answers to everything, providing absolute certainty, with everything straightforward; and consequently they no longer need to think about things, and that is why they are less stressed.

Many religious people say that it is not primarily religious ideas that help them, but rather, it is religious practice: prayer, meditation, congregation in a church.

So they might. Now I would disagree with what they say for two reasons. First, whether or not people are religious, they will indulge in what you might legitimately call spiritual activities all the time in order to relax – activities like gardening, going to a concert, visiting an art gallery, looking at pictures, walking in the country. These are all about stepping aside from life's tumults and going into a quiet place. People don't often describe these activities like this, though if they did, they might get richer benefits from them. A similar thing happens when a person goes into a church; it's nice and quiet and peaceful, and when you walk in the country it's nice and quiet and peaceful, so it produces the same kind of effect. But the killer blow in that argument is this: imagine an employment situation, in an office, where there is somebody middle ranking or junior whose job is insufficiently rewarded, and is uncertain of the future – they don't know whether they are going to keep their job, and they have never been given a pat on the back or been otherwise rewarded. Now that person would obviously be very stressed. But a person who knows there is a job for life, and who has a boss who says 'Well done', will feel appreciated. And if the person thinks there will be some kind of reward – an outing to Brighton at the end of the year, say – they will feel comfortable and secure. It's the idea that one is being recognized and rewarded and that the job is safe which makes that person feel good. Now the point about religion is that it gives you lollipops every time you go to church, every time you confess, every time you pray. Each time you're getting that reward, that sense of security. You are giving it to yourself of course, but it is a very big psychological prop. And the lack of psychological props like that is a crucial factor in stress, uncertainty, and having a sense of inadequacy or insecurity. So that would be my response. Prayer and meditation are no different, if you think about it, from when you watch a football match or listen to something on your iPod, or when you go to the theatre and get completely absorbed in what's happening on stage. In all these cases there is a similar sense of refreshment afterwards. If you look at church, and the ritual of church services, they are versions of theatre. They were once the only theatre that people had. And they offered the security and reward that reduces stress.

Given that religion seems to offer useful things to so many people, why is it so important to you to argue against it?

Well first, as just mentioned, there are many other things that, with far greater truth, can offer the kind of spiritual nourishment, solace and peace that people look for in religion. We can get this most especially in our relationships with others – if someone is very much in love and happy with the beloved. Or if someone belongs to a group of people who share their values, all in the group are going to get an enormous amount of positive feedback and a sense of security and worthwhile-ness from their belonging. Religion can obviously give that to people, but at the price of accepting and living by the ancient and distorting myths. The latter are not necessary for the former. Now a lot of people who become religious in adult life, having not been religious in earlier life, typically do so in moments of crisis. It may be because somebody has died, or a relationship has come to an end, or a job has been lost – and religion provides a quick fix of spiritual calories in response to that. So that is one reason: the false basis for the spiritual sustenance of life.

The other reason is this: if you look at the evidence for claims about the existence of deities, you see that they are as good or bad as theories about the existence of fairies and goblins; both sets of claims are epistemically the same. So if it is irrational to believe in fairies then it is irrational to believe in any supernatural entity: both kinds of beliefs are false, and if you live according to false beliefs, that is an intrinsically bad thing.

Also, history has shown repeatedly that religious organizations have on the whole been vastly more a force for ill than good. Of course, they have been a force for good in some respects: they've inspired people to do useful things; they have provided solace to people who are lonely and ill; they have encouraged charitable work. But on the whole, by far and away most human beings for most of history have been coerced and oppressed by the religious structures that have bound them in. If you look at the Christian tradition of morality with its overheated focus on matters of sex, marriage and reproduction, it has been very distorting and harmful. You only have to look at some of the agonies that people suffered because of the taboo about masturbation and premarital sex to see how dreadful an oppression it has been. It does harm. If you look at almost every conflict in the history of the last two millennia and in the world today, almost all have their roots directly or indirectly in the divisions between people caused by religion. And so if one could cleanse the world of religion we could go some way towards ending those conflicts.

Do you think it is possible to cleanse the world of religion?

Unfortunately it is not likely. People are innately superstitious, that's the bad news. I mean we know for straightforward reasons to do with the psychology of education that credulity is an evolutionary advantage for human beings. Small children have got to be prepared to believe anything they are told, because most of what they are told stops them from being eaten by tigers and burnt by fires, and so on. So credulity is a significant factor. That, by the way, is why 80 per cent of church schools are primary schools. All religions survive because they inculcate their faith in the young. If young people were not exposed to religious beliefs then they would be immune to them by the time they reached adulthood – the vast majority of them anyway. Also, the massive institutional investment that religions have in themselves and the fact that whole peoples, such as, for example, the nations of the Muslim world, are brought up thinking that the worst possible thing they could do is to deny the existence of God or to cease to be a votary of their faith. Apostasy is so terrible it is unthinkable. Some communities will stone people to death if they reject their beliefs; so what we have here is a very, very powerful force which is deeply ingrained. Therefore as representatives of the culture of science and reason, we have to hold the lantern high above the stormy waters of irrationality, and argue, and debate, and criticize, and teach, and hope for the best. I often say to people that it is tremendously important to fight for three things: humanism, secularism and naturalism. Humanism is the view that our ethics and political institutions must be premised upon our best understanding of human nature and the human condition. And that understanding is something which evolves through the negotiation that we have with ourselves about what it means to be human and what the best kind of society is, and what the good life is. Therefore humanism is an unfolding, ongoing process of trying to understand ourselves as we really are, and to identify the good on that basis. As you can see from that, there is no reference to any source of value from outside the world, imposed on us independently of what we are or know.

As for secularism: well the first secularists were churchmen who desired to be free of the temporal powers, thus giving rise to the principle of the separation of church and state. Thus you can be a religious person and a secularist. As I understand it, Rowan Williams is a secularist because he thinks the Church of England should be disestablished. So secularism is not atheism, but it does want the public domain to be neutral with respect to religious belief.

And then there is the third position: naturalism, explained above. Now it seems to me that the naturalistic view, the humanist view and the secularist view go well together, but they are not the same thing. Humanist ethics and naturalism are probably the two that most closely identify, because humanism naturally follows from naturalism; because if naturalism is true, then we are bound to only be able to refer to ourselves for our values.

John Gray is very critical of any belief in progress. He argues that humanism is just a shadow of Christianity, but that at least Christianity has this idea of original sin which can be interpreted as acknowledging that humanity is inherently flawed – an idea that humanism does not have.

Gray and I are diametrically opposed in our views about these matters. I had a debate recently with a canon of St Paul's at St Giles in the Fields about the origins of human rights. And he spoke as John Gray does about humanism in the Renaissance, and the idea of the importance of the individual, having Christian roots. But the case for what that is supposed to imply does not work. This is because if anyone stood up and expressed any of my kind of views about religion 400 years ago, he would have been burned at the stake. What we have managed to acquire over the last 400 years is freedom of speech and conscience. Freedom of speech is the fundamental human right because without it you cannot assert any other rights; you cannot stand up in a court of law to argue your case; you cannot have a free press to monitor and challenge a government and thus make the democratic process possible. So there can be no talk of human rights without free speech, and religion was and is and always will be against free speech. Religion is antipathetic to the idea of autonomous individuals. The idea of autonomy, the idea of rights, and the idea of a variety of different ways that people could try to live – which is very much at the heart of the liberal with a small 'l' outlook that you see in the thought of such as John Stuart Mill and Isaiah Berlin – is itself bound up with the idea that the individual does not lie under the iron law of a closed worldview, a closed morality with a definite and objective view of the right or wrong way of being human. The very idea of pluralism, the idea that there are many right and wrong ways of being human, is antipathetic to religious outlooks. For these reasons Gray has got it completely wrong about the origins of humanism, and as a result has got it wrong about the nature of humanism.

Think about the people that sat on Eleanor Roosevelt's committee which drafted the United Nations' Declaration of Human Rights. They were from all over the world and from different traditions, and yet there is not one mention of the deity or of any transcendental basis for the rights they identified in their document. They drafted a conception of rights which is fairly vague in itself, but which is meant to embrace everything required as a minimum for the possibility of living a good and flourishing life – security of the person, a right to life, freedom of conscience and speech, the right to privacy, a right to make choices about who you marry and whether to have children. These things are fundamental to any person throughout history and the world. To be secure, to be out of the rain, to have the opportunity to develop your human gifts, are just obvious claims that you would make wherever you live, from the jungles of Papua New Guinea to the island of Manhattan. And it has nothing to do with religion and it would not be possible to argue for any of these things if still you lived under the hegemony of religion.

Do you think there can be such a thing as a liberal Christian?

There are those who identify themselves as such, and who can do so because the protean and multiple nature of Christianity has allowed it to reinvent itself endlessly in the face of opposition. It reinvents itself over and over. If you walk into a parish church anywhere in England today during a Sunday morning service, you will get the kiss of friendship and people will shake hands with you, and you will hear a sermon about people starving in Sudan. But if you could go back 500 or 800 years you would see a very different picture indeed. You can see this if you look at the murals in a medieval church, with their images of the torments of hellfire for the damned, and the suffering Christ on the cross and the weeping Virgin Mary. These violent and oppressive images would be accompanied by sermons telling you that unless you keep to the narrow way which is steep and thorny and very hard, the devils that are all around you will snag you and carry you down to that hellfire. The whole thing is a battle – just look at the *Pilgrims Progress:* in it Christian has to fight his way to get to the gate of the city. Everywhere around you the dangers lurk, your own body is treacherous, it is occupied by devils – the lusts and the appetites, the desires and the laziness, everything about you is trying to kill your soul; you are in perpetual danger. It was a horribly frightening picture for the illiterate and impotent majorities of Christendom. That was Christianity for most of its existence until the great crisis in Europe in the sixteenth and seventeenth centuries, and especially thereafter when, as a result of the Reformation, it was no longer possible for sensible people who could read to take all this seriously. The Old Testament gives us a picture of a volcano God. He is a pillar of smoke by day and a fire on the mountain-top by night. He is violently jealous; if you follow other gods he will kill you – all who were not on Moses' side were swallowed up in their thousands, on one occasion, when the earth opened beneath their feet for punishment. Anybody reading that passage now should think 'This picture is not for me!' In the New Testament things are intended to be a little bit kinder and nicer. God is on the side of the underdog; the poor and meek will inherit the earth, and if you are rich you will not get into heaven. But even that has come to be reinterpreted now. Think about the modern age – nobody could possibly live the life painted as good in the New Testament. Indeed, if you tried to, you would get into trouble, especially if you had children, for we are told to give away all our possessions, to take no thought for the morrow, to repudiate our families if they will not do the same thing. As the opposite of what responsible contemporary life demands, such a morality is an impossibility. And, of course, there is nothing in the Bible about how much television you should watch or what the speed limit should be on motorways, because it is so distant from modern life and modern reality.

Even so, Christianity in some of its less conservative or ossified branches has tried to reinvent itself in an effort to accommodate itself to the new world. The Church of England gave up the doctrine of hell in the 1920s, the Roman Catholic Church is giving up the doctrine of limbo. Some churchmen accept homosexuality, others continue to condemn it. There is a constant attempt to try and accommodate themselves to a modern sensibility by some, a constant effort to turn the clock back by others. For St Paul, who invented Christianity, women had to keep quiet, cover their heads and sit at the back of the church, but now we can have women bishops. If that isn't reinvention I do not know what is. There is a constant moving of the goalposts in order to stay afloat.

There are examples of non-theistic, secular ideologies which have been incredibly destructive and manipulative: Nazism, Communism, fascism. Your liberal Christian might say: 'Atheism has done nothing to convince me that it is a better safeguard of humanity that theism.' Perhaps people are inherently destructive and controlling of each other and 500 years ago it was done in a religious way because that was the language of the time, whereas now it is done in a secular way because that is the language of our time. But actually to prioritize the non-theist or the naturalist point of view over the theist view is simply to be blind to the problem – the human component – of your own ideology.

Those points provide an opportunity for a very important answer, which is this: fascism and Stalinism are not themselves part of the Enlightenment or humanist tradition. They are part of the counter-enlightenment.

What they have in common with religion is that they are monolithic ideologies. They try to impose one framework which everybody has to conform to. So there is a great deal in common in Soviet Communism, fascism and religion. Now, monolithic societies – societies where everybody has got to dance to the same tune – are societies in which civil society organizations like the boy scouts, political parties, NGOs, charities, trade unions, and so on, cannot flourish because they are seen as threats to the monolith. It is only in societies which permit those kinds of organizations that all the very different needs, interests and desires of different people can be addressed and met. Western liberal democracies are characterized by their embrace of flourishing civil society institutions. You have groups that look after the interests of minorities and special needs constituencies, you have media watchdogs, you have all sorts of organizations, societies, bodies and groups lobbying, advocating, preserving, discussing, teaching, making, doing. So there are many different voices speaking up in society, and therefore there can be a rich debate and lots of opportunities for getting things done and for change. If you look at the picture of a modern liberal democracy you can see that there is an enormous amount of good work done within the framework of that society which benefits the individuals within it. Now, in a sense it is true that freedom of the individual and freedom of speech, democracy, accountability and transparency and so on are just myths, but they are very powerful and useful myths because they are about the aspirations that we define ourselves by, even if we have not got the full reality of them yet. But we have got a big enough percentage of each of them for it to be the case that each of us living here today has choices, possibilities and options which 500 years ago only aristocrats and the most senior clergymen had. Everybody else was in one way or another chained to their station in life and their place on the face of the earth. They were very limited in opportunities and they were bullied by circumstance. Well, we may still be bullied by circumstance, but in a much less direct way. Now we can stand up for ourselves, and there are institutions, and the rule of law, which protect us from arbitrary arrest and abuse of our rights. So the achievement of making most ordinary folks in our world aristocrats in comparison to people 500 years ago is an amazing one. And that is the result of the secular, humanistic outlook which has pushed all the monolithic ideologies and structures ever further back until they are just one among many competing claims.

There is a family of very important concepts in play here. One is pluralism: the recognition that people have a right to their own space for making choices that might not be shared by others. They might have preferences and interests that you do not share but it is up to you to tolerate them so that they tolerate you in return. So pluralism is a very important idea, and it carries the idea of tolerance as an essential concomitant. Another very important idea is autonomy: of being your own governor, the chooser of your own way. The opposite of autonomy is heteronomy, which means being governed by someone else's views and choices. It you are heteronomous you live a life that is being dictated by someone or something else, that is governed or directed by some force outside you. And given that 99 per cent of people living a heteronomous life will often be moving in a direction they don't want to go, they will constantly be chafing against it. Religion quintessentially seeks to impose a heteronomous life on people. If you think that there is a deity who directs your life and requires that you live a certain way, you are living heteronomously. Kant, in his famous essay *What is Enlightenment?*, says that: 'We live in an age of enlightenment not in the sense that we are enlightened, but in the sense that we have learned to strive for autonomy, and to make choices for ourselves.'

2

Giles Fraser

Do you have a working definition of the term religion?

It's a really difficult word to define because it presumes that you can find some common denominator for a load of different things. You know, it's like when people do the census and put down 'Jedi' or that sort of thing as their religion. They get away with it because you can't get a great definition of religion. It's more a family resemblance thing, you can see that different faiths share certain things in common but it's very difficult to say they all share one thing in common. Religion's a tricky term, and, in fact, it's even trickier than you might suppose because, surprisingly perhaps, some people you might instinctively categorize as religious would claim that they're not. For example there is a whole species of Christian theology, which is self-consciously anti-religious. There are, for example, a number of Christian theologians who say that Jesus was hostile to religion. Bonhoeffer, for instance talks about religion-*less* Christianity. What is religion-less Christianity? Well it's partly Christianity without an obsession with priests and churches and all that stuff that gets put into the category 'religion'. But there is also a side to Jesus where he is in direct opposition to the religious representatives of his day. So religion is a tricky old word really. I think you have to listen hard to the grammar of the particular expression of religious belief to see how it works in people's lives, to see what it means. You can't boil it down to an essence.

How do you define faith?

Well, I'm never very keen on definitions but I suppose the nearest equivalent is something like being in love. I remember the night before I got married, my brother took me out for a curry and he said: 'Are you sure you're doing the right thing, getting married?' You know, this is what brothers are supposed to do! And so he got a piece of paper and he said:

'Draw a line down the side and put down all the pluses and all the minuses for why this is a good thing, and so forth.' So you try and write down all the pluses, so 'She's great company', 'We have similar interests' and so on, and you make this whole list of things and then you suddenly realize that that list could never add up to justify what you're about to do – to get married. However poetic or intelligent or clever or in touch with your own emotions you are, the sum total of that list on the plus side could never equal 'I love this person and I'm going to marry her'. So there comes a point where what comes first is just *doing*, without the rationalizations, just the *doing* of love. And if you ask 'Could you fully justify exactly what you're doing?' well, the answer is sort of 'No, really, my justifications run out but this is just what I do.' Now that's the area of faith for me. So if I sit in a conversation with a pretty hard-core empiricist who says 'I'm only going to allow what's on this list as legitimate' – well, I'm stuffed you know? So what I do exceeds what's on the list. But then a whole range of things that we do exceeds what happens on that list. And I think, also, it has to do with some sense of otherness. There's a fantastic Emily Dickinson poem: *This world is not conclusion*. 'This world is not conclusion, a species stands beyond, invisible as music, but positive as sound; it beckons and it baffles . . .' and so on. It's to do with this whole idea of this 'other thing' than the empirical world. I mean I grew up as a hard-core leftie, empiricist, atheist, and when I went to university and did philosophy, initially, I bought the whole idea that the world could be described by a form of strict empiricism. But now, I'm a sort of failed empiricist simply because I look at that list and I think I cannot get out of that list all that I think is true about the world. That's where someone like A. C. Grayling and I would differ. He would think that everything you get is going to be on that list, but for me, there's more that I want to say, even if I don't know how to say it.

Would you describe the difference between you and A. C. Grayling as a leap of faith?

Yes. But, I mean, too many people use that as a cheap excuse for justifying whatever they like; so some might say: 'I'm anti-gay because hey it's faith!' So I worry about leaps of faith. But nonetheless, for me it starts with a sense that the empirical explanations of, or justifications for, the world in which I live, for everything about life, the universe and everything, don't succeed in describing everything that I want to say about the world, and that's the whole point about *This world is not conclusion*.

I mean, I grew up a firm atheist and see my religious faith as an act of rebellion. We're the first generation for centuries where this is a possibility. And it's very interesting how it's different now. It used to be the case that people's default position in the West was generally religious. But now the default position is secular. I think we're probably in an age where we are the first generation of people for whom this is true. And because the default position of the world in which we live is secular, religion becomes a completely different phenomenon. I rebel against the secular view because it fails to express all that I want to say about the world.

Do you think that this kind of leap of faith can be dangerous?

The big difference between liberals and conservatives in terms of religion across the board, and this is really important, is that liberals recognize that religion is a very dangerous thing and that you need to be careful, and thoughtful and that faith needs to be subject to lots of checks and balances. Whereas conservatives want to stoke it up a bit, they want to stoke up the passion in all sorts of different ways. They believe that faith gives you *carte blanche* to do what you like in its name. But then it is not just religious faith that needs policing, it is the whole irrational aspect of our lives. You know, if you go up Putney High Street on a Saturday night, most of the fights there will be over women. Passion, sex, love, all those things cause lots of fights. I think A. C. Grayling is a bit like Plato inasmuch in this *one* word as he wants to eliminate all the irrational aspects of life in order that everything is ordered and safe and so forth, but while passion is dangerous – it's also what makes us what we are.

You're talking about conservatives and liberals within a religious tradition?

Well I suppose I mean specifically liberals and conservatives within Christianity, within Anglicanism. But I think that is a crucial difference that goes across all religions. So there are those who believe that faith can provide a blank cheque for all sorts of moral and political positions, some dangerous. That's why religion needs policing with questions and checks and balances. Whereas the conservatives, or the radicals or however you want to put it, the people on that side of religion think that faith requires no checks or balances.

The other thing about faith for me is that, fundamentally, I see it as something that I am not able to get away from, rather than as the conclusion of any great logical argument. Put it this way, if I was going to sit in a seminar with Richard Dawkins, say, he and I could argue this whole thing out and the argument could fall his way extremely easily and I could walk away and think: 'Yes, he's right! But still, I can't get away from it that easily. And that is precisely because it's not something I can fully articulate. I just have a sense of this 'other' which has a sort of pull on me. I suppose he could and does explain that 'other' in other terms – psychology, etc. – but I think that's an unacceptable form of reductionism, and I'm not happy with that.

I talk quite a bit with people who think they might have a vocation to be a priest; I'm one of those people that selects priests to be priests. And one of the hallmarks of authenticity, for me, is the feeling that it just won't go away. If someone is feeling 'I don't want it to be there, I don't want to think about it, I wish it wasn't there, I wish I could get on with my life as an "X", but it just keeps on coming back and it slightly haunts me as this thing I should be doing, almost despite myself', I understand that. I mean, in a sense, I'd love to be doing something different in all sorts of ways. I'd love to be making so much money a year and flying off to Barbados. But it's just like being haunted by some call which one is not able to make complete sense of, but which is there in the scriptures. It's there in the way that you look at the world, and I think you have to give some credence to that call, to the fact that it won't leave you alone.

How does the other relate to an idea of God?

Well I guess the argument then becomes about how you form views about the other. Now for most religions the other is God. But I think we have to be really careful about thinking of God as a proper name for a thing. And I think that's really easy to do, to see God as if it's some object in the world. In fact, I think it's quite easy to demonstrate through traditional Christian theology that God is not a *thing* as such. If you trawled through the world, if you made a manifest of all the things that exist in the universe including tables and chairs and glasses and wine, there would not be on that list a thing called God. I think Thomas Aquinas says that. And his argument is that God cannot be both the creator of everything and something created – that is, something on the manifest. So he's not a *thing*; it's not as if once you've added up all these things, the furniture of the universe, you can say: 'Oh yes and plus one more thing.' No. God doesn't exist on that manifest of things that exist in the universe. And to that extent the atheists are right, there is no such thing as God and actually I think that can be seen straightforwardly in the Bible. I mean the great story about this in the Bible, it seems to me, is the story of the golden calf and Moses going up the mountain. This is the great story of religion I think: Moses travels up the mountain, and as he gets higher up the mountain, it gets cloudier and cloudier and cloudier. So the nearer to God he gets, the nearer to this 'other' he gets, the less able he is to see, the less able he is to know his way about. Meanwhile, what's happening down below is that people are making this thing called god – a golden calf – and it's like they're trying to make God into this thing, this concrete notion of the divine. So you've got this contrast, between the journey to the real divine which involves not being able to see or know one's way about, and, at the bottom of the mountain, the construction of a god that is very much a thing.

I mean why is the Bible so obsessed with idolatry? Idolatry is when we all want to have a really comfortable thing called god who is on our side and who we bow down before and so forth. And the whole argument about idolatry is about why you can't have an image of God, why you can't have even mental images and why you have to smash these images all the time. It's not thuggery: no it's much more interesting and profound than that. We can end up much more attached to our images of God, these depictions and so forth. Yet God will actually constantly exceed all of that, he – she – can't be captured and we find that profoundly hard to cope with.

I think that all this stuff about iconoclasm is actually really important. And it's even there in another sense in Marx. I used to be a Marxist and it's deep in the Marxist tradition. Lukacs called it reification. Marxists like him used to bang on about how capitalism makes people into things. And so in terms of religion, it is about being against God being reduced to a sort of 'thing'. And I think that certainly in the Christian tradition there's a huge hostility to God being cast as a thing. Yet there is also a real recognition about the way in which religious people are always tempted to do this, because it's much more comforting. You want to know what God looks like, you want know what God says, and the more insecure you are, the more you want this. This is the point about the modern world; fundamentalism is a feature. It's an absolutely crucial point to make about fundamentalism that it's an entirely modern, twenty-first-century phenomenon. The world is becoming more insecure, and global capitalism and so forth is creating such an insecure environment people need something to grab on to. It's like what happens on your first day at University. You know, you were the top of your class at school, you had your mum and dad and everything was fine, except then, you go away and you're told that all the stuff that you thought you knew you don't know any more, and you're no longer the top of your class, and you're away from all your mates and suddenly you're in an incredibly insecure environment. So what do a lot of these kids do? They join these hard-core conservative churches who will tell you that everything may be floating around and be very difficult but that the Church can give you a fixed anchor in your life.

Sam Harris in his book *The End of Faith* argues that there is no such thing as a religious moderate. And that those who legitimize the concept of God and the potency of the Word, are also responsible for legitimizing various literal or fundamental interpretations?

There are two points there, aren't there? One is that there's no such thing as a religious moderate and the other is that there are such things but that they are shields for fundamentalists. Now I don't agree with the first point, but I'm very sensitive to the second point, very sensitive. And sometimes

I think 'Why do I do what I do?' because I'm defending something which is being used by others to describe something I loathe. So that is one of the dark thoughts I have about religious moderates. But you see, on the other hand, I'm quite convinced that the most dangerous situation to get into would be to see the world (especially with the sort of geo-political stuff as it is) as a battle between those who have religion and those who don't have religion, where those who have religion are just defined as zealots. I think that there's a really important role for those who want to say we need to have better religion, we need to have religion that is capable of self-critical scrutiny; who understand that it's dangerous; who understand this passion; and who understand this potentially dangerous authority of the other which is un-checkable.

You converted to Christianity, but your background is Jewish. Why did you choose Christianity as opposed to Judaism or Islam?

Well partly, it's just the culture I was brought up in. But it was also something about the character or nature of Jesus. As you said, my family background is Jewish, but there's something about the character of Jesus which defined for me something about the other. I suppose it is that this other is bound up with what Jesus called 'good news'. There's something about what the world needs that is bound up in his teaching.

There's a great story about Jesus and the fisherman, and Jesus says to him 'Come follow me', and they drop their nets and they follow him. And I always think very hard about that story because he does not say 'Now let's just check what you believe before you come.' And I think what I did, as it were, was drop my metaphorical nets, follow and then think 'What the fuck am I doing?' Its not like I chose it but it chose me.

Most of the time I just didn't understand what was happening to me. Lots about my faith journey I didn't admit to others for a really long time. And initially, I wouldn't go to church and yet I was fascinated by it. For me, to start with, I would go to the library and read all this stuff and it was absolutely engrossing. But then, you know, you have to be a bit more open and honest about what makes you tick, but fundamentally, it was about responding to those words 'Come follow me' and not about having to get all your theology completely sussed beforehand. I mean, theology is a catch-up, always playing catch-up anyway. You don't have a perfect theology on which your facts are then built. Theology is always trying to make sense of that feeling of 'Fucking hell, what am I doing?'

Augustine says faith seeks an understanding of itself and theology is that process of faith seeking understanding. So I think: this is what I've been called to, and so, given that, how do I then understand where I am? How do I speak with honesty about what this means, even though it is a vulnerable position to be in because I haven't really got the language to describe it.

Is there an evangelical side to the work that you do?

Yes there is, but only inasmuch as I think being a bloody good salesman for liberal Christianity is a useful bit to do in a world where there is so much corrupting Christianity.

So you are speaking as much to corrupt Christians as you are to non-believers?

Yes, and I write often for corrupted Christians and that's why I write in the Church's trade journals. Sometimes I feel I'm the pin-up hate figure for evangelical Christians! But I write for others too. The writing I do for papers like the *Guardian* is me trying to say 'Look, I think you need to understand this better than you do' to people who look with puzzlement at religiosity and to try and articulate something of how there is such a thing as being religious where you're not actually a kind of alien.

Do you believe that the virgin birth actually happened?

As a Christian I am shaped by a set of texts from 2,000 years ago in which I find inspiration and meaning. These are texts which say a great deal that I believe about the nature of the divine. And it's not just about whether I believe or don't. These texts have shaped me. On the other hand, they were written in another age and all sorts of things come with that, you know. The authors of these texts had a completely different worldview to the worldview that I have. So there you go, but if the question is do I think that those things are meaningful and significant and interesting and important? Of course! Well, take the resurrection for instance. David Jenkins, the Bishop of Durham, was widely misunderstood when he said that it has to be seen as more than a conjuring trick with bones, but he's absolutely bloody right. The question isn't whether some strange abracadabra happened 2,000 years ago, but actually what that means, what that narrative means, and whether or not one is changed by it. And I think it has something to do with the triumph of hope, it has something to do with light and darkness and the triumph of light over darkness. It has to do with living in that light. There's a great many things you can say about the resurrection which don't require you to be so obsessive about literalism. But let's be clear: I believe in it. I absolutely do.

Rabbi Jonathan Sacks has said that religion has never been very good with power.

He's right! Now that's a good approach towards finding checks and balances in religion. If religion gives up power, then there would be a lot fewer things for people to complain about in relation to it. You know, if we give up the bishops in the House of Lords then that would help. But of course, it's not quite that clear, is it? Because the power that religion has is primarily often its influence, you know. If I ran a mosque full of 10,000 people, well my influence is my power. And you might argue that there should be a strong separation between church and state so that religion has no role in that regard, but it will still be powerful in other ways.

But my whole shtick, as I have said, is that religion is dangerous; I'm not trying to pretend that that's not the case. But, I suppose, one of the things I would say in order to defend where I am would be in terms of strategy. From a pragmatic point of view, I'm ten times more useful than an A. C. Grayling or a Richard Dawkins. Because their dismissal of religion means that they are not going to be able to speak to these people. I believe we need to have *better* religion, and to get this, we need to dialogue theologically with all the problematic aspects of faith. And to make a difference, this is a vital process. You can't simply say: 'Well screw you lot, you're all bonkers', because that isn't going to do anything, is it? That would achieve nothing. But proper engagement with Muslims, proper interfaith dialogue, and proper discussion about the nature of faith, is really important and will help. But it can only really happen between people who understand what it is to have this itch that you can't scratch, which is the nature of God.

What do you think of those people who say they don't prescribe to any specific organized religion, but prefer to call themselves spiritual?

That's bollocks! Spirituality is religion that's been mugged by capitalism; which is to say that it sort of just reduces everything to choice. 'Spirituality' just takes the ascetic patina of religion: you know, saying 'I like to burn a few joss-sticks' or 'I like crosses, they look very nice and rather alternative', or 'I want to live in a church that's made to look like my comfortable flat'. Spirituality often acts as though you can go through all these sorts of different bits of faith and that you can take one thing or another. It's as if you can choose between them like you were in some sort of supermarket of ideas, and all that matters is whether they make you feel better about yourself. It's a form of self-help or therapy. Now Christianity, and all religions in fact, often deliberately challenges the view of the 'I' being at the centre of life, you know; it says that the 'I' is *not* at the centre of things. But with this spirituality stuff, the 'I' is firmly at the centre of things.

Spirituality becomes a fashion accessory to the successful urban life. No, I loathe spirituality, and in fact, historically there never was such a thing. Spirituality is a very twentieth-century phenomenon. There never used to be such a thing as spirituality; there was always Christian spirituality or Muslim spirituality or Jewish spirituality but there was no such thing as spirituality as such, it's a false extrapolation. I mean, I think part of it, historically, comes from William James' 1905 book *Varieties of Religious Experience*. I think that is one of the most dangerous books ever. I hate it because it is what invented something called 'religion'. I would say 1905 is when religion was invented. And from this, spirituality arose as the aesthetics of religion.

Would you say this was important in relation to an issue like creationism or intelligent design?

Well, intelligent design, I mean, how intelligent is that?! It's stupid! I can't bring myself to talk about it really.

Where do you think it comes from?

Well, in a sense it's about sex. I mean, why would you want to defend the literal truth of Genesis? Because you're trying to defend traditional sexual roles in relation to Adam and Eve! What's going on here relates to the whole structure of 'the family' that American conservatives bang on about. It says 'Here is a man and here is a woman, they're the ones that get together and this is how it happens.' It makes gender and sexuality all very clear and simple, because after all, 'This is Genesis so this is the nature of things of creation.' So to take it literally is to underline a traditional take on sexual morality. But in the end, I don't know; I can't get inside the heads of people who think the world was created in seven days and that fossils were added to confuse us. I mean what is that? It's just ridiculous.

The other thing about creationism or intelligent design is that it's actually a kind of revenge. This is because there is a problem with the scientific worldview which constantly gives Christianity a right kicking. And this is that, actually, it can't quite finish off intelligent design. Now, I am happy to say that, as intelligent people, we can all believe in Darwin, I'm sure that's absolutely the case. The problem is the nature of scientific truth itself, in that it's difficult to prove something once and for all, to prove it definitively because everything is always a theory that can be overturned by another. So if you put up something preposterous like intelligent design it's very difficult for it to be conclusively defeated.

You are defining the scientific method as relying on something that is always just a theory which, potentially, could therefore always be replaced by another theory. So there is a kind of doubt at the heart of any scientific theory. Do you see a parallel between that and your kind of theology which also has a doubt at the heart of what it perceives to be true?

No, it's not like that. Let's go back to the analogy with love. In those terms, when I go for what's on that list it's a 'performative action', OK? I say I will marry this person and I love this person and that's it, it's done, 100 per cent. It's not a theory that I may change or not change at will. I'm in it completely. The stuff that's weak for me is the link between how I get to that 100 per cent commitment from my reasoning. You know, various people will say: 'Well, there's a gap here between how much evidence there is on this list and how much you are prepared to dive in.' But once I'm in, I'm in. It's the same with religion: once you're in, you're in 100 per cent. It's like with marriage: you might have all sorts of questions when you get married, but we all know that when you're in, you're in 100 per cent. So there's a gap between the ability to provide rational evidence for a commitment and the act of being in 100 per cent. It's different to scientific reasoning, because there the percentage of truth in your theory is related to the reasoning for that theory, and so it isn't the same. Whereas for me, if I was proportionally committed to Christianity only inasmuch as I believe that there is evidence for it, then that could be a problem, as in some ways there is only a small amount of evidence for it. You can't expect faith to work in terms of kind of scientific tests that are measurable and repeatable and so on.

Do you find your faith psychologically helpful?

Well, that is not the purpose of it. It may be helpful but that's not the point of it. It's a complicated question; its purpose is not to be helpful and people get that wrong quite a bit. I guess that idea comes from this spirituality thing. The question people ask is always: 'How can all this help me?' It's as if they are saying 'Well let's take all the little bits that help me, that make me feel better about myself', but it's not always helpful, I mean sometimes it's a pain in the arse. For me, sometimes it's unhelpful, you know, in terms of what I'd like to do with my life. But it's stuck there like a bloody great big rock that I can't ignore. But even though being helpful is not its point, I think it can sometimes be helpful. And I think it's simply to do with the fact that religion has various different things that I think make people happy. Again, this is not its function, it just happens. It brings people together, it congregates them; it gets them to do things.

What does your role as a priest give you?

I think it's a fantastic job. Why? Because people come and talk to me about amazing things in their life that they wouldn't go and talk to other people about, and I find that hugely satisfying. The other night I had a couple round at my house, and for about a year I've been going for long walks along the river with them because their first pregnancy was terminated as a result of a terrible hereditary disease. But now they've had this new baby, it's been born and it's absolutely fantastic, and they've called the baby Grace and they are going to get it christened on Sunday. It's a privilege to be a part of a story like that. So simply for that reason, if for no other, it would be really tough to imagine doing anything else.

3

Rowan Williams

Do you have a definition of the term religion?

A working definition, I think, would have to be a set of habits: habits of speaking, habits of imagining, habits of behaving physically. Habits which are intended to anchor you in relation to something invisible, incomprehensible, and challenging.

And how does that relate to definitions of things like faith, or belief?

Well, it has to do with the shape that these habits take; these habits are formed by the stories people tell which are basic to their experience. Your relationship to those stories becomes a relationship of trust. You say, OK, I want to find myself in relation to that story. I trust that story to help me grow. These habits are keeping me in touch with that story, so that's how I grow in truthfulness.

How did your religious habits begin?

I grew up in a Welsh Presbyterian community and so I got taken to chapel, and that was it for some years. But then, when I was a teenager, we moved house, and I discovered the local parish church, which had a different kind of worship, a different kind of atmosphere. That's partly because it was quite a high church: music, drama and the rest of it played a very great part in the worship. This is, I think, why I talk about habit, and the *physical* side of religion. And, I was lucky in having a parish priest who thought that faith was about growing up, and he always struck me as a deeply grown-up man. He had a sort of emotional and spiritual maturity to him, and that must have rubbed off in some way. I must have been about 14 when I had some kind of breakthrough, in here (*gestures to self*). It's not just about words, but it's about developing a sense of a relationship with something, someone, who's enough like a person to be able to talk to in these terms, and yet, enough not like a person for you to need to be very careful about what you are saying. I suppose also it had to do with discovering certain aspects of the Eastern Christian tradition – that helped, and discovering certain kinds of poetry helped. And then somewhere around the age of 20 there was a sense that yes, actually this is gripping, something's taking over me.

And your academic interest?

That developed at around the same time I suppose. I suddenly thought, its really interesting seeing how people try to talk about this. I wanted to know, what are the criteria, what are the standards that make sensible religious language? Why can you get a sense of religious language that's corrupt and stupid? The whole history of theology, which I taught for over 20 years, is, in a sense, all about that. Theology is often about: 'What does a stupid religious statement sound like?' I know that some people would no doubt say: 'All religious statements are stupid!' But you know, those of us on the inside don't necessarily think that. We therefore need criteria to say: 'What *are* stupid statements?' And, in my academic work, especially when I was teaching at Cambridge, I got more and more interested in this question of: 'How do you really know it's God you're talking about?' And it's about developing a habit of that reigning up before you go so far as to say: 'Yes, this is *God* we're talking about; it's not just a cosmic leprechaun, it's not just a kind of big mirror in the sky: it's God.'

Can you tell us something about the God you believe in as opposed to the God of other religions?

I'll try, yes. I'm a Christian as you may have noticed! They still expect that from Archbishops of Canterbury! That means I believe in God as a trinity. This is one of those ideas that tends to produce a sort of glazing over sometimes. But for me it came alive when I was first thinking about faith as a teenager and then again when I taught it. What it's saying is that the word 'God' isn't the name of an individual, somewhere else, in heaven. God is the name given to whatever that life is out of which everything else is generated. And the character of that life is the relationship between the Father, the Son and the Holy Spirit. It's a rather inadequate shorthand for saying the life out of which everything else comes is a life which, if you like, breathes out and breathes in, and relates to itself, folds back on itself. I tend to reach sometimes for musical images here. It's like a three-note chord, it's something which is already plural, and which flows back and forth within itself; and out of that comes everything else. And we say Father, Son and Holy Spirit, because in the history of Christianity, in the Bible, these words and these images are what we are given. There's the aspect of that life which gives out: so that's the Father, there's the aspect which communicates and responds: so that's the Son, and there's the aspect which binds those two together and then opens up the relationship to everything else, and that's the breath, which means the Spirit. So that's the God that I believe in, and that's the kind of basis, though not necessarily in those words, on which I preach every Sunday. Now the difference between that and other conceptions of God is best understood by going to the two different ends of the 'religious spectrum'. Look at the difference between that and Buddhism. I've always thought Buddhism is the next best thing, and I've learned a lot from Buddhists. A Buddhist will say: 'At the end of the day there is no *thing* that you are relating to outside yourself.' The practice of religion, the habit of religion is so, if you like, *gathering* in itself, in consciousness, that all the selfish, distracting, corrupting bits of your emotion are purified all the time. They might call it that luminous emptiness and so out of that, for a Buddhist, flows compassion. I think that's wonderful, but it's not quite true. Because when you get to the luminous emptiness stuff, I want to say, yes, that's also Christian love, but it's not just emptiness; there is, somehow, a subject and object. And then at the other end of the spectrum, there is the difference between Christianity and, say, Islam. The Muslim says 'God is God. You mustn't associate anything else with God. God is absolutely different, absolutely one.' The biggest sin for a Muslim is associating something else with God in their doctrine. And again, I think: 'Yes, bang on.' But the Muslim would go on to say: 'Therefore forget this Father, Son and Holy Spirit nonsense. There's one God, one great cosmic mind saying, "do what I tell you and it will be fine".' And the disagreement there is that we align ourselves with the life of God. But it's God's *own life* that dwells in us, which 'makes us possible'. And that relationship doesn't just come out of obedience; it's about going into a lasting relationship of intimacy. So, those are the sorts of differences.

How do you respond to the argument that there is no evidence for belief in God?

Well this is very difficult isn't it? Because religious commitment, like most forms of serious commitment, isn't something you just come to at the end of a process that you can terminate. Why is anybody a socialist? If you're not a dogmatic, scientific Marxist, why are you a socialist? Why does anyone get married? Why might you want to perform Bach rather than Mozart? Faith is where something comes together for you, where you say: 'On the basis of the form of the world, the form of the situation, I'm driven towards the best resolution that I can find.' But if I were asked about evidence for being religious at all, I'd first put in the caveat that you shouldn't expect it to be like a proof for something like the existence of the Loch Ness monster. To answer the question: 'Is there a Loch Ness monster or not?' you can look at the various bits of evidence and say: 'Well probably not.' But the question, 'Is there a God or not?' doesn't work quite like that. Now there's a perfectly real question about the nature of that energy which sustains the universe. Is it enough to say, 'Well, it's just a self-explanatory system', or do you have to say 'something *energizes* the elements of the universe'? It's at least a good question to ask. At school, in science lessons, when you start talking about the Big Bang, sooner or later most of us will think, well, did anybody 'press the switch'? Of course, that's not a watertight argument, but there's a sort of instinctive drive to ask: 'Does the whole universe not depend on some energizing material?' So that's one way which I think the idea of God can *begin* to make sense. The other way, of course, is completely chaotic, messy and intuitive. And it's about asking: 'What do you say about the lives of people who are used to living with God?' Do they look like more or less human lives to me? That's where you get almost into an endless exchange of anecdotes. Some might say; 'Oh come on – Osama Bin Laden, does that look like a human life?' Maybe not. Or you say: 'Yes, but Desmond Tutu, *that* looks pretty human to me. That looks more than averagely human; Osama Bin Laden looks less than averagely human.' So you have to weigh that up.

How do you think God relates to people of other faiths and to people of no faith?

Well, the God I believe in is just *there*. And that life, that energy, that three-fold energy just goes on – it penetrates and sustains us breath by breath. Nobody can fail to be related to that God, because it's his gift that keeps the whole thing going. So within that framework, the Christian faith would say that because of all sorts of complicated historical reasons – a particular place, a particular country, a particular language, the Holy Land, the people of Israel, the person of Jesus – things suddenly came together. And so you can say: 'That's where it comes through, that's where the whole thing suddenly comes to light.' And, I would have to say, as a Christian, that without that, we wouldn't know what God really was. So, does God never come through at all elsewhere? Well, he must do – there's a lot of him around! And it would be deeply surprising if Buddhism, Hinduism, Sikhism, Islam, let alone Judaism hadn't got something to say. The fascinating thing about interfaith dialogue is that you can encounter something completely strange, and then sometimes, sometimes you want to say, 'That sounds very familiar, I can do business with that' – even with a Buddhist. So, it's not as if somewhere up there, there is a God who looks down at the world and says: 'I think I'm going to talk to *those* people, and

I'm not going to talk to *those* people. I think I'm going to reveal myself *here* because I like the look of them, and I will ignore the rest.' On the contrary I think that God's intelligent, loving presence soaks through them. And in this particular circumstance, in the biblical history, in Jesus it came through most fully and made the decisive difference; but in all the others it's throbbing under the surface, throbbing away, and comes to the surface in different degrees. And that's what makes a really lively interaction between faiths.

Can we talk about the concepts of hell and Judgement? You rarely hear those words in the liberal Anglican tradition these days. But in a radio interview about the environment you said, talking about the world's leaders: 'Those who have the challenge put before them, but not only the challenge, but the evidence for it, and don't respond, bear a very heavy responsibility before God.' What did you mean by that?

Well, I'm rather in favour of hell, but bear with me for a moment! I think it comes down, again, to habits. If you get into the habit of living profound untruthfulness, what's that like? Project that. If you live with deep illusions about yourself, other people, about the nature of the world you're in, then you bump into reality. What if (I don't know if this ever happens), but what if you sort of got stuck like that? That's hell for me, being in this state of perpetual untruthfulness.

What about after death?

Well again, it's not God saying: 'You've not done very well, off you go to hell.' It's much more me on Judgement Day coming face to face with God and thinking: 'Have I been lying?' – as the character in Dostoyevsky said: 'I've been lying all my life.' So then what? Well, I believe in a loving God, and that *could* mean that if I am prepared to say: 'I've been lying all my life, oh God, sorry!' I might have some growing to do. But what if I said: 'No I can't face that, I can't'; I can't admit that'? Well then I'm stuck. That's hell for me, that sort of frozenness.

So you would characterize it in moral terms, not in doctrinal terms?

I don't think God condemns anybody just for thinking things. The question has to be: what sort of a person have you made yourself? Is that sort of a person capable of facing the truth? Think of Elgar's *Dream of Gerontius*, which is based on Cardinal Newman's poem. There, after death, the soul finally comes face to face with God and says: 'Take me away, I can't stand it.' And the 'taking away' is part of the mercy of God. But in terms of my comments about leaders and the environment that you referred to, there are two things. One is: acts have consequences. Your choices make you a certain kind of person, and you need to keep a pretty clear-weather eye on what sort of a person your choices are making you. The second is: among those choices are choices about how you affect this world – literally, the environment you're in. And people who collude in all sorts of fantasies about the endlessness of our resources, and believe that technology can just fix it, well that's just lying. And people who nurture that lie and stop other people fixing it – well, I meant what I said earlier, they've got a heavy responsibility. They will come face to face one day with the truth which will say to them: 'OK, so why didn't you tell people the truth?'

What are your ambitions for religion?

Ambitions? That's an odd word to use in this context, but I see why you're asking. I don't know if I would say I have ambitions for religion. I have profound hopes that what I do becomes interesting, and engages people in life. There's a great phrase in John's Gospel: 'I've come that they may have life, and have it in abundance'. Somehow I hope to act by my faith in such a way that that statement, 'they may have life in abundance' doesn't sound ridiculous. But of course you know, prima facie, when somebody walks past a church on a Sunday morning, with raindrops streaming off the flying buttresses, and a six-month-old harvest festival poster hanging by a drawing pin on the notice board, and five elderly figures huddling their way into it, it can take a while to make the connection! But my ambition is to try and make that sort of remark plausible. Which means, going back to where I started, we have to keep telling the stories about those in whom it looks as if it's in abundance, Desmond Tutu and so on. I sometimes talk about a woman called Etty Hillesum. She died in Auschwitz, when she was 27. She was a Dutch Jew, who left behind her a great bundle of journals and letters which were all published a few years ago. And, I don't know why, or what it is about her, but I can read those and say: 'Yes *this* is life in abundance.' And she was a very free spirit – her private life wouldn't necessarily fit with strict Christian morals as they say! She taught Russian literature and was not at all conventionally religious. But what you see in her journals, as the Nazi occupation of Holland proceeds, is her gradually coming to terms with being Jewish, and with the inescapability of God. And it's very strange, she says at one point: 'I've always said I don't believe in God, but here I am kneeling. I'm not quite sure what I'm *kneeling* to, what I'm talking to, I just know that I've got to go down on my knees.' And later, just as she's about to go off on the transports to Auschwitz, she says: 'Somebody's got to take responsibility for God and I suppose it's got to be me.' To be there, at the centre of that, to feel, to love, have faith, and decide to take responsibility for that. I think it's that phrase that sums up what I mean.

Is it important to you to evangelize?

Yes, I suppose it is. I *do* want to convince people, but at the same time I need to recognize the very intuitive, unpredictable nature of how people begin to see things. The worst thing I could do is to try and manipulate people into it. But I'm happy to talk about it.

Do you think it's possible to change people's minds?

Well, it's possible that people's minds can change; but that isn't quite the same thing. I was asked by a group of evangelical Christians from Africa a couple of years ago, how many people had I brought into living faith in Jesus Christ? It was very clear to them that I was a gutless Western liberal. And I said 'Well, I'm not sure, because *God* brings people to living faith in Jesus Christ, not me or you. I can tell you about a couple of people that I sat with as their minds changed, as they moved bit by bit towards faith over a longish period. And, as part of that journey they shared conversations with me. And I think of one person who was baptized on her deathbed, and one Buddhist, finding their way back into Christianity.' Well, these may not be great 'conversions' in a sense, but I think of them as that – they got there in the end. Though, of course, I'm not at all sure of what part I played.

A great number of churches, mosques, synagogues, have been accused of being manipulative, abusive, exploitative and intolerant. Aside from the question of whether or not they make up a majority of any religious community, why do you consider Church important for an understanding of, or a relationship with, God?

Religion is a very explosive thing. When it goes wrong, it goes very wrong. And if it doesn't make you more human, it does make you less human – Desmond Tutu and Osama Bin Laden again. But why do we need Church? Well, let's distinguish for a moment between the Church as an institution, with archbishops and all of that, and the Church as a community. As I read the Bible, God's way of getting everyone through is not just by giving a set of instructions from heaven that anybody can pick up and read. God comes through in the life of these people, these tribes of Israel. And it's in the law, the working out of how to live together, that God reveals Himself. In the Old Testament the message that comes through is: 'God has chosen you, and given you the law so that the nature of God will be made known in the community'. So for example, in Deuteronomy God says: 'You've got to be good to the strangers and the aliens, because, when you were strangers and aliens, I took care of you.' So, what sort of a God do we believe in? We believe in the God who likes strangers and aliens. Or again:

don't commit adultery: I'm a faithful God. Don't favour the rich over the poor: I'm a God of justice and equity. These patterns, they're not just arbitrary laws, they're asking: 'What sort of life is a sustainable life?' So you can't get away from the idea of relationships in community being part of knowing God. It's the same in the New Testament. But instead of the old model, the nation, Jesus says, in effect: 'If you want to belong with the people of God, well, all you really need to do is just trust what I tell you and hang around.' This is what is known as 'repent and believe the gospel'. So from the first, Jesus relates to a group of people – that group of people which started out as a bundle of North Country artisans in a backward province. But gradually this group grows, it gets to the capital city, it moves out to include non-Jews as well as Jews and then you're on the road to a worldwide community: the Church. And the word used in the New Testament – sorry this is anorak stuff in a way, but it's not wholly unimportant – is *ecclesia*. The word actually means a 'citizens' assembly'. It's the gathering of people where you make decisions about your common life. And then grafted on to that is the big metaphor in the New Testament of the Body of Christ. Just as in the body different bits contribute to each other, and there's a 'flow' throughout the body, so in this community there's a flow. And what's given to you, is given to *you* so you can give it to *them*. And so it becomes a sort of pass-the-parcel. Then to round that off, the institution, if you like, inevitably comes on top of that. When you've got common life, you've got to organize means of communication, the places you meet, the people who convene the meetings, and then you're on the road to the establishment, the institution. But all the time throughout the history of the Church you have a kind of circling back where people ask: 'Look, hang on, haven't we got the institution a bit out of proportion? Shouldn't we be asking the fundamental questions?' Whether it's St Francis in the Middle Ages, or the Reformation, or various things happening now, people are always going back to that.

How do you relate to the Bible and those aspects of biblical tradition which might be unpalatable for a contemporary mindset, whether it's on issues of homosexuality, or God's vengeance, wrath and jealousy? And how do you relate to the idea of miracles, the resurrection and the virgin birth?

Well, first there's no reading of the Bible that isn't in some way selective. Even the most ardent fundamentalist is actually being selective. So the question is: 'What's the principle of selection?' The problem I think a lot of fundamentalists have is that they treat the Bible as a flat surface. It's *all* from God, it's *all* inspired, and the inspiration *all* works at exactly the same level. So if it says at the beginning of the Book of Job, 'there was a man in the land of Uz whose name was Job', it means there *was* a man in the land of Uz whose name was Job, end of story. So if anybody weakly, and liberally says: 'Yes but hang on, isn't this meant to be some sort of *novel*?' then wrath descends! Now, it's the 'flat surface' that I object to. Because I think, both the Old Testament and the New Testament in their context are focused collections. You draw together a huge cluster of very varied documents: law-codes, histories, novels, songs, and you say these are all together because, taken as a whole, what they give you is a picture of God's engagement with this human community. I used to say to students: 'St Paul didn't *think* he was writing the New Testament. He was just writing letters, you know: "Dear so and so . . .".' And so, just like most of us probably wouldn't like to be on oath about everything we put in letters, let alone emails, neither would Paul. Thank goodness Paul didn't do email! So there's an exploratory element to these texts. And one of the things I love about St Paul in the New Testament is that he'll show his workings. He will say: 'Yes that's a problem; well what I think is this, I think this because so and so, and no, hang on, hang on, um, no, this is, this is the argument, now look it's, it's about . . .' and so on. There's a famous bit about women wearing hats in church. He says: 'It's because of the angels, the angels, it's because, you know, women's long hair distracts angels who might be around, it's um, yes, well, I don't know actually.' And then at the end of the chapter he says: 'Look, if anybody wants to argue all I've got to say is, we don't do it OK? Next question!' Now I think that's inspired, not quite in the fundamentalist sense, but because it shows St Paul trying to bring to bear a huge vision on some very local matters. He doesn't always do it terribly clearly, or coherently, but what you get from it is a sense of just how driving and powerful the vision is that makes him wrestle like that. In the letter to the Romans, there are three whole chapters, nine, ten and eleven, asking: 'So what's happened to the Jews in this story? Has God forgotten about the Jews?' And Paul's a Jew, and it matters to him, and he just agonizes. I've found these chapters terribly difficult, but also very moving because again he's just saying: 'Oh, I don't know how to deal with this.' And what we've got therefore is this tremendous testimony to the pressure on him, to what's hit him. It would be awful if the New Testament were full of neat questions and answers. So, what I'm trying to get at is, we look at the Bible as a variety of texts drawn together with a focus. Paul is worried about all these sorts of things ultimately because he wants to know: 'What *difference* did Jesus make?' He has to ask this even when he's got to apply it to the question of why women should cover their heads in church. He has to go a long way to get there, and so it's not wholly surprising that he doesn't get it clear in one go. So, I would say to the fundamentalist (in fact I do say to the fundamentalist from time to time) 'Step back a bit, and instead of the flat surface think of a landscape. You're coming into a world where the light falls in on things in a new way. There's a lot to discover.' Karl Barth, the greatest theologian of the twentieth century, talked about the 'strange new world' of the Bible and he wrote this great commentary on the Epistle to the Romans, just after the First World War. Essentially, he said: 'Look, we've got it all wrong; the German Churches have got it all wrong. We made a complete pig's ear of Christian reaction to the war, and we covered ourselves with shame in the war, in supporting militarism and oppression.' Then he asks: 'So where do we go now? Well let's start opening the Bible again and see if we've got something to learn.' I think that's wonderful. That's one of the great books of the twentieth century.

As for miracles, well, there are a number of different kinds of question here: because part of what you're dealing with in the Bible is, if you like, folklore material. So when it says in the book of Joshua: 'The sun stood still that little bit longer so that Joshua could finish slaughtering the Amalekites' well, the jury's out on that! It's folklore, and there's lots of that. This is because you're dealing with texts that are looking back hundreds, even thousands of years and so they just have that kind of legendary character. Of course, that's *not* to say there's no basis for the outline of the story. But, to take a parallel that interests me a lot, it's a bit like how the sixth century in Britain is re-imagined in our own literature, chronicle, and folklore through the Arthurian legend. There's something there, certainly, at the beginning, when you can pare it down to some basic things. But what that something has done is to *make possible* a great chain of imaginative elaboration. And I think we rather trivialize it actually if we imagine it's all got to be viewed as *Times*-style reporting. Now that means that when you're dealing with the sun standing still over the valley in Ajalon, or a plague of gnats, or whatever, frankly not a lot hangs on whether that's historically accurate or not. However, when you're looking at the New Testament, it's slightly different: you're not dealing with folkloric documents; you're dealing with texts that are written at most only 65 to 70 years after the death of Jesus. And they have been written in an environment where there are lots of living witnesses around. It was quite a small world in some ways. That means I feel obliged to take them a bit more seriously as something like exact history. For instance, certainly in terms of the resurrection, I'm unashamedly conservative about that. I think the tomb was empty, I don't understand it, but, you know, there it is. And for me it's quite clear from the texts as they stand that nobody was expecting it. It's the oddest single thing about the narratives of the resurrection. You read the stories of the crucifixion, and all the way the evangelists says: 'Now this happened so as to fulfil what the prophet had said.'

As if they were saying: 'We could have expected this.' And then it comes to the resurrection and there's a kind of difficulty with what to say about this. There is some very confused reporting, as if something quite unexpected and un-cope-able with is in the middle of it. So I don't have any objection in principle to miracle at all. And, I am committed to believing in the resurrection as a miracle, and feel I've got to entertain therefore what is said about the miracles of Jesus, the healing miracles especially.

Some people argue that living your life based on an irrational belief or a leap of faith can be dangerous.

Well yes. Next question!

Does religion need policing?

By whom? By rational people? Show me some. I think it's the definition of rational that's difficult. I think one of the problems we've got is that in Europe we inherit this eighteenth-century idea that we all know what a rational argument looks like, what a reasonable person sounds like. They are a bit like us. And that's led to a very sharp differentiation between rational beliefs and irrational beliefs. Now I would say an irrational belief, ultimately, is one that not only has no evidence for it, but also one which makes no attempt to cohere with a picture of how the world generally works. Religious philosophers since the beginning have at least had a good try at making their beliefs cohere with the way the world actually works, even when they've talked about miracle. They've wanted to say, like St Augustine: 'It's not that there are no causes and effects in the world, it's just that there are some causes that we don't fully understand.' So there's not a kind of head-on collision with reasonable argument. But if you're asking: 'Is religious belief dangerous?' Well I think the answer probably has to be yes, as I said earlier. You're dealing with such big things and such uncontrollable things, that, as I said, if it doesn't make you *more* human, it may make you *less* human. Jonathan Smith, a very interesting American scholar of religion, a secularized Jew gave a course of lectures years ago, which I came down from Oxford to London to hear. And he said: 'Don't imagine religion is always nice'; it was just after the Jonestown mass suicide. Religion isn't necessarily nice. It's serious, it's deep, it's mysterious, but it's not automatically nice. And I think you get some sense of that in the Bible from time to time. So I would say don't pin your faith on *religion*. Faith is about the reality of God, religion expresses this commitment. Religion in and of itself is not always good for you, because you've got to ask: 'What kind?' And that's where there do have to be some kind of cross-checks between what looks humane, and even what looks reasonable from time to time – cross-checks, not policing; and that's why cross-frontier conversations are important.

4

Lewis and Matthew Wolpert

Do each of you have working definitions of the term religion?

LW: Religion is for people who believe that there is something extra in the universe, that doesn't fit with science. They believe that there is some creator, something spiritual that is not definable. For me, religion is totally related to the idea of God. Though of course there are many religions which don't have a specific God. But I'm a nice Jewish boy, well actually, a not so nice Jewish boy! Because I just don't believe a word of it.

MW: Well for me, the word 'religion' has got quite a negative connotation. You know, when I think of religion, I think of a fixed set of laws and so on. Going back a bit, I was very involved in a church for about 15 years, but I came out of it about two or three years ago and so now I'm much more liberal in my views. So in terms of religion, I quite often have a negative association with that, but in terms of belief, well I grew up adopting quite a lot of my dad's views in terms of atheism, but then when I was about 18 or 19 I had some kind of religious experiences when I was taking drugs at the same time, and I was kind of mixed up, but that was when I started to believe in something. Because up to that point I didn't believe in ghosts, ESP or anything, and that was obviously quite like my dad.

LW: Yes, and also there is the Jewish aspect in my life, with all its rules. I mean, my mother died because I didn't get married in a synagogue. I could tell you stories of my family. When I was younger, when I went back to South Africa, my mother said: 'You did promise to marry a Jewish girl didn't you?' And I said: 'No, I don't remember that.' And so they went in to mourning for three days, and at the end of that I said to my mother: 'You know this has had a very negative effect? Your older brother couldn't have children because he married a non-Jewish woman, and they had to wait until your mother died before they could get married.' 'Yes,' said my mother, 'and they didn't have the decency to wait until Polly – their older sister – had died'! So that's my background. I was quite religious until a certain age, and I prayed to God asking him things like 'Where have I left my cricket bat?' And because he didn't help me find it, I gave it up! It just didn't make any sense to me, and I didn't like going to synagogue or anything like that.

How do you define belief?

LW: It means to believe in causes about which we cannot be absolutely sure. We all need explanations for things which affect our lives, and for many people, religion provides that. God punishes and rewards, and so a belief in him gives answers and explanations for why things happen.

MW: For me, a belief in God definitely gives meaning. The biggest issue for me was that when I believed in nothing, it led me into a kind of *Waiting for Godot* nihilism, which is pretty depressing. But through some very clear, definite experiences, I started to believe in God. And the good thing about belief in God is that it does provide some sort of meaning. If you believe that everything is in your hands; that puts an incredible amount of pressure on you. And so you can end up feeling that your whole destiny is in your own hands. And that's not actually true even if you don't believe in God because at any point a piano could drop on you, or you could die suddenly, or get paralysed. You're not in control. So to believe that there is somebody up there looking out for you, and to believe that God is good, that there is ultimately a good force in control of the universe is helpful.

Is there a danger in such a belief?

LW: It depends how it affects people's behaviour. When a church starts to interfere, or when religious people start to interfere with what other people believe, then I feel very strongly about it. I'm very against the Catholic Church on contraception and their idea that the fertilized egg is a human being and so forth. But I have never tried to persuade Matthew not to be religious. It's helped him a great deal. People asked me if I was upset that he was religious, and I said: 'Not at all.' If people want to believe these things, as long as they don't interfere with other people, well that's fine.

MW: The church I ended up in was very fundamentalist. Not fundamentalist in the American sense, like Waco, or George Bush. It was not politically right wing. It was more about taking the Bible very literally, and about converting other people. So the chief scriptures that they believed in were the ones that spoke about saving the lost, and making disciples of all nations and so on. And so I would constantly try and convert every member of my family. Every Christmas I would give them a Bible! In the end, though, I think my church was more of a kind of a cult. And it could be very frustrating; for instance, I believed dad was going to hell.

In fact, everybody was going to hell: Catholics, Protestants, everybody outside of my church. We used to have discussions about whether Mahatma Gandhi would make it, and you know, maybe he would just scrape in. Whereas now, I'm not sure, I don't know what God wants. I want everyone to go to heaven, I've always wanted that, but I felt like God was telling me that this wasn't the situation; and that God understood why people had to go to hell and that he was righteous and so on. And my church had all sorts of arguments to justify those positions, and I would adopt those. But now I believe that God loves my dad.

You have both spoken about how religion has either been helpful or unhelpful to you, and you both seem to agree that in general terms it can be both helpful and unhelpful for people depending on the situation. But, presumably Lewis, you would agree that it is a statement of fact that God does not exist?

LW: Yes.

And you, Matthew, would agree that it is a statement of fact that God does exist?

MW: I believe that he exists. But I can't prove it either way. I can only go on what I believe in my experience.

LW: My position is that there is no evidence for God.

MW: But I would say that my dad does have a belief. He believes in science which goes beyond the rational, because he believes that ultimately science can explain everything.

LW: Well, I've always said that there's a little bit it wouldn't explain.

MW: You take circumstantial evidence as predicting what is going to happen in the future, and so I would say that science, to a degree, is your religion.

Lewis, what, if any, are the unexamined assumptions or presuppositions on which the scientific method rests?

LW: None.

Doesn't it rest on the assumption that there is no God?

LW: No, certainly not. You don't make that assumption whatsoever. You just look for evidence and internal consistency; either you can explain things or you can't.

So how do you deal with things you can't explain?

LW: Well, I suppose we are not doing very well with consciousness at the moment, but you just have to be patient. Maybe we will understand it eventually, maybe we won't, but you don't need God to do that. Some things are very complicated. I mean, did you ever see a fly make a mistake landing on the edge of a teacup? No. And look how small that brain is! So our brains are very complicated. The thing is, we're investigating it, but whether we will get there or not I have no idea. We just have to be patient.

Do you have a view on spirituality?

LW: Well, I think Matthew's spiritual. Aren't you?

MW: Well, I wouldn't use the word mainly because it has kind of New-Agey associations with it. In the past, when I was in the church, if people used the word spiritual, I always thought it was a bit of a cop out.

LW: A friend of mine who is a painter claims to have seen ghosts three times. She's a highly intelligent woman and she claims to have seen ghosts, and I am sure that in her experience they were very real, but that doesn't mean to say there are ghosts. A lot of people have very strange experiences; though *I* don't on the whole.

Hypothetically, if you had an experience like that, how would you respond?

LW: Well, I'd think I was going slightly mad. Something has gone wrong with my brain. Of course, if you do surveys, you will find that quite a significant percentage of the public have had experiences that they can't account for. There was one time when I was thinking about a friend of mine in America, and the next day he phoned me, yet I hadn't spoken to him for six months. And so we worked out that it took one day for the message to get across the ocean! No, but seriously, these things don't perturb me one bit.

Do you think it is possible to rationally argue someone round to not believing in God?

LW: Oh, you can't persuade people. You can't persuade people to change their views. Rupert Sheldrake, the scientist, believes in telepathy and things and I've had debates with him about this, but you'd never persuade him to change his mind. And it's rubbish! He hasn't got good evidence. It's all about evidence, reliable evidence. It's like homoeopathy; homoeopathy might work because of the placebo effect, but the idea that water has a memory is just nonsense.

Are you tolerant of your dad's view?
MW: Definitely more now than I was when I was in the church. Because there is less pressure now to convert him, because my views have changed.

Do you think that your dad would be better off if he came round to your way of thinking?
MW: I think ultimately everyone would benefit.

LW: Why would they benefit?

MW: From a relationship with God?

LW: Yes.

MW: Well look, I am speaking from my own belief here, and I do have doubts, but I think God is good, and it's like drinking water . . .

LW: Do you think he influences things all the time? Has he affected your life directly?

MW: Definitely sometimes. There are definitely some times when I can feel it. You could say he does it all the time, but I can definitely think back to certain moments of my life where I can absolutely feel that God was there. And so having a relationship with God meets a very fundamental need.

LW: I have argued that religion is probably in our genes. Spirituality, or believing that there is 'something more' is something that comes quite naturally to us. Why? Well consider the following: if you take LSD, you then have these extraordinary experiences. Well it can't be the molecule in the LSD that does that; there must be something in the brain which is there already, and which is just activated by the drug.

My argument is that we are basically primed to have these supernatural beliefs. Because I think, as Matthew rightly points out, that it makes people feel better. People who are religious are on the whole healthier and do better. There is no society that didn't have some sort of religious belief. It's in our brains.

So if it is hardwired into us, why don't you have religious beliefs?
LW: I didn't say it was hardwired. I think we can escape it. But the blunt answer is we don't know really how the brain works. The brain is just weird! I have dreams which are so extraordinary, but I am not doing anything consciously to create that.

Richard Dawkins would disagree with you about the nature of religion. He sees it as malign.

LW: Yes, I don't agree with that. I don't know why Richard is so militant about this; we've never really had a discussion on this particular issue. We certainly are both atheists, but I am not anti-religious. I'm certainly against the church interfering in other people's lives; I'm militant on that, particularly, as I said, on the belief that the egg is a human being and being against contraception and all that.

MW: When I used to read him, he would really wind me up, but I saw him the other day on his television programme *The Root of all Evil*. And when he went to Jerusalem to talk to that Muslim guy who just laid into him, for the first time I was on Richard Dawkins' side. I could relate to the Muslim guy as well, because I was a bit like that. But for the first time I felt a bit more sympathetic towards Richard Dawkins. When I used to read his books it felt like a constant attack on my faith. But I have changed my mind, I think, because from my point of view, I felt God had put me in that church and had said 'This is where I want you' but I felt like I had a kind of combative relationship with God and so I felt kind of forced into it. At the same time, because I loved God I was willing to trust him, but it was a real battle. So I was in this church for a very long time, then I left it and then came back, and then I started to see things in the church that I didn't agree with. And my trust in God began to grow, I started to be less scared of him and more trusting, and as I did that, I saw stuff in the church that I really didn't agree with, but at the same time I thought 'Well who am I?' I thought the leaders seemed more righteous and like they knew what they were doing. But after having these doubts and concerns, there was then a kind of mini-reformation – you know Martin Luther pinning that thing to the door – there was a kind of mini one of those in my church where a lot of stuff got exposed. And from my point of view, it was God showing me that the kind of Christianity that is very literal can just lead to things like vanity. I really think that if Jesus had come back and come into my church, then he would probably have ended up being kicked out.

How do you relate that to the fact that people believe in different gods?

MW: Well, when I was in the church, I very much believed that the Bible was the truth, that Jesus was the way, the truth and the light, and that other religions were basically false. Whereas now, basically, I am still very drawn to the Bible, and I have looked at other religions and to me the Bible still stands head and shoulders above the rest. The central conceit of God sending his son to earth, that he loves you so much he is willing to send his son to die for you, and whatever else you believe, just that central conceit is very powerful. The God of the Bible is very passionate; he doesn't just stand back but he gets very involved, and I am still very attracted to that.

John Gray would call that story a myth which perhaps answers a basic human need.

LW: I'm not a good enough anthropologist to really explain what is going on with these kinds of things. There's a lovely story which I put in my book. Pascal Boyer was at a dinner in Cambridge, and he was telling them about these people who he had studied in Africa who thought that they flew at night and the head of the college asked 'How could people believe such bizarre things?' And Pascal didn't have the courage to tell them that these people knew about the Christian religion, and were very puzzled to know why eating a bit of fruit in the garden could produce such a disaster!

What about the question of miracles, such as the resurrection?

MW: I don't have a problem with believing in miracles, I mean if God exists and he created the universe then doing miracles is hardly a big deal. The first issue is whether God exists, and if he does then miracles are not really a big thing in that respect.

LW: I'd like some evidence for miracles. If you could turn the pond on Hampstead Heath into good wine, well that would impress me! But the evidence for miracles is few and far between. You know, if someone was dead, and God suddenly announced that he was going to resurrect them, well that would make everything perfectly clear. There would be no problem if God decided to show us some miracles according to his powers, but he just doesn't bother to do so. As David Hume said, unless the evidence for something is so strong that to not believe it would be ridiculous, then belief in such things is nonsensical.

MW: I am still very drawn towards the Bible, but I won't try and justify it really now. You know when dad says things about miracles or whatever; I'm not so concerned about justifying it because I think that's God's battle. But also, I think there are scientific arguments against science as it were. Like the fact that there is no way that DNA could have come about through evolution. That is my understanding anyway.

That's interesting, Anthony Flew the philosopher, who was an atheist, has now come out as a 'deist' for exactly that reason: he says that the emergence of DNA could not have come about through evolution.

LW: Well philosophers are clever, but they contribute zero to anything.

Because philosophy is not about the way the world works. They are not scientists, they are clever performers. Other than David Hume, no philosopher has contributed anything to our understanding of the world. Hume at least was about truth and he was against religion; well he wasn't against religion, but he said that it was not unreasonable to think that there could be a creator though he couldn't make any suppositions about the nature of that creator. But as for Anthony Flew, I mean, how boring can he be! What does he know about it?

MW: But even Richard Dawkins in his book would say that we don't know how DNA came about.

LW: Well yes, but there are models.

MW: Who was that bloke that said they came by aliens? Was it Francis Crick?

LW: Yes, the idea that it came from outer space.

MW: Which shows how desperate scientists are.

LW: The origin of life is quite tricky, there's no question about that. There are a lot of people working on it; it's very interesting. Before DNA and RNA what was there? Now I'm not a good chemist, though it will be resolved.

Do you have a view on the anthropic principle? Could you explain it?

LW: Yes, well it's the idea that all the constants in the universe seem specially organized for life to occur; though I am out of my depth with theoretical physics. Biology is interesting, it's amazing, but there is no reason to believe that there is any designer. It drives me mad all that 'intelligent design'; though it's true that there are some very big problems.

So you're saying there is no reason to believe in an intelligent designer, and so would you also say that there is not an intelligent designer? Do those two statements logically follow?

LW: Well there's no evidence for an intelligent designer.

So would you say there therefore isn't one?

LW: Well, look, there's no evidence for fairies, so I on the whole would say there is no such thing as fairies, no. Unless there's evidence for something, it doesn't exist. It would be such an extraordinary thing to have an intelligent designer. I mean, here you've got this God, you don't know where God comes from, he has all these powers, though he hasn't done any miracles lately; I mean: what's he doing?

MW: If you found, every morning, at the bottom of your garden, little fairy dresses, but no evidence of anything else, what would you think?

LW: Well that would be a beginning!

Do you have a moral or ethical stance? A way that you live your life or would prefer that other people live their lives?

LW: I don't think I think like that. I just take each case as it comes. Just don't interfere with other people, leave other people alone and just don't interfere if they're not interfering with anything else. But I'm not very moralistic on that. I think on the whole that people should be allowed to do what they like, as long as they not interfering with anyone else. So when it comes to the ethical things in relation to biology I'm very permissive; though you have to think about the child, particularly with genetics and so forth.

In terms of outlook, Matthew, it seems that your father's view allows you yours, but your view, at least at one point in your life, would not have allowed his.

MW: Well, I would have allowed it. From my point of view, I would never have forced anyone. I mean I was a bit confused about things like abortion and sex change operations and so on. Though probably if my leaders had come out strongly on something I might have followed them, but I was never really sure about telling other people what to do. So I never forced it on anybody else. But I would have believed it would have been better for the whole world to be Christian. Whereas now I pretty much agree with my dad that we should just live and let live. But I do also think that people love Jesus, whether they know it or not. So people who love truth or, for instance, Mahatma Gandhi is probably a better example of a Christian than any Christians I have actually met. At least he actually practised non-violence and I don't really know of many Christians outside of the famous ones that have actually practised non-violence. There was this Muslim guy who we were trying to convert in Jerusalem (I was at a church in Jerusalem for a year as I was doing a degree in Hebrew); he used to look after mentally and physically disabled children in a home in Palestine and he had very little money. And one of the rich Christians from my church offered to adopt him and take him back to America. But he said 'How could I leave these kids?' and looking back on it that certainly seems more Christian than what the rich Christian was doing. There was a lot of hypocrisy in our church.

Though presumably the Muslim would answer that by saying: 'No I'm not more of a Christian, I am a Muslim, and if you respect my lifestyle then perhaps you should convert to Islam'?

MW: I do see what you mean, but when I look at Muhammad by comparison to Jesus, well I see Muhammad as a warrior, which I don't like.

LW: I'm very against the Muslim's suppression of women, this idea that they have to cover themselves and so forth; it's really terrible.

MW: I think there are atheists who love God, and there's lots of Christians who ruin it. There was a gay march, and there were lots of Christians shouting; 'You faggot! You're killing Christ!' And the homosexuals were walking along the street just being joyful, and so if God looked at this scene, whose side would he really be on?

You spoke earlier of God being a God of love. What do you make of something like the 2004 Tsunami, a natural disaster where God does not intervene?

MW: The bottom line is I don't know. It's like the end of the book of Job; there is the simple issue of how can you possibly believe in the face of all this suffering.

LW: I have heard a religious person say that it is the earth relieving itself.

MW: I don't know how to respond to that. I suppose the argument can only be that God can see the big picture and we only see a little part. Though people do often scoff at that and I can see why. But I believe that God has been fair to me, so I can only really deal with that. I can only assume that God has been fair to everybody else in some way, because why would God be fair to me and not to everybody else?

LW: But when one's converted to believing in God there are suddenly no constraints on what God can do and what he believes in, so you can have anything you like.

MW: In terms of what he can do?

LW: Yes, there are no constraints and that's wonderful in terms of your beliefs.

MW: Well there are some constraints, if he's evil . . .

LW: So long as he's not evil he can do anything.

MW: Well that's what the Bible says about him. It says nothing is impossible for God.

Lewis, when you listen to Matthew speak like this, do you have no opinions or value judgements?

LW: I'm absolutely against organized religion interfering in people's lives. Take stem cells for example: the idea that the early embryos are human beings comes from religion, and it's just nonsense. I don't care what other people believe; as long as it doesn't interfere.

In your everyday life, does your faith, Matthew, and your lack of it, Lewis, does it affect your relationship?

LW: Not dramatically.

MW: We used to talk about it a lot more, we used to have lots of discussions about it, but I feel now that we've pretty much covered all the territory. We've been over and over it so we don't really need to talk about it now.

5

Don Cupitt

Do you have a working definition of the term religion?

Yes. I've tried to prove that in recent religion there's been a massive switch towards 'life', which we now speak of in the same way we used to speak of God. I've done three books about the word 'life' in modern speech. I've been trying to prove that since about the time of Wordsworth, and especially since the Second World War, people have come to speak of life, and their own immediate engagement with life, in religious terms. So religion is our attempt to come to terms with the fundamental limits of life. Which are three: temporality, contingency and finitude. Or in popular language: time, chance and death. These limits of life are all around us all the time and we can't even begin to feel that we might think them away. *We can't think away time, we can't think away contingency, and we can't think away finitude, death.*

So in my view, religion is our attempt, in symbolic language, to strike a bargain with life, to make it possible to live, and to make life bearable despite its radical uncertainty and contingency. It is our attempt to deal with the fact that we may die at any time and so we don't know how to make long-term plans, the fact that everything happens only once and there's no retakes, and the fact that any project we undertake is vulnerable and so we can never get complete control of our own lives. So I now see religion in much more humanistic terms. In Britain we've moved over from an absolute monarchy to democracy. The queer thing is that in America, though Americans have grasped the importance of democracy in politics, they haven't understood it in religion. In religion they still think the cosmos is an absolute monarchy, with an absolute monarch who rules everything and allows you no right of appeal or reply or anything, and they think that's normal. It's very hard to persuade people to democratize their religious thought so that God is dispersed into people, and comes down into religious language.

And what I found in 1998 when I did this basic work on the word 'life', was that I didn't know what my own religious beliefs were. But I found that the language in which I talked about life was much more effective and vivid than the language in which I talked about God. In more general terms, in present-day English I find only 30 or so vivid and interesting God-idioms still surviving at all in popular speech. Whereas there are over 250 life-idioms, and the life-idioms are much more powerful than the God-idioms.

Could you give some examples?

'He took all that life could throw at him and endured'; 'a sin against life'; 'trust in life'; 'committed to life'; 'what life says'; 'what life teaches us'; 'the university of life'. These astounding expressions show that modern people, since about the 1850s – you first see it coming out in impressionist paintings – began to think that just ordinary life is itself a religion. The beginning of this, historically, is in the fifteenth century and in the Reformation, when religion comes out of the monastery and into the home. Instead of 'the religious life' being the life of monks and nuns, the religious life becomes about ordinary people living in the world. One of my favourite early examples of this is in the church at Lowick, Northamptonshire, not far from Cambridge, where a couple called the Greenes in 1420 signed a contract with the carvers for their tomb images to be put in the local church. And they specified that they must hold hands; in fact you can go to see this now, and they're both wide awake! So here is a secular, anti-Christian affirmation that marriage itself has a kind of eternity in it. They're lying on their tomb, wide awake, holding hands. Whereas, of course, technically in Christian thought, you're supposed to be separate. Marriage has been ended at death, and husband and wife go separately to judgement. They're no longer married. This is the beginning of a lay protest in favour of this world, and in favour of humanism, developing within Christianity itself. There are about three such tombs in England. And it's already happening under Luther, its beginning to happen in sixteenth-century Dutch painting with the work of Pieter Bruegel, it's very conspicuous in the letters of van Gogh. And even in Tolstoy's *War and Peace*, the character Pierre says 'God is life, and to love life is to love God'. So the real completion of Christianity arrives when you no longer need the Church. And instead, you have the courage to engage directly with life. It takes faith to believe that you can live. To have the courage to accept contingent life; contingent being is all there is.

Is this a religion without God?

Yes, of course. Since about 1980 I've argued that the metaphysical side of God is not tenable any longer. 'God' is best understood as Kant understood it: as a spiritual ideal. So to say that God's heart beats is to say that love is God. In chapter four of the First Epistle of St John, there is the famous discussion where it's said that God is love. In the New Testament it's said explicitly that loving God and loving your neighbour are one and the same thing. Love itself goes beyond all; it has a slightly transcendent quality about it. The Victorian world is full of it. Love with a capital 'L' is all over the hymn books. People have never noticed that this demythologized, non-realist notion of God has been part of Christianity for some centuries now. But when I made it explicit, it finished my career. It's there in the books, and people couldn't see it. They were singing it on Sundays in church, but failed to see what the language implied.

That finished your career in the Church as a minister?

Oh, of course. Nobody would come out explicitly in support of me. What I was saying was that the whole supernatural world is over, there is only this world. You must no longer believe in a hidden spiritual world; you must no longer think that your real life is second to a spiritual life inside you, as it were. You must be 100 per cent committed to contingency and to this life, even though in another 10 or 20 years' time you'll be extinct. You have to face the fact that you're hurtling into extinction at top speed, and there's nothing you can do about it. All life is radically uncertain, and there is no guarantee you'll complete any project you undertake. But that's how you've got to live, and that's the religious life. You've got to make it the *religious* life.

And this is the final state of the development of Christianity. Church Christianity is dead, it's finished. It stopped in the French revolution, when the *ancien régime* came to an end. Once you get liberal democracy, you are democratizing this-worldly religion that accepts contingency. The point about democracy is that it's politics without any grand finale. There is no conclusion. Democracy is piecemeal adjustment for ever. And that's what religion will be from now on, just piecemeal adjustment to life. Just a way of making life worth living.

Do you see this as an inevitable process in other parts of the world, the Middle East and the wider Islamic world?

Of course, yes; when the Islamic world finally accepts things like feminism, which will prevail in the end. You know damn well you can't defeat feminism, it will win. And although American weapons are terrible,

American culture is far more powerful. American cinema and television are far more important and interesting than American warplanes and tanks. And they're going to prevail. What persuaded me of this irreversibly though was visiting modern China and seeing how enthusiastically they're absorbing Western culture and forgetting the past. But, you see, it broadly happens in the Arab world too, when the ordinary people get a chance. They don't want the Mullahs to be sitting on them for ever; they want freedom. All over the world people are turning from God to life. I often use the example of how, when a young person dies tragically nowadays, everybody pays tribute by saying: 'She loved life'. 'She was full of life', that kind of thing. Nobody says she loved God. When did you last hear a recently dead person praised by saying they loved God? You don't. 'They loved life', that's what is said. When a Baptist deacon was killed on the 7th of July last year, in London, his friends, and his ultra-fundamentalist Baptist church, said they were going to arrange a celebration of his life. And that was what they said for the media. There was no Christian language, just the new language of life. Funeral and memorial services are celebrations of life.

Do you think the occurrence of fundamentalism is an inherent by-product of democracy?

Well, I don't know. I would argue that Roman Catholicism and fundamentalism have also moved over to life-centred outlooks. Osama Bin Laden is dead right when he says: 'The West loves life, I love death.' His kind of religion is oriented towards death, but I think *we're* now irreversibly committed to life.

So you think that his kind of religion is doomed?

Oh yes! What I describe as a religion of life is post-Christianity, but it's still Christianity. It's the kingdom of God, to which Christianity looked forward. And you can read my stuff as post-ecclesiastical kingdom Christianity if you want or simply as a decentred, globalized, religious humanism. I don't mind, I don't care about the labels. We don't know enough about the historical Jesus to make him any longer the centre of a religion. And in any case, I want to destroy all national and religious identities of the type we've already seen. I want an end to traditional identity; I want people to be free of that sort of burden of the past. If you're a Jew or an Arab, you know what it is to carry a huge chip on your shoulder all your life. Forget identity, it's a waste of time. I don't just mean Christianity; I want to attack the whole notion of defending some sort of local religious or ethnic identity. It seems clear to me that you're at odds with it all your life. I personally welcome globalization and postmodernism; I like the fact that I have to be translated when my books are published, even in America! The English language is decentred, English identity is decentred. There's no such thing as English national culture any longer. That's why the little red flags that fly in the World Cup are so silly really. England is decentred and I like it. I don't want a traditional identity any more.

We're going that way, because I think biology – the future of life – is increasingly taking over as the most important science. In the early twentieth century it was physics. I think in the twenty-first century it's biology. This is because the environmental crisis and so on makes us aware that the very survival of life on earth is under threat. And, of course, we also belong now to a single world-conversation. From about 1980, the ring of satellites around the world was complete and human beings began to take part in a single conversation.

Amazingly, my books about the English life-idioms have gone into Chinese and they're very popular because new idioms in one language spread straight to another. So I would argue that there is now a single world-conversation of humanity, with only rather small fanatical groups outside. This issue with fundamentalism is over what philosophers call 'foundationalism'. From Descartes onwards, it's been widely believed that you can only overcome scepticism and nihilism by positing some secure foundations for thought, some dogmatic starting points for thought. Descartes found it in the *Cogito*, religious fundamentalism finds it in religious authority. But that simply makes you a servant – somebody else's servant – and I want a free religion. I insist that faith is doing without any fundamentals or certainties. The classic example of this kind of faith is the four-year-old child learning to ride a two-wheeled bike, or learning to swim. You have the courage to go out on your own, and somehow, you stay up, you stay afloat – you can do without that parental hand. That's what faith is now: the ability to bear the foundationlessness, the constant shifts and uncertainties of modern life. For me, that means that, whereas in the past, the true religious believer was like a soldier, fitting into a preexistent framework of rules and authority, now, the believer should be like an artist. We should be happy to start with a blank canvas, just a chaos of experience, out of which we've got to make our own lives as something like works of art.

So, my notion of religion wants to leave behind all the existing world religions and look for a purely affirmative religion of life. I'm very insistent in ethics now that I cut out all the penal stuff, all the negative side. I'm looking for a form of ethics which concentrates simply on revaluing life. And it has to be purely affirmative without any condemning or censuring. So I want to forget the whole traditional notion of religion as a means of social control and a structure of authority. I want to get rid of that. I want to make the most radically free form of religion there's ever been.

Bishop Richard Harries has, in the past, criticized you and the Sea of Faith movement for embodying little more than a kind of shame-faced atheism. How would you distinguish your views from straightforward atheism?

Well, the bishop is not a free man, and you can't be a bishop and tell the truth. You can't be a bishop and say what you really think! You can see this with Rowan Williams. He knows damn well that the evangelicals are talking nonsense, and that all this anti-gay hysteria is unchristian. But he somehow can't convey a liberal position while being a bishop. Because he thinks his juridical role inhibits his freedom of speech. The same is true of the present Pope. The institutions are spiritually destructive to the people who serve them. That's why I think church Christianity is over. You can't be completely honest as a bishop. You have to make a clear distinction between what you really think, and what you have to say institutionally. As for Richard Harries, well he's talking institutionally. They don't make you a bishop unless they're sure you're a safe pair of hands, i.e. that you'll never say anything interesting.

The Shia tradition of Islam, for instance, could be seen as radically anti-authoritarian – given the idea of the occultation of the twelfth Imam means that there can be no absolute authority. The rise of Khomeini and the other Ayatollahs is a bizarre paradox in that sense. Would you say that Islam actually has a theoretical basis, which gives it the potential for resisting these kinds of institutional problems that you see in the Christian Church?

Yes, well it is a lay religion of course, and in some respects it's more modern than Christianity. In its early centuries it looked as if it was ahead of Christianity spiritually and intellectually. But now, I'd say not, because it hasn't managed to internalize God. The very posture for prayer, and the fact that it's a male religion, shows that it's objectifying God. What unites believers is not their shared freedom, but their common subjugation; a subjugation to all types of authority. A religion in which we all prostrate ourselves before authority, where it is believed that this is what makes us strong, is, to me, abominable. The psychological structure of the religion is a male and military one. I think we need to feminize religion, not ultra-masculinize it.

There are strands in Islamic thought I admire very much, even to this day. Look at the films of Abbas Kiarostami. He can make films which show you how beautiful peasant life in a Muslim village can be. His work has a kind of beauty and dignity about it. But at a popular level, Islam cannot cope with modernity, because it cannot cope with the critical thinking that has given us modern science and modern historical thinking. Islam doesn't understand historical change. It doesn't understand the way in which truth is kept alive by being continuously reinterpreted. It's the 'theatre director' problem – you know? To keep a text alive you have to continuously make new things out of it. Whereas Islam tries to take the fundamentalist view that the Qur'an is the absolute language of God, and that God himself thinks in Arabic. But that's a crazy view of language.

All the scriptural religions have this problem, I think. In Christianity, people wanted to make a radical distinction between 'sacred letters' and 'human letters', to use the Oxford language. But you can't make such a distinction because it's quite wrong. I can only say that there's one lot of letters; human and sacred all together. You can't say that in the world of sacred letters, the language of God, all meaning is eternally fixed and nothing is ever changed; whereas here, in the world of human letters, the meanings of words are constantly shifting. On the contrary, religious texts are as open to reinterpretation as any other texts that survive over time. So fundamentalism rests on illusions, basically, about language, and about historical change. Oddly enough it's not science that's the most fundamental threat to religion; it's the modern understanding of history and language. People miss the point about science really. Perhaps Darwinism is the scientific theory that comes closest to seeing how meanings change over time because the genetic code itself is a kind of text which evolves and shifts over time. Indeed, the belief in the fixity of species against which Darwin struggled is very like the belief in the fixity of linguistic meaning in fundamentalism. There are some very interesting parallels there.

What do you understand by the numinous?

The numinous? Well, there can be mysterious depths in art, but art is purely human. There can be mysterious depths in holiness and religion but these are also purely human. So I don't accept that there is a *sui generis* concept of the sacred which distinguishes religion absolutely. This point was made long ago by William James. There is no distinctive religious emotion. For me, the sublime in nature is largely the place for traditional religious awe as it was in Wordsworth. Nowadays I read a lot of Wordsworth, and in some ways, Wordsworth in his best years was very close to us – during the 1790s, early 1800s. His sense of the life of the body and the emotions and feelings and his response to nature was much like ours.

Do you have a theory as to why *The Da Vinci Code* has been such a success?

It's because, although critical thinking is fundamental to the West and we all depend on it everyday, most people hate it. Most people, like Prince Charles, will reluctantly admit that there is such a thing as conventional, orthodox, horrible medicine, but what they really like is superstitious, wish-fulfilment, fantasy medicine. We have forgotten how things work. In the nineteenth century you could look at a thing like the steam engine and more or less see how it worked and feel how it worked. Nowadays people just carry on their wrists things that they don't understand at all, like a quartz watch. They haven't a clue how it works, and they're not even *curious* about how it works. Everything is made as user friendly as possible so they don't have to think. Whereas the eighteenth-century gentleman knew about the connection between barometric pressure and future weather; nowadays the BBC leaves the isobars off the weather forecast because it's too intellectually demanding for people to know that there's such a thing as air pressure any longer. Dumbing down has gone to amazing lengths and many people now have little capacity for critical thinking and no awareness of scientific theory and so on. Perhaps it now depends on just a few hundred, or a few thousand people to keep up the standards, to struggle to maintain the line between science and non-science, between critical thinking and pre-critical thinking. But in the case of *The Da Vinci Code*, people obviously have no idea of historical evidence. They've never looked at the New Testament with the eye of a critical historian. Even though they sort of feel that a new drug ought to be tested before it's prescribed for people, or a new plane ought to be tested rigorously before people fly in it, they won't test *ideas*. They've no idea how you check statements about the Virgin Mary or something. So people read *The Da Vinci Code* and think: 'Gosh, there might be something in it!' They believe they've somehow been taught new information. But if people actually compared what's in the Gospels, or looked up the most elementary aspects of Christian theology, they would know that Mary herself was a composite figure made up of Mary Magdalene, out of whom Jesus had cast demons and who was supposedly witness to the resurrection, and a different character, the woman that was a sinner who anointed Jesus' feet and wiped them with her hair. It was this that started a long historical process of gradually eroticizing the relationship of Jesus and Mary. You can see it in Titian's painting *Noli Me Tangere*, as Jesus recoils gracefully from the beautiful Mary. So Dan Brown is sitting in that long tradition of creating a fictional Mary as a sort of erotic subtext to the Gospels. But people have forgotten all the lower criticism stuff about the manuscripts and the Gospels and how you compare the Gospels and so on. If you look at a children's nativity play you'll see that people are still working in a medieval way, adding together all four Gospels without any critical assessment. So they add together the nativity stories of Matthew and Luke and just assume that a composite narrative made of both is true. Well that's the way of medieval thought. But you don't expect a modern law court or a modern journalist to operate like that.

You have written about there being a difference between what people think they believe and what they actually believe.

Yes. I argue that it's often been said that our language is wiser than we are. The popular idioms of ordinary speech give you access to a more serious level of thinking than what people say. On the surface, people will profess allegiance to hundreds of different religions, but deep down, in ordinary language, there's a surprising consensus about what I call this religion of life. Some say that all the major world religions can be found in Britain, some of them with hundreds of different sects, and that there are something like 1,500 new religious movements. So if you put them all together you'd be able to find about 2,000 distinct religious movements. I'd say: 'Yes, but actually our common idiomatic English contains a common philosophy which is surprisingly strongly marked. And there is a sense in which that's a more profound and interesting guide to what people really think, because the idioms in ordinary language spread in a kind of Darwinian way. For example the quote 'Get a life', which originated it seems in America in the late 1980s. The earliest reference to it I've found is American, in 1989. And that spread all around the world very quickly. Why? Because it expressed a new sense that we ought to have a better quality of life. We've got to live more intensely and so we ought to 'get a life'; it's a terrific phrase. But the use of that phrase indicates common public feelings, ideas that people share. Well, they might be the best clue to what we all really believe.

Do you have a view on spirituality?

Yes. Well, that's a complicated story. I define spirituality as a personal religious style, and I'm in favour of that. But if spirituality means there's some kind of second ghost world alongside this world, then I violently oppose it. So I'm happy with spirituality in the sense of a personal religious style. Nowadays, we all have to make our own religion out of ourselves as we struggle with the great questions of life. Struggle to come to terms with the way life slips away. We have to deal with the incompleteness of our ability to ever understand anything. But there's no creed in my religion, although there's a common religious agenda that we all have to face. But we'll solve it in different ways, and we'll develop our own take on the great questions, our own view of them, our own response to them, and our own spiritual style. I would argue for that instead of religious law and a standard Christian ethics. I want a very plural religious scene in which different people make different kinds of contributions. This is what St Paul always envisaged. So there isn't in my view a standard right or wrong for the whole human race. Rather, everyone should find what they're good at and find their own take on life. People should be eclectic in their working out of a religious outlook. I've suggested new religious practices that people could try, like looking at clouds, watching time pass, meditating with your eyes open, or engaging in art and music. I have suggested new forms of meditation and prayer and so on. But I've never said yes to anything standard. Nothing's compulsory in my religion; it's up to you to discover your own take and to cope in your own way with the thought of your own death.

How does you religion fit with our secular capitalist society?

Well, our society is still, surprisingly, a Christian society. And one of the advantages of capitalism is that it innovates and changes constantly. It does it in a way that makes us constantly aware of the motion of life; its aimless restlessness; its ceaseless discontent. Capitalism has to keep us continually wanting more, dissatisfied and open to change. I don't want a stagnating traditional society like in ancient Egypt in which nothing changes, as it were. I want us to accept a fluid world, rather than have a constant religious nostalgia for a changeless and static world.

I've just written a book called *Impossible Loves*. It takes up a theme from Derrida that love is impossible because we always want a more complete knowledge of the other and a more perfect possession and security than life will ever allow us. Love always demands more than you can have. But in a sense, that's a good thing; that's part of religion itself and part of capitalism. We're always hungry for more, hungry for life itself; we're never satisfied. So I accept a certain amount of bitter-sweetness and discontent. This idea appears in Wim Wenders' film *Wings of Desire*, where the chap has a choice between being a sexless angel in eternal bliss for ever, or being a mortal human being who lives only once, but is able to know human sex and love and the bitter-sweet transience of life, and he chooses to be human. That's correct, I believe in that; that's my religion.

6

Muhammad Yusaf Al Hussaini

Do you have a working definition of the term religion?
Well, in Arabic, the words that are used for faith and religion are closely interlinked. And the word for religion is *din* and it is the same word used in Hebrew and so the religious courts in the Jewish community are the *beth din* or 'the houses of religion'. And in Islam *din* encapsulates quite a holistic way of life. I know that the other great religions talk in terms of a holistic way of life representing the inner and the outer and so on, and this is very much the Islamic position, but there is a great deal of emphasis within the Judeo-Islamic tradition on *din* as an expression of day-to-day ordinary living. So if you were to take it back to its Latin root *'religio'*, something that is binding, then certainly *din* overlaps with that. It is the concept of a working way of life in communion with God that is lived and springs out from the heart of faith. Now faith is something that is related to religion. And faith in Islam is called *iman* and there have been various notions of what faith is down the ages. Now, one of our greatest scholars, Al-Ghazali, was pretty much Islam's Augustine and Thomas Aquinas rolled into one. And his definition of faith was a light that is cast into the soul of the believer, almost undeservedly and by God's agency alone, like the Christian idea of grace that is transformative. And so that transformative act results in the believer becoming a different kind of creature, and that new creature needs to find a new way of expressing their new relationship with God. And the language, if you like, through which that expression is given is *din*, which is religion. Namely, life lived entirely for the sake of God such that every act of every day is a work of worship. So it is a holistic representation of the relationship between God and man expressed in day-to-day living.

Can you define God, as Islam sees it?

The Islamic contribution would be to define God first of all as being a personal God, and being the one and the same God that has been known to the prophets of Israel. The Qur'an explicitly defines the Islamic God as being one and the same person as the God of the Jewish people. And He is a person with a personality and a personhood like you and I, and that person is the same person as the God known to Abraham to Jesus to Isaac and to Ishmael, to all the prophets. And the Islamic definition of prophets extends outside of the Israelite genealogy. Some Islamic traditions talk of 12 times 12,000 prophets, and other traditions talk about 240,000 prophets. So there is a universal concept of a God that is being made known to man, and this person has very specific characteristics of omnipotence, omniscience; personal characteristics such as you and I have; but whereas by our very nature as creatures we are contingent and dependent and finite, this person is infinite. And that is where differences of understanding, or perhaps misunderstandings, can arise. This notion of God as a personal God is a really important thing to bring forth because it is not very evident from the perception you get of Islam at the present time. But the Islamic concept of God is very, very strictly that of a single, indivisible and uniate person, and in that respect we are 100 per cent in agreement with our Jewish sisters and brothers. I think there would be some differences of understanding with regard to the Christian understanding of God as a community of three persons in dynamic trinity. We would see God very distinctly as being uniate.

In Islam, is God the creator?

Yes. He is the origin of all things. Look at it in terms of the ontological argument for God's existence, which is basically an argument based on contingency. This says there has to have been a prime, greater thing which is greater than all the greatest things we can know about or don't know about who caused all these things to come into being. And so by definition God must exist according to the ontological argument, though of course your philosophers will take issue with that. One particular Islamic contribution that has been made to the four arguments for God relates to the teleological argument. And this arises very much from the heart of the Qur'an, because in the Qur'an the word *ayah*, which means the verses or statements of the Qur'an, also means sign, miracle, indication. And signs arise out of creation as much as out of scripture. So there is an absolutely seamless continuity between the majesty of creation and the majesty of God's revelation in word. So, for Muslims, there is a repeated Qur'anic injunction or refrain which says: 'These signs are evident to people who have understanding' or variously 'to people who contemplate'. So we are commended to contemplate the majesty of creation and from that to have some kind of sense of how this complexity, this beauty, this tremendous vivid diversity of creation can only have come into being by the agency of some agent that contains all these dimensions of infinitude, complexity and diversity within him. And that really cuts to the heart of how Muslims understand God as being not only a uniate person but also an omnipotent person. A person that has certain overlapping characteristics with us, but who at the same time is way, way, way outside the bounds by which we are constrained as human beings. And so whereas our Christian brothers and sisters might well talk about God in terms of being an indwelling spirit, that perhaps is slightly foreign to orthodox mainstream Sunni teaching; though such a notion of God indwelling as *wahdat al-wujud* (unity of person between the creator and creature) is probably expressed more within the Sufi mystic tradition within Islam, which certainly talks about the notion of communion between the essence of the human self and the essence of the divine self. But certainly within the orthodox Sunni tradition, God's unknowability is one of his characteristics.

Scientists like Lewis Wolpert identify a problem in relation to the idea of God: the lack of persuasive evidence for his existence.

Well, on the one hand Islam is a reasonable religion – i.e. one that is open to reason. And while we recognize the ultimate unknowability, as finite creatures, of the infinite in God's person, we do also recognize that, as Ibn Rushd Averroes says: while the canons of true faith are not built upon human reasons, they cannot be opposed to reason. And that is a position that the Islamic rationalists maintained and which was supported by the Jewish rationalists like Maimonides and his disciples. So I fully believe that religion cannot be unreasonable and irrational and stupid. On the other hand, we talk about *fides quaerens intellectum*: faith seeking understanding. And I am persuaded by Augustine's view on the mystery of the Trinity. He says in the opening passage of *De Trinitate* that he wrote the book in response to those that have a perverse and excessive love of reason rather than depending upon the grace of faith. I think that by its very nature, science has its limitations – you know, you get into string theory and you're lost. We can do Hooke's Law, we can do the gas equations, we can start to look at theoretical physics and talk about quarks and quantum mechanics. But when you get into higher mathematical string theory you are just starting to get lost. And scientists who hold to the canons of higher physics are making up three-letter acronyms all the time for little macro-molecular interactions that you can't really prove. And yet we find these things to be reasonable and useful. And so, for a person of faith, for whom

God is a person that is ultimately unknowable in his entirety in much the same way as my wife will be ultimately unknowable in her entirety, the idea that religion must somehow be subject to a higher level of evidence than that which we would apply to our understanding of higher mathematics and theories surrounding the Big Bang and so on just doesn't seem entirely fair. And it also undermines, in a really clear and basic way, one of the essential things that protect religion from fundamentalism, and that is a sense of our own humility and our own sense that ultimately we cannot approximate to the divine. I believe the Qur'an, for example, just as a believing Christian will believe the Bible to have a sense in which it is the word of God. I do not believe that my human approximation, my understanding of that divine, is in any way complete or perfect. Whereas a Muslim Wahhabi in Medina with his highly anthropomorphic understanding of God, or a literalist in St Helen's, Bishopsgate, or a fundamentalist church in the Midwest would say they do have that perfect understanding. I think that is almost idolatrous. What is really striking is that you talk to them and they will say 'Oh no, obviously you can't know everything, but we're still right.' So what we really have is a case where secularists are trying to force us into a position where we have to identify with fundamentalists, whereas the essence of true faith is to recognize our humility and our limitations in relation to the divine.

Would you talk a little about the Qur'an?

Certainly. First of all, Islam teaches that the idea of revelation is intimately bound up with the concept of prophethood. So as I have said, God in Islam is a good God, a righteous God and not a God that punishes undeservedly; and so one of the key moral principles that underpins Islamic thinking is the idea that God's revelation is superabundant. We've talked about the superabundance of God's signs in creation and in his revelation, and there is a superabundance of prophetic revelation: thousands of prophets of all races, of every community. According to the Qur'an every community has been sent its messengers. And alongside the messengers, in many cases, have come those who are not just *naby*, i.e. prophets, but the subcategory of *rusul* – messengers who have come with a scripture. And among the scriptures that are referred to in the Qur'an there are the *suhuf* – the scrolls given to the prophet Abraham; then there is the *Torah* which is the law of Moses, and there is the *injil* which some would say is a corruption of *evangelion*, the Greek for gospel. Do you know about the 'red letter Bibles' where the very words of Jesus are marked out in red letters in contradistinction to the black of, say, Paul's epistles? Well Muslims would perhaps see some concept of a Gospel being Jesus' very words. So there is the *ingun* given to the prophet Jesus, and then there is the Qur'an, which is the revelation given by God through the agency of the prophet Muhammad. Just as we would see a seamless unity in prophethood, we would also see a seamless unity in the books of revelation. And in Islam one speaks of the *al-lawh al-mahfouz* – the inscribed tablet in heaven, from which all these portions of revelation proceed. So in Islam the Qur'an is seen as being an element or part of God's wider eternal inscribed revelation. It is seen as being inextricably bound up with God's essence, it is God's very word. So whereas Muslims make a clear distinction between secondary revelation – namely the words of the prophet: we would see, for example, the Gospels of the evangelists as being secondary revelations. They are narratives about the works of Jesus and his teachings and so on by other people, by other apostles. But God's very word 'Thou shalt not kill' as described in the commandments of the Torah, or God's very word as set down in the Qur'an, is deemed to be primary revelation, and for us that is inextricably an attribute of divinity. And to this day, orthodox Islamic teaching regards the Qur'an as being the eternal and uncreated attribute of God; and so it is forbidden to desecrate the Qur'an for that reason, because it would be a desecration of God himself. A lot of Christians would say that there is a parallel with the Trinity here because they would say 'Well, Christians believe in God having attributes that are witnessed in three persons: the Father, Son and Holy Spirit. You Muslims see the word as being embodied in a book – the Qur'an – whereas we perceive the word becoming flesh in Jesus Christ.'

Part of the debate in medieval times between the *Mu'utazilites* and the Asharites over the question of the uncreated nature of the Qur'an was that it might imply there was some aspect of polytheism being introduced.

The *sifat* controversy. This controversy about the attributes of God was one that nearly split apart the Islamic *Ummah* in its early stages. And the effects of the outcome of that controversy are something we are feeling even today. The *Mu'utazilites*, the rationalists, they lost the argument. And their teachings in regard to the createdness or the uncreatedness of the Qur'an related to their emphasis on God's absolute and indivisible monotheism which meant that he couldn't have additional attributes that pluralize that uniate essence. And there were also arguments around the importance of free will versus the predestinarian thinking of orthodox Sunni Muslims. There were arguments around the introduction of Aristotelian philosophical thinking into the ways that we read the Qur'an. And because the *Mu'utazilites* lost, Islam lost that whole heritage of scholastic pluralism, and that whole tradition of scholastic enquiry. It was difficult, when I was doing my seminarian training for my Imamate, because theology to this day has been prohibited since the *Mu'utazilite* contro-versy. Because the *Mu'utazilites* advanced what was seen as a dangerously rationalist approach to the understanding of Islam. And with their loss the doors of interpretation or *ijtihad* were closed. And the effects of that are being felt in the global polity to this day.

You have been talking about Islam's contribution to an understanding of God, which seems to imply that there can be a very real dialogue between religions. There are clearly other Muslims who do not have the same degree of tolerance for other faiths. And in the Qur'an itself there seem to be conflicting messages about whether people of other faiths are to be respected, or whether they are infidels.

There are a number of really important issues there. First of all, in regard to the issue of how Islam saw itself at the time of the ministry of the Prophet himself in relation to the other recognized, valid people of scrip-ture: the Jews and the Christians. That is a really complex story from the point of view of Islamic history. And there are two strands that emerge from it. The first is the inclusive strand that talks about the gift of monotheism to the human tradition and experience. It brings the elimi-nation of multiple warring or rival tribal deities. You know, you read in the Old Testament of Baal of the Moabites or Moloch of the Ammonites and 'my god versus your god' mentality backing up tribal conflict and warfare and so on. The gift of monotheism is to eliminate these petty tribal conflicts and to institute the notion of the one God who is father to us all regardless of race or creed or gender or nation or any other personal characteristic. And yet that message which has been conveyed by prophets and through the scholars of the Talmud and the scholars of the Islamic tradition through the medieval period has been lost to a very great extent by the more modern and exclusivist tradition. And this latter exclusivist tradition is the one which talks about a supersession of the traditions that come before it by Islam, which abrogates the foregoing faiths of Judaism and Christianity. You know, Christianity claims to be in continuity with Judaism and reveres the ancient covenant with the people of Israel, but for similarly supersessionist-minded Christians, Christ was the final revela-tion and the final fulfilment of the expectations of the Jewish people and so these stiff-necked Jews who refuse to accept him are a problem. And likewise within Islam, during the time of the Prophet there is clear evi-dence that there was frustration amongst the early Muslims at the refusal of Jews, especially, not to acknowledge the credentials of the Prophet. And even during the time of the Prophet there is the classic case of the treat-ment of the Jewish tribes in the city of Medina. So when the Prophet emigrated from Mecca to Medina he established within Medina the first embryonic Islamic state, within which there was a pluralist *sahifa*, which Orientalists have called 'the constitution of Medina' and which established and guaranteed freedom of religion for the non-Muslim communities. And it was really a tribal covenant between the various tribes – both Muslim and non-Muslim – that allowed Jews to be ruled by their own law, to have their places of worship respected and so on. And there were other treaties signed such as the famous treaty signed with the Christians of *Najran* respecting their religious liberties, and there is the covenant that exists to this day with the monks of St Catherine's monastery in Sinai, which says that no cross shall ever be defiled, and that their rights and privileges shall be respected until the day of judgement. So it is all very inclusive, but at the same time, during that period, there were allegations of treachery by the Jewish tribes, who were said to be acting in cahoots with the Meccans and so on, so they attacked the Jewish tribes. Eight hundred men were beheaded, the women and children were sold into slavery and other Jewish tribes were exiled from the whole area. This taking place in the lifetime of the Prophet has led to a kind of Janus-faced approach towards people of scripture. On the one hand there is this concept that 'we believe in what was sent down to us and what was sent down to Abraham, Isaac, Ishmael and all the other tribes', and 'whosoever believes in God and behaves with righteousness then in the last days there shall be no fear upon them'. That seems to be a very powerful tradition on the one hand and yet on the other hand there seems to be a sense in which Islam is a supersession, a completion, a perfection, and therefore the previous communities are at best politely redundant and at worst actively dangerous. And that is the dichotomy that continues to this very day.

How current a dichotomy is that really, do you think? Is it a genuinely live issue affecting the spread of fundamentalist or extremist positions in Muslim communities today?

One of the things to consider is the identification of religion with a sense of tribal identity. In this increasingly globalized world there seem to be forces that are out of our control and that are impinging upon the familiar and the safe. And also there is a sense within the Muslim community of externalizing problems that we don't want to face. Now, when I lived and worked and studied in the Middle East you would see this all the time. People would say: 'The reason I can't make ends meet, the reason I can't send my son to the school I want to, the reason we live in such depressed circumstances isn't because of internal issues to do with our dictatorial government or economic problems or the fact that the state of Singapore produces more manufactured goods than the whole of the Middle East put together. Well they aren't intrinsic issues to do with us; they are to do with external issues like the crusader Zionist conspiracy.' And you see this right here in Britain as well. People say: 'The reason why there is Islamo-phobia, the reason that we have stuff daubed on the walls of our mosques, the reason that our women are name-called and harassed isn't because there have been instances on university campuses where Muslim students have actively threatened Jewish students or because there have been suicide bombs going off on the London tube and there is a genuine sense of fear within the wider community; it is just because they hate us. We have a truth that they are envious of and it is all part of God's plan because God put it into his scriptures that "my people will be oppressed and bullied".' And you take that and you transplant it into Dayton, Tennessee, you know, where you've got isolated fundamentalist evangelical commu-nities that feel their whole world cracking up under the oppression of liberal, homosexual, materialistic values, and then you can really see how communities need a sense of security and safety by growing inwards and clinging on to a feeling of certainty. And in the case of Islam, Muslims haven't taken ownership of our blood-spattered passages of scriptures in the same way as other faiths have done. So, for example, if you go to the book of Joshua, there is that famous passage when the Israelites cross the river Jordan into Jericho and Joshua and the armies of Israel put every living thing to the sword: men, women, children, cattle, sheep and donkeys. Now the Jewish rabbis have stated very clearly down the ages that this was a historical event at that time, these enemies no longer exist, they are not valid, and this passage should not be cited as behaviour to be emu-lated. Whereas for Muslims we are in a culture where the doors of *ijtihad* have been closed – speculative reason, theology, is not allowed. I mean, when I was at the seminary at Al-Azhar in Cairo, which is the bastion of Sunni orthodoxy, we used to sit in these great big lecture halls and the lecturer would read his lecture out, and every time he mentioned the *Mu'utazilites*, just as after a mention of the Prophet you would say 'Peace be upon him', he would say 'l'anahum Allah', 'God has cursed them'! So there is no sense of a critical approach to scripture. There is no context for passages like the famous sword verse which says 'Kill them after the pro-hibited months have passed' or the passage where Christians are referred to as being 'nearest in love to the believers' but where in the same verse, there is a reference to the Jews being 'the worst of enemies to the believ-ers'. And without an appreciation of Islamic scholarship, in this world where material is very freely available through print and the internet but without a notion of commentary behind it, then, as the Chief Rabbi Jonathan Sacks puts it, 'Scripture without tradition and commentary to provide a context for it, is like nuclear fuel without protection.' And what we find in the Muslim world today is a whole generation of people who have no access to Islamic scholarship and who have no access to orthodox Islamic scholarship let alone any medieval scholarship which could give them an access to a religion that is more diverse and heterogeneous and contradictory. You get instead, people picking up these verses out of context and using them out of context. This is bad enough in a Protestant fundamentalist tradition, but in an Islamic context it leads to bombs going off on the tube, and that is the fundamental issue within the Muslim community.

It has been argued that one of the problems with the Islamic world, internally, is that the vast majority of mosques and madrassas that are built today are built with money that comes from Saudi Arabia, which has a Wahhabi tradition that is particularly literalist. Is that one of the reason why there is this limited availability of views?

Wahhabism has a crude anthropomorphism in its approach to scripture, so a reference to God's arm means his hand; it can't be seen in any allegorical sense. So if that sort of crudity is applied to the understanding of the divine person can you imagine how crude the interpretations of things like *jihad* or notions of the status of women as expressed in the Qur'an is? There is no sense of cultural or historical context. It is just 'This is how it is.' Seventh-century understandings of Shariah in a brutal desert environment are to be applied wholesale wherever you are in the world. It is quite striking to see in various bits of Africa that, like Catholicism in Latin America, it's fused with local tradition and local custom even though they don't like to admit it. You know, Islam in the Indian subcontinent is intimately bound up with the richness and diversity of religion within that geographical area and likewise in Africa and South East Asia and so on.

Do you think that religious moderates, by legitimizing the concept of God and the potency of the Word, in some way legitimize various literal interpretations?

Well I know there are people like Richard Dawkins who would say that you cannot be intellectually honest and a person of faith at the same time. And if you were to buy into understandings of scripture as being true, including understandings of creation, then you either accept it as it stands – so, you know: 5,000 and however many years ago and six 24-hour periods – or you are being intellectually dishonest. But I don't buy that. I think that is putting us in a box, I think both parties are trying to put us in a box. The fundamental way that people like me would see our relationship with God relates back to the beginning of our conversation. A person is unbelievably complex; you can be married to a person for 30 or 40 years and still be discovering new things about them all the time.

Can you imagine how that must be multiplied with an infinite being whose concept of justice is outside of our ken? So to try and put God in a box in a way that fundamentalists try to do, in a way that has never been the case, historically, with religion is wrong – I mean the whole notion of the medieval Mass was something deeply mysterious and in many ways inaccessible – is not on. The concept of God as mystery is something the fundamentalists feel deeply uncomfortable about. They like the idea of the canon of the Bible in the King James translation being *it*. No ifs, ands or buts; no variant readings; no complexities about canon or diversities of understanding. The certainties to which fundamentalists cling in this day and age are very modern ideas.

Why is religion important for you?

Well, I'm probably the worst person to ask. Because my relationship with God is a bit like the relationship you might have with an uncle or senior member of the family that you're sort of not talking to! God and me, we don't get on. He's kind of like my dad: he's always been there, he's always got a finger in my life, and he's always guiding and moving things in my life. But it is not a sort of sweet, cosy relationship, for me – that is a purely personal perspective. And I guess that because of this ambivalent, bitter-sweet relationship, my approach to Islam has kind of taken on a very easy going, matter of fact attitude. There's a really good film, *Le Grand Voyage* by Ismaël Ferroukhi, that sort of captures the essence of how most Arab Muslims see religion as opposed to these really zealous Afghans and others. The majority of people in the Middle East are not raving funda-mentalists. They are people who are deeply cynical about Islam. They will be deeply respectful of the faith, but then they will still knock back a Johnny Walker on the quiet, and they don't fast, and they don't pray and they are sick of seeing on the TV the guy with the great long beard shout-ing at them. They respect that as being kind of the embarrassing grand-parent whom they love dearly and whom they have to have in the family, and life wouldn't be the same without them. You can't live without it, but it still drives you mad. And this ambivalence of approach to religion is common among Muslims, certainly in the countries that I have lived and grown up and studied in, but is something that is completely lost in some of the communities in Britain. This is particularly the case with something like the South Asian community, because there has always been a sense of inferiority amongst them by comparison to the Arabs because quite often they feel they have been relegated to a second-class status within the Muslim world. They are not Arabic-speaking and they don't really have access to Islamic scholarship because Arabic continues to be the language of Islamic scholarship and so this body of traditional scholarship is quite often hidden from many people. And so, as a result, this community treats their religion very, very, very seriously. They are a second-generation immigrant community here; it is an identity that defines them, setting them apart from the white host community, and it is a religion that gives them a sense of pride and identity that they do not have as Asians or, say, Pakistanis.

Do you think that a lack of integration is a significant problem in Britain?

In Britain, the issue of integration is complicated. You've got to integrate communities first with each other. We have in this country a situation where my father's generation, the first generation, came to this country as economic migrants. And in many ways the Muslim community's history and pattern very much follows that of the Jewish community. We even live in the same parts of London. The Jews lived in the East End, they migrated north. But the concerns that both Muslims and Jewish immigrants have faced – from meat slaughter to marrying out – can be very similar. The fundamental difference, however, is that whereas the Jewish community came with their rabbis and their scholars and their religious apparatus, we didn't. And instead what happened was that our fathers and our grand-parents came here as economic migrants, not as Muslim scholars. And they came here with an attitude that said 'We're here to get on; keep your head down, don't break the law and we are all ultimately going to jump on a plane and go home.' But they stayed on and they spawned a second gen-eration. And because Dad always thinks of home as being 8,000 miles away, and because dad and his friends have chosen to live in ghettos (to put it bluntly), the second generation has not been able to integrate. Socially, they may or may not have a large number of white English friends but their contact with the host community has been pretty nega-tive. They perceive the attitude of the white host community to be: 'You're good enough to be my friend but if you dare try and date my sister, well my mum and my dad won't have a Paki being bought home.' So this sense of alienation leads them to feel uncomfortable around other communities and institutions that might not fully accept them. But they also feel uncomfortable around their own community institutions because the mosque committees are completely dominated by first generation immi-grants who are increasingly elderly and who have sat on those committees year after year and who won't give room to the younger generation and who still have mosques that give the sermon in Urdu, not in Arabic, let alone English. They are really just transplanted from the Kashmir or wherever they come from. And instead you get these sort of younger people who are looking for an identity which they don't find with their parents and they don't find with their host community and instead they do find it through things like someone saying to them: 'My older brother knows this Egyptian guy, Abu something or other, who preaches at the Finsbury Park mosque; why don't you come along?' And then this Abu Hamza guy provides him with an identity. He is no longer a Bangladeshi guy or a Pakistani; he's a Muslim, and he's part of something bigger. And if you want to understand Islamic fundamentalism, you must understand that there is no doctrine behind it. It isn't like Communism, it isn't an ideology. What it is, is an extremely heterogeneous, anarchic, chaotic beast which draws upon elements in the Qur'an from this 'internet Qur'an culture' which doesn't have any depth of scholarship. It picks up vague elements of that and then combines it with local issues. So in Israel/Palestine it is about the occupation of land, for Bin Laden and his crowd it is a question of the violation of the sacred territory of the Arabian peninsula by the presence of infidel troops on it. For Muslims in this country it is an issue of identity. So there are different determinants, and the determinants here are seeking an identity that they find in a particular street culture that picks up on all the stuff that is going on in Chechnya and Palestine and elsewhere. And whereas in Harlem young African-American men will find an identity, perhaps through the Nation of Islam or through gangs or street culture, Muslims in this country find their own street culture based around militaristic videos and wearing combat gear and Arab clothes and going to mosques and hanging out with the lads and blowing themselves up on the tube. And this kind of street culture is something that is very specific to this country and to the Western milieu. And unless the government and Muslim institutions can start to take ownership of the distinctiveness of extremism in this country and culture and the determinants of it, we are still going to have more of the same problem. It is not going to be solved just by foreign policy issues. There are real fundamental issues of the lack of integration between the first generation and the second generation, let alone the integration between the Muslim community and the rest of the country.

It seems that you are saying that one of the core problems that Muslims face in Britain is a sense of rootlessness, dislocation and severance from tradition. And so suddenly the internet, which has become a pseudo-authority for everyone in the world, has become a Qur'anic authority but without context. And the charismatic preacher has become a source of authority given the lack of qualified teachers.

In Britain that is very much the case. The first generation is not a generation of *ulama* scholars and they are not able to provide the much needed context from which to appreciate the many approaches to the Qur'an. And it's all part of this third world bureaucratic culture; I mean, the

Muslim Council of Britain is a creaking South Asian institution that is incredibly hierarchical. It works on the principle of personal patronage and things only get done by having the ear of the Secretary General. Can you imagine how impossible it is for young people on the streets in Bradford or Leicester or in the East End of London to get the ear of the Secretary General in order to raise issues? And the parallels between Islamic fundamentalism and the convulsions going on in Christian fundamentalism are really striking. When I was at university, I had Catholic friends who would say 'The Catholic priest would never talk to me, he never had time for me, he never explained who Jesus was, he never explained what the Bible was. I grew up, I went to communion, I did all the things my mother told me to and I hated it. And then I come to university, I find the Christian Union, and I find a charismatic, powerful, strong, demagogue-like conservative evangelical preacher who sets it all out very simply with beautifully presented services which are well organized and well regimented and with lots of activities to get involved with' and so you get drawn into that culture of religion. It is a way of life which fills up your timetable and gives you a sense of person and identity.

So is religion dangerous?

It can be. Well, is sex dangerous? Religion and sex are only as dangerous as people choose to make them. Religion can be a mechanism for most purely and most truly expressing our love for one another, but it can also be a mechanism for rape and for violation and humiliation of the other. And there are parallels with other really fundamental elements of our humanity – our sexuality, our need to belong, our need for family, companionship and friendship. All these things have incredibly dangerous aspects to them. Islam and brotherhood are intimately bound up. If there are two words that really summarize what Islam is about, certainly in the present day, it is monotheism on the one hand and brotherhood on the other. There is a sense in which I carry this invisible card and I've seen that this invisible card, like a Platinum American Express, open doors to me. One of the things I have always felt very strongly about is the persecution of Christian minorities in Muslim countries, because as part of a Muslim minority in this country I have been on the receiving end of a similar kind of thing. But I was on a train in Egypt and I bumped into some Muslim Egyptian guys doing their national service and there were some Coptic Christians there too, but because I was a Muslim, because I was one of the club, or one of the boys, I clearly got a sense of how I was being drawn into the Muslim guys' circle. I was being looked after and taken care of, whereas these Christians were kind of invisible. I think Copts are something like 15 per cent of the Egyptian population so Islam is overwhelmingly dominant in Egyptian culture and the glories of Islamic civilization are widely touted, meaning that the Copts are almost non-existent in regard to the public discourse that goes on around them. There is a sense in which Muslims feel that by being part of this international brotherhood you are truly part of a tribe that is in solidarity with one another. If something happens in Ramallah then there are demonstrations in Jakarta, there are bombs going off in Pakistan. The solidarity of the Muslim *ummah* is pretty much unparalleled. But where you have a tribe, there always has to be a sense in which the tribe is held together by exclusion. And if you go to a conservative evangelical church, or a conservative mosque – there's a church in Bishopsgate and the guy who runs it is an ex-army officer and it's almost like the First Battalion St Helen's Regiment, you know? – there is a sense of pride, and a sense of 'us' and 'us having the truth against all the error of non-believers and Muslims and Jews, but most especially, the error of other Christians' is very keen. And there is a way in which we Muslims are like these pioneers with their wagons in a circle defending against the marauding Indians; there is a sense in the Muslim community in which we do that. And in the course of all of this, the complexities of Islam, the contradictions of Islam, the sense in which there are so many things in Islamic thinking and doctrine which are not worked out, so many problems with Hadith that are forged or weak upon which our Shariah is based, so many issues upon which our teaching is based that need to be challenged, all these hard truths are subjugated to the overriding principle of protecting the tribe and the unassailable truths of belief and self-belief which define and defend the tribe. And so somebody who does the unspeakable thing of washing dirty laundry in public will get a bloody hard time.

How do you view non-belief?

Non-belief is difficult for a Muslim to grasp in many ways, because the lack of belief in God is seen as a religious identification with a humanist religious belief. When people say that they don't believe in God that does not mean they don't believe in anything, it means they believe in something else. For instance, they believe in the power of the human spirit, and that the human spirit is a force for good. And I would say that just as there is truth in religions outside of the monotheistic, Abrahamic traditions that are explicitly acknowledged in the Qur'an, there is truth and goodness in a belief system that is humanist and that focuses upon what I would see as the divine residing within the human soul. There is an extremely negative or pejorative way in which believers talk about atheists and non-believers and non-believing people. I think that everybody has a deeply inherent sense of their own idea of what is valuable, what is worthy, what really matters in life that goes beyond the extraneous elements of everyday living. And I would say that there is great validity and worth within that.

Someone like Giles Fraser would agree with much of what you're saying, but he believes, ultimately, that Christianity is better, or more right. Presumably you have that same feeling with regard to Islam?

Well, there is a question as to what kind of approach you take towards people of different faiths and different beliefs, including people who are non-theistic in their religious belief. And there are some who would try to be all things to all men and say that there are many paths and good luck to them. That is a valid approach that some of the Eastern religions take and it is also an approach that many liberal Anglicans take. There is another approach that is exclusivist and monopolistic of the truth, and you will get that in mosques in Finsbury Park, you'll get it in Wahhabi mosques around the Middle East, you'll get it in conservative evangelical churches and so on. There is, however, an approach that says there are fundamental truths that we share in common that matter and that are absolutely central and important, but there are also differences of belief between us that must be honestly acknowledged. And what is so essential, and what some or many interfaith people fail to do, is to honour the differences of belief. And this is not just about disagreeing, rather it is about honouring and seeking to understand the basis of that disagreement instead of just saying 'Oh we've got lots of common ground; we do and believe lots of the same things.' And I think that Giles will ultimately, naturally, see the expression of God's word in flesh, in the person of Jesus Christ. That is a view that I would disagree with. But as far as I am concerned, we agree on the really fundamental issues about God as a good personal being; the fundamental issue relating to the way that we should live with one another and honour and respect one another as brothers and sisters. They are not just as people that we are willing to coexist with, which some conservative Muslims and evangelicals would say, but rather, we need really to engage and feel that they are valid human beings and not a different species to us – and the Qur'an says very clearly to all mankind 'I created you from a single soul, male and female and made you into nations and tribes that you may come to know and understand one another.' And in order to be able to move into that relationship we need to have a clear sense in which we respect the differences but also recognize that the things we agree on are so significant. There is no sense, for me, that Giles is going to burn in the hereafter. It is all very well for conservative Muslims and conservative evangelicals to say: 'Yes we're happy to sit round the table together and make decisions about faith-based schools or banning the teaching of homosexuality by local authorities or stopping a particular TV programme from being broadcast, but that ultimately we understand each other – you think I'm going to fry and I think you're going to fry.' Well, Britain can't cohere as a nation while these marriages of convenience constitute the way that the Muslim community or conservative evangelicals exist in relation to one another. These marriages of convenience remind me of that line from *1984*: 'You and me under the chestnut tree, I sold you and you sold me.' And it is the basis upon which some leading organizations in the Muslim community in Britain interact with the British government and with other communities.

If you look at someone like the Ayatollah Sistani in Iraq, he has played an enormous role in preventing the Shias in Iraq from entering into violent conflict and has said that Iraq needs to be a democracy and so on. Now he is clearly a highly qualified, well-regarded and experienced cleric, and someone that could show that Islam is not an anathema to liberal values. But then recently he came out and said homosexuals should be stoned.

Well I think this is right at the core of our conversation with regard to approaches to scripture. We need to take ownership of scripture – all of it; including the stuff about Joshua slaughtering every living thing; including the stuff about the killing of infidels and the beating of wives. We have to take ownership of the really nasty, bloody, historical circumstances in which these scriptures came to be written. We have got to take ownership of the fact that people who are practising homosexuals are stoned and beaten and slaughtered, that women are beaten, that slavery is permissible and so on. Until the Muslim community and the other faith communities can start to be honest about scripture we will continue to have these shocking inconsistencies of scripture's application.

So you are saying that it is still acceptable and popular in America and the Middle East to preach homophobia, whereas if you start preaching slavery no one is going to take you seriously, but unless you do both you are hypocrite?

Exactly right. There is that verse in Genesis that was used to justify slavery, and the Bible was the basis upon which the institution of slavery was continued. And slavery was an inherited institution for Europeans, which they got from the Arabs. The Arabs had been enslaving African people for centuries before the West got involved. So this issue of cherry picking from scripture is something that liberals and fundamentalists do with equal disingenuity. And until people really start to take ownership of what scripture is and what it is about, and start to apply the same arguments

about slavery being a thing of its time to these passages that relate to sexuality, and do so in an intellectually honest way which comes to an intellectually consistent outcome with all of these sentiments, then my respect
for such judgements is very constrained – because these readings in reality
seem to be motivated in large part by the pragmatic political circumstances which prevail at a particular time. You know, racism was a perfectly good thing for the Mormons and the Southern Baptists to be
involved in when it bolstered up the Church and increased their revenue
and increased their numbers, but now it is a good thing for them to reject.
So I just want people to be honest and consistent. And that is why labels
like 'moderate' and 'liberal' or 'fundamentalist' are not helpful. The core
thing for me, in my bitter experience with *fatwas* being passed against me
by extremists, is that people are just honest. I want the whole story not just
half of it. And I think people like Richard Dawkins have a point there, and
we need to answer that point and we need to study together, Christians,
Jews and Muslims. There is a practice at the St Ethelburga's centre on
Bishopsgate where Christians, Jews and Muslims sit together and they
study their own scripture, and I have been pretty much the main Muslim
input to that. And what you see emerging is a really interesting dynamic.
Because instead of the Christians or the Muslims saying 'This is it, this is
how it is', you have Christians reading the Muslim texts and saying 'Well,
from my Christian understanding this is how this sounds to me.' And
what emerges is this kind of really interesting situation where I see my
faith reflected in the words of another. And if this was to be done on a
much wider basis, first with other people of faith, but also with people
who have a non-theistic faith, humanists and the like, then we would
begin to open those closed doors of *ijtihad* in the Muslim community and
really start to challenge the basis of people who say 'Well this is how it is,
this is why I blew myself up.' And you can also, in that same process, really
start to engage with social issues like community cohesion, the Israel-
Palestine issue and so on. If you look at the video of one of the suicide
bombers in London it was all: 'My brothers! My hurt! You hurt me! You
hurt my family! You blew them up!' You could feel this guy's heartfelt and
sincere rage, but he had no sense of being able to see beyond his own pain
and see what Muslims were doing to people in places like Darfur. The
Muslim country, Indonesia, invaded Christian East Timor, built illegal set-
tlements, illegally occupied their land, and committed genocide on a scale
that wiped out a third of the male population. But you don't see Christian
suicide bombers. So what is different about Islam? And why is it that
Muslims feel they have a monopoly on feeling aggrieved? And that can
only happen when we start to engage with the fundamental mechanism by
which Muslims engage with the divine and that is our sacred texts. But to

go back a bit, this desire for input from others really can extend to non-theists too. I am a scientist by undergraduate training, and I did my post-graduate training in medical sciences before I moved into the Imamate, and I have a high regard and a deep esteem for the scientific method. And the contribution that scientists have to make to challenging issues of faith is something that must be welcomed and embraced. And I think people like Dawkins, whatever people of faith might think of him, are to be welcomed. And the methodology and rigour that he applies in his work is to be welcomed as an approach to faith. But we must also acknowledge the limitations. You know, his computer models are just models, and we all know the great mathematical dictum that no model is true, but some models are useful. And there is a utility to Dawkins' approach, but it is to be circumscribed by the fact that science is not the arbiter of truth. In the medieval period it was Aristotelian philosophy that was the arbiter. And you found Christians, Jews and Muslims talking to one another, and they were talking past one another because they didn't agree about really fundamental axioms concerning which scriptures were valid. You know 'Is the Talmud an authority or is the Qur'an the authority?' They were different. The things that they did use as an axiom of common ground were the canons of Aristotelian Greek philosophy. But nobody believes in the eternal spheres any more. And just as Aristotelian philosophy has its limitations, I think natural philosophy has its limitations, but it is useful and to be embraced, and Dawkins makes a good contribution to that.

7

Tariq Ramadan

Do you have a working definition of the term religion?
I have many. But I suppose fundamentally it is: the structured way in which we connect to God according to what He is asking us to do.

And how does that relate to a word like faith? What does faith mean for you?
Faith is the natural aspiration for Him, or for something which is beyond what we see. And religion is the way He has of telling us how to keep this faith vivid. So faith could be alive and could be dead, or covered by many other things in our life. Sometimes emotions cover spirituality, sometimes problems will hide spirituality. So religion is the way to remind us of Him. As human beings, we can forget, and because of this we need something to help us to remember; so religion is the structured way to keep us connected, whereas our natural state is to forget.

How does the word belief relate to the word faith?
Faith is the state of your heart when you believe in Him. So faith is really to believe, but faith is the substantive of the verbal way of putting it which is 'I believe in' or 'I have faith'. So to believe is what you are doing; faith is what you are getting.

And so do you have a working definition of the term God? And a sense of what that means and how that's understood and communicated in the world?
In the Islamic tradition you cannot say anything of God except for what He says of Himself. But there is a spark in all of us, in our natural state, which is the quest for meaning. And every human being has this, whatever his or her personal or community situation is. In far-off tribal communi-

ties you will still find this quest for meaning. For us, this comes from God. He is the One. An entity which is beyond any imaginative description, nothing is like Him. So whatever you try to compose out of your imagination will not be Him. He is beyond all this, but He tells us that He is first, and so He is. Then He gives us some of His qualities in order that we, through our reason and understanding, can have, not a definition, but an understanding of Him. You understand *that* He is and *who* He is, but you cannot define *what* He is.

So understanding him is an experience which can never be communicated because that would be to fit him into words?

Well, it's more than an experience; it's really a state of being. What I mean by that is that you cannot describe everything you experience with your faith or your beliefs; these are things which are very deep and personal experiences. But as He reveals books and reveals himself He tells us that He is the Most Merciful. And I cannot define what it is to be the most merciful, but I can become closer to him by understanding what mercy is. And He tells us about His qualities and He relates these qualities of His own to potential qualities in us. So by coming close to the meaning of mercy I come close to Him. I cannot define who He is, but I can be closer to Him. So it's really a question of proximity much more than definition. I can never define God, but I can feel if I am close or far.

Presumably God lets us know about him primarily through the Qur'an?

Well, He does it through all the revelation throughout history – the Torah, the New Testament, and some Muslim scholars would say that even in texts like the Baghavad Gita, He reveals Himself somewhere . . .

So that is still the case in texts that emerge from polytheistic traditions?

Yes, because sometimes that spark that we have inside us can produce that coming back to Him as the One in other ways. Even if it does this by speaking in the wrong way – and for Muslims, polytheism is the wrong way – still, there is something that comes from the same spark; it is the wrong answer to the same natural source. We always have an answer. In fact, if someone tells you 'I don't believe in God', or 'There is no God', or 'I don't believe in anything', well this itself is a belief. Belief is always there; to think that you don't believe is to believe in something nonetheless.

Someone like Richard Dawkins would be very critical of that view. He would argue that there is a difference between religious beliefs, which he would say are unprovable, and scientific beliefs for which there is empirical evidence. Or someone like A. C. Grayling would even reject

the term 'atheist'; he prefers to call himself a naturalist as he does not want to give away any ground to the notion of God. If, as you say, that spark is in all of us, and if that kind of quest for meaning is in all of us, what do you think is going on with individuals like these who claim to have absolutely no religious faith?

I think it is important first to realize that whatever you do with your life you will find yourself looking for an answer. Every one of us has a question, and so we end up looking for answers. This answer could come through your work, through drama, or aesthetics or whatever. All of these provide potential answers. At the end of the day, you are just giving meaning to your life. For us as Muslims, following this cycle of prophetic traditions, we can see that throughout human history God has repeatedly come back to us and sent revelation. So for us the way of getting back to him is to respond to that spark in us and to that revelation that he sent to welcome us. This is why we recognize that it is God who provides the answers. But if you don't recognize those revelations, at some point, you will recognize something else. As someone has put it, 'Your heart is never empty'. You will always fill it with something; if you don't have God, you will have something else. If you don't recognize the revelations, you will put something else there. In the end, you won't find an adult human being who isn't trying to give meaning to his or her life. This is even the case, for example, with someone like Sartre, the French philosopher, or Camus. They say that life is absurd, that it has no meaning; they take the existential position by saying that life has no answer. But even Sartre said, 'I have to give an answer'. And this is exactly what I am saying: the question is always there and you make what you want out of it.

Doesn't this, then, beg another question? Presumably you would say that Islam is the purest or the highest way of responding to that quest for meaning. Is it? And if so, why is it important that other people are persuaded to that point of view?

I wouldn't put it like that. Why am I a Muslim? Because I think it is the latest revelation confirming all the others. At the end of the day, what is important for me is the question of sincerity and consistency. So, what is going to be the future and destiny of a sincere Christian? The only thing I can say as a Muslim is that God knows best. This is the same even if someone says to me 'I don't believe in God'. What is really important to me is that faith is visible, and it is visible through your behaviour, through the way you act in life. I have many friends who are atheists, they don't believe, but they are more consistent in their ethics than many Muslims within my spiritual community. Of course, recognizing the One is the highest level of our commitment towards Him, but the way we act with what He has given us – our mind, our body, our heart – is something which must also be taken into account. So for me, Islam is the latest revelation, it is the one that recognizes and confirms all the others, but I would never seek to judge other people beyond their consistency and sincerity. I am trying to be consistent with what I believe and to be sincere, and so if I can see that someone is a sincere Christian, a sincere Jew, a sincere Buddhist or a sincere atheist, and if they are consistent in their ethics and behaviour, then I cannot judge them further. So the job of converting people is, I think, totally wrong. It is a wrong understanding of Islam to try and convert people; at the end of the day it is only God's job to do that.

But surely one of the things that Christianity and Islam have in common far more than any other faith is that evangelism is an important duty?

I think that is often understood to be the case by many Muslims, but I don't think that it should be. This is one of the traditional concepts within the Islamic tradition that I want to change. My point is that now, in this time of globalization, our main duty is simply to bear witness and give testimony. We have to bear witness to God's message before other people – and what I mean by this is what I was saying before: we have to be consistent. We spread our message simply by explaining it to others, by bearing witness. Now to convert people, all this business of having missions here, or the kind of Christian and Muslim missions that happened in Africa, is, for me, a perverted way to deal with our religion. Everything that happened under colonization, or the way that Christian or Muslim NGOs might only help you if you listen to their message, is a perverted way of dealing with our religion. I would never, never say that as a Muslim you have to convert people. You have to make your message clear, but to make the message clear is not only to speak about it, but it is to live it, to experience the ethical dimension of it. And this is why, for example, the world for me, and especially countries in the West, are spaces of testimony. And I ask the same from Christians and Jews; bear witness in your ethics. Even if you say you don't believe in anything, you will still have ethics, and I want to see these in your actions, I want to see them incarnated in your life. That's it. It's no more than that. But it is difficult to make it clear for fellow Muslims because some of them just count the number of converts and say 'OK, it is the fastest growing religion in Europe because all the people are converting', but I think that's dangerous.

In your book *Western Muslims and the Future of Islam* you say that it is important to be both Western and a Muslim, and it seems that there are some significant differences between Muslims who choose to live and integrate in the West, and Muslims who live within the Muslim world itself.

Abdelwahab El Affendi has said that there is a surprisingly high level of atheism in the Muslim world and it often seems that there is more focus on outward conformity to the faith rather than true inward belief. What is your view of the state of Muslims within the Muslim world?

It seems to me that we are facing something in the Muslim community, not only in the West, but within the Islamic countries as well, that has a very formalistic way of speaking about or dealing with our religion. So it focuses on the outward forms; it believes that simply saying the *Shehada* is enough and that you only need to say you believe and that will be enough. Even in our teaching we speak about the formalistic elements, the five pillars and so on. But this is the problem: often, people are not told what the meaning of the *Shehada* is; they go straight to the second stage and ask how to pray, rather than first asking why. It is a purely technical approach. And there are two reasons for this: the first is simply because there is too great a focus on the appearance of our faith, but the second has to do with the relationship between the West and the Arabs. Muslims today perceive themselves as targeted and they believe that we need to fight the West, so the religion becomes seen as just a set of orders rather than anything that goes to the heart of the teaching; there is just a focus on the differences which show why we are not like those in the West. And I think this is very dangerous as it means we end up defining ourselves or our religion as simply being against something, or that we only define our religion in terms of the form and not the substance. But many people are now being attracted to Sufism, because Sufism is concerned with the substance, the meaning of the faith. What I am trying to do is show that there is more to Islam than just the legal aspect; there is the spiritual dimension too. My book on the life of the Prophet focuses on spiritual teaching for today; it goes back to the essence of the faith rather than being about confrontation or being against something else. I am trying to show that, for example, Muslim identity is not about opposing something else, but rather it should be about the blossoming of something that comes from within. Yet there is a great deal of hypocrisy around, and it is a kind of sickness within our communities, and there is also a victim mentality that has arisen, and I don't like it. When I deal with the Muslim community I can feel how much the people are affected by this, but they don't know how to get out of it. So I think we need a positive discourse that recognizes this sickness and looks for some positive solutions.

You said you had written a book about the Prophet. Now, when you were speaking about what religion was earlier, you immediately referred to God, but when we spoke to Dr Azzam Tamimi about religion, his primary reaction was to speak about it in terms of the Prophet and he went on to speak about the controversial cartoons depicting and mocking the Prophet that were initially published in the Danish newspaper *Jyllands Posten*. Now, some time ago, Ziauddin Sardar wrote despairingly in the *New Statesman* about what he terms 'the fetishisation of the prophet'. In other words, he was saying that the Prophet has almost become for Muslims what Jesus is for Christians: i.e. virtually God incarnate. He argued that this overwhelming focus on the material world through the life of the Prophet has distorted Islam. Would you agree with that?

That could be the case. But the problem is that this will always happen when you have a personal relationship to someone, and what we were always taught was to have a personal relationship to him. He is an example and he is a model. It is exactly like a text; a text can nurture your intelligence or it can imprison it. It is not the fault of the text, but rather, it is your mind. These days, people often say that if Muslims recognize that the Qur'an is not the very word of God then they will be liberated. But that is totally wrong; it's not the text that imprisons the mind, it's the way it is read. And, of course, you can have exactly the same dogmatic approach to reading something like Marxist literature for instance. With the way we look at the Prophet it's exactly the same. You have people who have a way of dealing with him which means they literally look at his life and say 'This is the only way' and they idealize him and the people around him; you know, they believe that there was this ideal period of time in the past: and all cultures have this, it is part of the way that civilizations build themselves – by referring back to an ideal age. The point is to say 'Ok, he is the way towards God' but as the Chinese prophet puts it, 'When the wise man is pointing to the moon, it is the fool who is looking at the finger.' So this is the point. The Prophet is only the way, he is not the end. I think that this is really important. But I will often quote this proverb to a Muslim, and they will say 'Why are you quoting a Chinese proverb rather than an Islamic one?' but actually it is an Islamic Chinese proverb. And the point is that the Prophet was only a man. So this is why the way that we deal with him is so important. It is the revelation, the message that is important. But I have written a book about him because he is still the right introduction to Islam, because he was a man and a messenger at the same time. It's much more of an introduction to Islam than to the Qur'an, which is a very difficult book. This is particularly the case when it comes, not just to the spiritual dimension, but to the legal one. And also, of course, the text is not presented in a chronological way. It is a very difficult text to deal with. But with the Prophet's life, you can take a chronological approach, and you can understand what happened at the time in order to put things into context. You can have both the human and the spiritual dimension. And it is the exemplarity of the Prophet and the humanity of the man which helps us teach Islam to both Muslims and non-Muslims. And when you understand the humanity of the man, you can understand that sometimes he was wrong. But we always have to be cautious though; we have to avoid, as Muslims, just talking about the Prophet, because in the end he is only the finger pointing the way.

Could we talk about the nature of authority in Islam? Dr Tamimi says that because there is no formal hierarchy in Sunnism, and even less so in Shiism – contemporary Iran being an exception rather than a rule – much religious authority, and by implication political authority, has to derive from what might be termed 'the consensus of the community' – so people bestow authority on you by following you. Now the trouble with that, it seems, is that it leaves religion open to the power of very charismatic individuals who are in the right place at the right time. The most striking and depressing example of this might be Osama Bin Laden. He has little legal or theological training, but is still able to gather a great big following. Where do you think true authority lies within Islam?

Well, first of all, I don't think Osama Bin Laden has great authority; he has no great powers, and I don't think there is a huge number of people following him. And I really think that the people who are involved in all this business are on the margin of the margin.

Well, there may not necessarily be a large number of people who are actually active members of al-Qaeda, but is there not a wider sense that many people feel that Bin Laden is speaking for or acting on behalf of Muslims?

I really don't think this is the case. People can emotionally support the fact that he is against the West, but this is not a religious recognition. As to the question of authority, I think what you have said is true. I am always saying that within the Muslim community and in Islamic majority countries we are facing a crisis of authority. This was an asset at the beginning – the lack of central authority helped Muslims to come together with different ideas, to have more diversity, and the fact that we had more than 18 schools of law in the first two centuries was really an asset. It meant there was a real intellectual life, which allowed for legal creativity amongst scholars and real respect for each other. But a problem occurs when you cannot manage this, because things become too complex and there emerges a wider range of questions and challenges which derives from a wider geographical reality. When you cannot manage this diversity it becomes chaotic, and this is what we have today, because we don't have a central voice. And I think that we are changing what was an asset to something which is now a liability and we have to tackle the issue and ask ourselves how we can do that. So the problem for me is not someone like Osama Bin Laden, because I really think he has no religious authority. But, still, at a different level, at an international level, there is a lack of voices that are able to speak for the mainstream or to accept that there is diversity, and that there is a way of speaking about Islam which recognizes that there is no uniformity. There is now an international platform for Muslim scholars, and it may not be working very well, but you at least have attempts to create those platforms. And I think this is going to be the way forward. It won't be at the international level first, but rather the national one. I think that, for example, in the UK, or in Morocco, or in the Islamic majority countries, it is important to create platforms where scholars coming from different traditions, different schools of law, can just sit down and create a united platform of different voices, and to try to promote something that is at least a vocal presence in opposition to the vocal presence of the radicals. And yes, charisma cannot be the main thing that underlies who deals with political issues and sometimes with religious issues. This is a problem at both the national level and the international level. Now, I don't think we have to go towards a church. But we have to go towards something that can manage this diversity rather than create divisions, which is what we have at the moment.

Where can this management come from? What, in your opinion is the right, or ideal source of authority?

In religious terms, it should come really from the Muslim scholars. But the other book that I am working on now is called *Radical Reform*, or *Radical Ijtihad*. For years I have been working in this field saying that because we have new challenges and new questions, we have to come up with new answers. After 20 years of working in this field I still ask 'Why is it that for over one-and-a-half centuries we have been talking about *ijtihad*, and yet we have not seen any results?' And I think that the answer is that we have been speaking about *ijtihad* within the field of Islamic jurisprudence and not coming to it through the fundamentals. And I think we need the fundamentals when it comes to answers to the contemporary world because we cannot just rely on Muslim scholars. So, if it's only about the way you practise, the way you pray and all that, then you only need the Muslim scholars. But now, when it comes to answers to contemporary questions – the economy, society, medicine – you can't rely on the scholars. You need platforms for scholars of the texts and also scholars of the contexts all together and at the same level. And so I am proposing a shift in the centre of authority and power within the Muslim frame of reference. And I know it is going to be controversial, but I really think it is the only way. You have to say 'You cannot come with your own ethics of economics and speak about Islamic economics, because there is no Islamic economics.' There is economics, and there is an Islamic ethics within relation to economics, but you need people who specialize in economics in order to get the right picture so that you can then come to the issue with the right ethics. But if it is only scholars of the texts who speak, then you will just simplify the context because they won't know what they are talking about. You cannot specialize in both skills at the same time. I really think we need a radical shift here, because at the moment the Muslim scholars keep their authority, and this is fine when it comes to questions of daily practice, but not when we need to find new answers for new challenges.

Looking at the issue of authority from another point of view, you have a campaign on your website demanding a moratorium on the death penalty and stoning in the Islamic world, and you say that the reason you are campaigning for a moratorium rather than outright abolition is that you acknowledge the texts do allow for this punishment in theory, but the phrase you use is that this is 'almost never applicable now' . . .
Well, this is the phrase that the scholars use. And my point is really to say that we all agree now that the conditions are not there; now if the conditions were to come back – which I don't think they will – then that's fine, let's speak about it. But don't keep saying that 'it could be', because it isn't.

But nonetheless, the implication there is that you recognize the legitimacy of the Shariah in its entirety – complex as it is – as a source of law. Now someone like Abdelwahab El Affendi would say that while he does think that people should live in accordance with those principles, it should be an entirely personal decision, and should not be mandated or legislated for at a national or international level. Would you say that a reformed and contextually sensitive Shariah should be enforced like this?
The problem with this, for me, is that the starting point of the discussion is wrong. I am not defining Shariah as a legal corpus of Islamic law. For me, in the Qur'an, Shariah is defined as 'the way'. The most important thing for me is the objectives of the law. These objectives are justice, equality, and so on. So to try to be faithful to these objectives is to be truly within the Shariah. For example, I live in Britain, and in Britain there is a law that tells me that all should be equal before the law, and so this is my Shariah, because it is following the objective of 'the way'. But of course, we do have these legal texts too, and what I am saying with the moratorium is that you cannot deny that the texts exist, and if you deny that then you

will alienate 99 per cent of Muslims. So we have to read the texts in the light of the objectives. Because the objective is justice; to read the texts whilst ignoring our conditions is to betray both the text itself and its objectives. We must understand that the texts were revealed in a specific time, and that the relationship between the text and the context helped us to extract the objectives, which were justice and so on. And so now, we still have to read the text in the light of our specific contemporary context in order to keep getting closer to the objectives. So it is a dialectical process between text and context. I would never deny the texts themselves, but I would deny that they are being implemented in the right way in specific contexts today.

So would you say that the way it is often implemented now in places like Saudi Arabia or under the Taliban ignores this context and is purely formalistic?

Indeed, it is formalistic, and because it is only formalistic without taking into account of the objectives it is a betrayal, it is pure injustice.

What is your ambition for Islam? You wrote an article saying you were worried about a 'them versus us' mentality developing with the recent debate of the veil, and the Danish cartoons and so on. So how would you like to see Islam develop in the West and globally, and in relation to that, how do you think it is actually going?

Well, we are going through a crisis, but it is a necessary crisis and it cannot be avoided. Islam is a new presence in both Western Europe and in the West. The perception now is that we have two separate entities, and this is wrong but it is there nonetheless. The 'clash of civilizations' may be a wrong approach, in one sense, but you cannot deny psychologically that the idea is there in our minds. So the point for me, really, is first to address the issue and say, well what can we do to combat that? And my aim is to help Muslims be able to remain true to their own principles, but also to face the challenges of our contemporary world. But I don't want Muslims simply to adapt, but rather to contribute to the societies we are in. Integration is the first step, but it is important to give something as well. Because when you are prepared to give, people won't always be asking you where you come from. If you are perceived as a problem, people will always be asking where you come from, but if you give something back, you won't be perceived as a problem. I always use the footballer Zinedine Zidane as an example. Because he gives something to the French team, no one says 'Well, you know, he comes from Algeria . . .' We forget where he came from, because he is giving something back. So the future for Muslims is to contribute, and to be a force for change, and not only to adapt. And this is the problem I have talked about with many Muslim scholars; they only talk about adapting, whereas I think that our world needs change, radical change in many fields. You know, between the time that we woke up this morning and the time when we go to sleep tonight, 100,000 people will die as a result of injustice, because they are starving. So this world needs to be changed. But we must not think, as Muslims, that we can do this exclusively by ourselves. I think that, as we are living together, we can build bridges with people who have the same approach from the Christian, Jewish, atheist, Buddhist or Hindu traditions and say that we can do something together. But a lot of people think we cannot do this because we have different ethics. But Hans Küng has this idea of Global Ethics, and I think he is right even though he was speaking very far from the grassroots of his own faith. The only answer to globalization is to have these local initiatives, and this may be paradoxical, but it is the only way.

Finally, could you speak a little bit about your own religious journey? How has your faith and your relationship with it developed? How would your life change if you woke up tomorrow and found that you had lost your faith?

The central dimension for me is, as I said, the quest for meaning. But of course, sometimes, you can find that you doubt yourself, and you ask Him and you ask yourself questions, and you examine your life. This can happen even after prayer – and when you pray it means you are with Him – you can still find yourself asking these questions; you know 'What does it all mean?' One of the most important authors for me when I was a teenager and when I was teaching French literature was the French poet Rimbaud because 'Why?' was the central question of his work. And I have this question whether I feel close to Him, or far from Him. And you see this with everyone; even when people speak about their work, what is always behind it is the question for meaning. If you go to my website you will see that in every single article, the question is there. 'Why do we love?' 'Why are we doing this?' It is the true question. But coming from a very religious family, a family that was very active in this field, I think it was quite difficult for me, as what people from the outside might have assumed was quite natural for me was actually a real inner conflict surrounding the question 'Why?' But you have to build something out of this and it breeds humility. 'Why?' is the best question for remaining humble; because you cannot find the answer straight away, and you will never find the definitive answer. Even if you are close to Him, he will still send you this question in order to help you to remain humble. For me the worst weakness of people is not lying, not doing something bad, but being arrogant. A human being who is arrogant is dangerous, because anything could happen.

8

John Gray

Do you have a working definition of the term religion?

Well, you see one of the things I think is that the term religion is itself part of the problem that needs attacking or questioning. People who write about religion tend to interpret it as meaning some kind of supernatural belief. And of course many nowadays are very hostile to supernatural religion. And they think that by exploring supernatural belief they've got religion. Now I think that view is wrong. This mainly relates to the idea of religion as a force in human affairs or as something that touches the human need for meaning in life, and that has galvanized politics and history for the last few centuries.

In the twentieth century, the strongest, most politically powerful and also the most humanly destructive movements were not animated by supernatural belief, but rather by other kinds of belief or faith which we commonly call secular. I mean here not only Communism, both in its Leninist and Stalinist forms, but also Nazism, which was strongly hostile to Western religion, particularly Judaism, but also Christianity. Yet it had a kind of faith system of its own which involved the idea that by the use of science human beings could be improved. It was bullshit science, but it was science in their eyes, which made them believe that they could create a new human being. This pseudo-science told them that most of the human species was inferior or flawed and should therefore be got rid of or used as slaves. But once that had been done, they thought they could create a new human being.

By the way, this ambition – just as a little historical footnote – was not just restricted to the Nazis. In the early 1920s in the Soviet Union, Stalin employed a former tsarist horse-breeder called Ilya Ivanov to run experiments with 'volunteers' and apes in the belief that they could generate a super-species of human. Stalin went on record as saying that what he wanted from this was a new breed of soldier who would need not much sleep or much food and would lack the human responses of pity and distress that even hardened soldiers have. This sort of aspiration of using science to generate a higher species was very powerful in the twentieth century, and a lot of people subscribed to it.

So, in other words, my analysis is something like this: the underlying human phenomenon, of which religion – in the ordinary sense of the term – is part, is what you might call a need for faith, but this does not have to mean faith in a supernatural sense.

Do you have a working definition of faith or of belief?

Well obviously, we all need beliefs of some kind. If you're in a courtroom you need to have beliefs about evidence, about whether the person who's being tried is guilty or innocent. But in terms of what we're talking about now, in relation to myth, you have to understand that myths are not simply primitive theories. There is a sort of nineteenth-century idea which is still very strong in writers like Daniel Dennett and maybe A. C. Grayling that myths are unworked-out theories; that once science comes along you can dispense with myths; I think that's a complete mistake. Myths are narratives which have the characteristic that human beings who enter into them or, so to speak, 'internalize' them, get meaning in their lives. The goal of the myth is to provide meaning. In other words, what a myth gives you if you subscribe to it is a structure of meaning in your life which can survive the accidents and misfortunes of ordinary human existence.

And if you think of religion in its broadest sense as having myth at its core, then you can see many of the secular movements of the twentieth century were based on myths really. These myths were very powerful and in the cases of both Nazism and Stalinism, although they were very different in certain respects, they both expressed a powerful secular myth of the last 200 or 300 years, which was that by using science humanity can create a future for itself which would be better than anything that's ever existed in the past. With Communism the idea was that everybody was to enjoy it, at least once you got rid of the bourgeoisie and various other remnants from the past, but in principle the whole human species could enjoy it; in Nazism only a small section of the human species could enjoy it, and this new species that they were going to create would enjoy it even more. And that's a myth. Why is it a myth? Well first of all it doesn't correspond to any knowledge, or rather, any real knowledge, that they had at the time. This is a very important thing because science had become a vehicle for myth, by which I mean that they used pseudo-science, even though the best science of the time said it was all cobblers, to support the need for meaning and to project a future better than anything in the past.

There are similar beliefs like this today. I would argue that there are no rational grounds for thinking that in core ethical or political matters, the future of the species is going to be any better than in the past. In certain respects, of course, the growth of knowledge makes things better: we have anaesthetic dentistry; we live longer; we have better health care; we have drains and sewers, which they didn't have in Dickens's day. So we've left that behind – at least in the rich parts of the world – and that's a sort of direct spin-off of technological progress which itself is a direct spin-off of the growth of knowledge. But in ethical and political matters the twentieth century was a time of mass murder, and of mass enslavement – slavery came back but it was called socialist construction or *lebensraum*. The old evils of slavery were there on an even bigger scale than before. And now we've got torture coming back, so the belief that in ethics and in politics the future can be made better than anything in the past is a myth. But it gives meaning to the lives of those who enter into it. I don't know how many times someone has said to me: 'If I thought that, John, I wouldn't be able to get up in the morning.' And often, the people who say this call themselves rationalists. They say that they're led by reason, but they're not led by reason, they're led by an emotional need for myth. It is a sort of secular myth. It's like Christianity: if you talk to Christian believers and press them a little bit, they say: 'Well, if I really didn't believe that Jesus rose from the dead, and that when I die I will meet my loved ones then life would be meaningless: I couldn't go on.' Now there's obviously need for that kind of belief. But in my view there's no essential difference between that and the secular belief of someone who says: 'Well, if I really believed that tyranny would come back, that anarchy would come back, that torture would come back, and that genocide would come back as it did in the twentieth century on an enormous scale, I just wouldn't be able to take it.' Well, that demonstrates a need for myth.

So the thing that is interesting to explore, is how this need, which is manifested in religion in its broadest sense – and that includes both these powerful secular movements and also certain attitudes to science – shows that what may be hardwired in humans is not supernatural belief but rather the need for myth. This means that even if you trample on the supernatural part of it, somehow discrediting, de-legitimizing or repressing supernatural belief, you can pretty well guarantee that something else will emerge, be it Communism or Scientology, both of which claim to be scientific, to take its place. And whatever that might be, it will still express this fundamental need for myth or meaning. So the more fundamental question that needs addressing is not religion, but rather this issue of faith, belief or myth.

What is your personal interest in exploring these myths?

I think the myths that prevail now are shallow myths. I'm not a religious believer, and maybe I am unusual, as I just don't seem to have as urgent a need for myth as many people do. But the traditional religious myths are in some ways deeper than the secular myths. For example, the biblical myth in Genesis says, rather like the Greek myth of Prometheus, that knowledge can be dangerous. This doesn't mean that you should stop knowing things, but rather, knowledge doesn't just liberate us, it can also be very, very dangerous or ambiguous, and it can enslave us. Now that, it seems to me, is a kind of profound myth about human experience. Whereas contemporary myth, which has attached itself to science and the Enlightenment, believes basically only that knowledge can liberate us from past evils. Well, the reason that that is a shallow myth is brought out by the examples I have given of Nazism and Stalinism. This is because they use knowledge, or what they think is knowledge, to pursue their goals and to pursue their values whether they are benign or genocidal. And they often use their knowledge, which was sometimes real knowledge, as when they used it to create their bombs or whatever, in the pursuit of mythic goals. But myth in general has, of course, re-entered politics to some extent now with the role of Christian fundamentalism in America and a type of Islamic apocalypticism in the Middle East. And these are based on very ancient myths; we're not now talking about twentieth-century secular myths, we're talking about straight-out religious fundamentalist apocalyptic myths. How many secular thinkers of the twentieth century predicted that? Very few!

You speak of Genesis as a myth. Some Christians would agree. But a Christian fundamentalist would not. Do you think this is a result of the twenty-first-century fundamentalists in some way, perhaps unconsciously, adopting a scientific or 'scientistic' approach to reading texts?

Yes, absolutely, and it is not just about texts. I mean creationism is a pseudo-science. It is complete bullshit but it is in the mode of science. Science is the dominant form of knowledge in our culture and it is also the dominant form of authority. So if you are a fundamentalist Christian you can say 'Well we can demonstrate that there are holes in Darwin, and we can show that Creationism is science' but this is all nonsense as far as I can tell. And this is similar to their attitude to text. But of course, not all religions have fundamentalism of this literalist or scripturalist kind. Hinduism doesn't; Buddhism doesn't.

Do you think it is possible to have a rationalism or a science without myth or without belief?

Well there have been rationalists all around the European tradition who, historically speaking, believed that one should apply reason to human affairs and do the best you can to live life using reason, so it is possible, but it is very difficult for us. And I will give you an example: think of the Stoics or the Epicureans. They were strong rationalists but they didn't believe in progress in ethics and politics. They thought that human history was cyclical; they thought that individuals could make their lives better by being more reasonable and not being dogged by irrational fears and so on. So they thought that human life could be happier if it was in some ways more rational, but they didn't believe in progress. And why didn't they think like that? Well I think Christianity is responsible, its underlying need to believe that human history is meaningful. This is a belief that the Greeks and the Romans didn't have. Read Homer, read Lucretius, read Seneca, read any of the Greek Tragedians. Did they believe that human history had an overall meaning? Definitely not! It never even occurred to them. That came out of Christianity. It came out of the idea that Human history is a universal drama of redemption. And this is a distinctively Christian view. It is not in Judaism, Hinduism, Buddhism or Shintoism. So is it possible to have science without this kind of faith? Definitely! Is it possible to have philosophy without it? Definitely!

There are one or two examples even after the Christian era – Hume got close in some ways, as did Spinoza and Freud. You can find a few thinkers who didn't subscribe to a myth of progress. In the case of Hume that was because he didn't so much reject Christianity as step outside of it. He just sort of ignored it, and that wasn't easy in Scotland in that time; he lost a lot of professorships and had other professional difficulties as a result. And of course, he had to exercise a good deal of caution in what he wrote. But in his basic outlook I think he was a pagan. He didn't subscribe to an idea of progress. There were a lot of historians at that time in England saying God was at work making English liberty ever more wonderful, and he said that that was just rubbish, that it was down to chance. He tried to identify specific chance events in human history. Now you couldn't think like that if you were any kind of Christian or secular believer. You would think that there was some kind of underlying mechanism making England wonderful, just like the American Neo-Cons believe now, or the French did in the eighteenth century. No, he saw it as a series of accidents. It is a pagan view rather like the ancient histories of Tacitus or Herodotus where they recognized the role of fortune, not providence.

It sounds similar to Tolstoy's view in *War and Peace.*

Absolutely right, and that was written at a time when Tolstoy was heavily influenced by Schopenhauer. And the reason why Schopenhauer is still so heretical is that he thinks that human history is meaningless. Now you could say that Nietzsche thought that, but he thought that it could be made meaningful by these supermen, which is frankly ridiculous. But Schopenhauer had a huge impact on a number of writers: Tolstoy, Turgenev, Hardy, Conrad, Proust. What was so provocative in his work was that he said that there is no reason to think that human history has any overall meaning or structure.

How do moral values relate to myth?

Think of the Stoics, the Romans, the ancient Greeks, the ancient Indians, the ancient Chinese. None of them had a belief in progress, but didn't they think that there were important values or human goods that should be protected? It's a bit like when they said in the nineteenth century: 'If you give up Christianity, why don't you just go out and rape everybody? Why not just rape and murder and indulge in unmentionable devices?' But why should you go out and do that? What would you do?

I am not preaching or sermonizing to people. But nonetheless, giving up the secular myths could enable people to have a clearer idea of what they value, what gives them fulfilment. They won't end up wanting to run around getting drunk and raping and mugging people, but they will actually be able to ask themselves: 'Well what do I want to do with my life? What do I find meaning in?' And they will find lots of things because, unlike Christians and secular humanists, I think the capacity for meaning is ingrained or hardwired in people. The Stoics and the Epicureans and the Daoists and all of these people who didn't believe in anything like Christianity, still, I believe, lived happy and meaningful lives. And the vast majority of humans who've ever lived didn't subscribe to any thesis – they didn't have literature and philosophy, they didn't have Christianity – you know, people in pre-history and so on. And did they all have meaningless lives sitting about tormented by nihilism? Nonsense!

And if you go further back and look at the hunter-gatherers, did they live bad lives? There might have been certain elements of insecurity in their lives, but I don't think their lives were in general blighted by a lack of belief. So the need for belief, I think, in the sense of a radiant future or of a god or whatever, is not hardwired into us. But in a culture which has been shaped by Christianity and its secular surrogates, it is very difficult for people to shake it off. And it is also very difficult for people to notice it. The majority of philosophers haven't studied religion, so they are not aware that many of their secular tropes come from religion.

Do you have a view on God?

I have no such beliefs. My general approach is to avoid beliefs – in this sense – as much as possible. I mean obviously I have beliefs about things like when the train might leave. But I want to avoid beliefs in the sense we have been talking about. I remember an interview with Graham Greene in which he was talking about being Catholic and about how he used to study theology with a famous Jesuit for two years, and he said: 'There came a crucial point where he gave me a completely knockdown argument for the existence of God.' And the interviewer said: 'What was that?' And Greene replied: 'I can't remember!' Isn't that great? It shows that argument is not the key. Another story I like is about P. G. Wodehouse. He was interviewed on television towards the end of his life and he was asked: 'Mr Wodehouse, do you have any religious beliefs?' and he replied: 'It's frightfully hard to tell!' I think that is absolutely wonderful because what it identifies is the elusiveness or the obscurity of belief or faith. It is a bit like Keats's idea of negative capability that he talks about in his letters, where he talks about 'the irritable demand for certainty'. Why not just accept uncertainty? That is the attitude I recommend and that I try to practise myself in as many areas as I can.

Do you have a view as to a society, or way of relating to each other that is better than another?

No. There are some that are bad, that we should avoid in the sense that they embody important human evils that we know from history and experience are bad. So theocracy is bad for various reasons, it always involves repression and stultification; totalitarianism is bad and so on. But apart from those, there are many different forms in which humans can live well and I wouldn't want to prescribe them. I'm not a Salvationist. To me the most destructive people in the world are these Protestant missionaries who descend on these tribes who have been living perfectly happily for thousands of years, or, to take a different example, think of the Chinese cultural revolution. These secular or religious Salvationists that descend on communities and impose their ridiculous, childish, silly, preposterous, ludicrous, comical view of human salvation on them can often have an enormous cost to the people concerned. I find that contemptible.

Do you have an idea why such behaviour seems to recur?

Yes. A certain type of faith requires others who live well without it to be subordinated. In other words, if something gives meaning to your life, if you believe that your life has been turned round by the Christian God and there are people in a remote Amazonian rainforest who have never heard of him or want nothing to do with it, then you are likely to conclude that there must be something wrong with them. Because if they carry on living well without that faith, it undermines your faith. If others can live well without it, why can't you? So it sort of relativizes your faith. But remember, not all religions are like this; most religions throughout human history have not been missionary religions. Hinduism, Buddhism, Shintoism and Daoism are not missionary religions, the Greek and Roman cults weren't; normally when they arrived somewhere they incorporated the local gods into their pantheon. They didn't bother too much about them. So this need might not be absolutely universal.

Dr Fraser Watts and Archbishop Rowan Williams have said that they are not particularly interested in evangelizing, and that they see the mission of the Church as being more about things like interfaith dialogue and so on. So it does seem that in some forms of Christianity at least, this evangelism is dying out.

I would go slightly further than that. And I learnt this from the reaction to my book *Straw Dogs*, at least in Britain and some other European countries. Many Christian thinkers now are more sceptical about the missionary project than secular people. Now I'll tell you why I think that is: it is because Christians, not American fundamentalist missionaries, but Christians in England, other European countries and so on, have had more opportunities to interrogate their myths. They have been forced to do this by the mockery of a secular world. Therefore they know that they are myths, they know that they are not truths in the sense of scientific truths. Whereas secular humanists are in the driving seat in Britain – if you are Richard Dawkins or someone like that, you won't admit that you are governed by any myths as you have never been forced to interrogate them. But Christians since Pascal or even St Augustine have interrogated their myths. And I have actually found, at least in Britain, that some practising Christians have a more sceptical and enquiring attitude to their beliefs, and perceive them to be in some sense myths, and don't want to impose them on anyone. I think that is a much more intelligent and subtle way of thinking than most secular humanists and it brings out the fact that they are much further ahead of the game than most secular humanists.

Can you identify some of the myths you think secular humanists live by?

Well, the main one is the myth of progress in ethics and politics; obviously there is progress in science and technology. The myth of progress means that there is a possibility of a kind of cumulative advance over time where each generation inherits the political and ethical achievements of the last one. In the ancient world nobody believed that. They thought that you could have peace but it would be lost, and you could have freedom but it would trickle away. Now, this doesn't mean that you should just give it up. If you were a Stoic you would try and make it last as long as possible so that people could benefit from it and enjoy and cherish it and so on, but in the end it would trickle away. Why? Because that is what history is like.

And what makes me so certain that secular myths are all basic varieties of the same thing – even if they spread to non-Western contexts – is that they all have the structure of Christian myths. They don't have the structure of Animist myths, or Shinto myths, or Hindu myths. You know, Hindu myths are about things like the unending cycle of the whole universe; that is the way they see the world. You would never find a secular myth like that; I can't think of one anyway. To look at it from another aspect, George Bush talks about destroying evil. But that is a very unorthodox view for a Christian. An Augustinian, at least, would say nobody can destroy evil. It is sort of there, and you can fight it, you can resist it but you can't destroy it. And I actually think that part of the decay of contemporary culture is in the idea, which secular people also have, that there would not be evil if it were not for ignorance; that if people were better educated they would not behave badly. Well, where did the Holocaust occur? Not amongst hunter-gatherers! Rather it occurred in one of the most highly educated cultures of modern Europe. I think the idea of destroying evil has reappeared in the heterodox, unorthodox form of Christianity that modern Bushite Christian fundamentalists represent. But this idea is also present within secularism. They believe that we can destroy evil by enlightenment, by knowledge and by educating people so that they don't have these terrible tendencies. That is absurd in my view because what we call 'evil' is a whole range of human behaviours or tendencies which might well someday have a scientific explanation, but even with a scientific explanation they won't be eradicated, because the people who get the explanation will be the same old animals. The Nazis used modern scientific, psychological knowledge about mass meetings and propaganda in order to pursue their goals. But it is an incorrigible illusion amongst secular humanists that somehow if you have more knowledge people will be better. When I've said that scientific knowledge has been used for different purposes, both good and bad, I've often had people say 'Ah yes, but when we get a better knowledge of human psychology and society things will be better.' But who will get this knowledge and how will they use it? It is the same as the way that knowledge which emerges in the physical sciences can be used to develop weapons or to cure diseases. Why do I say this? Well it has already happened. It's not as if there was no

Nazism, or there is no example of propaganda in liberal societies; you know, Fox News or whatever. But it is an incorrigible illusion. I have talked to an awful lot of highly intelligent, very moderate secular humanists, but they all say 'If we had more knowledge, this wouldn't happen.'

Do you have useful myths that you articulate and that you live by?

I don't think individuals can invent myths for themselves; rather, I think one just finds myths in the large compendium of humanity's imagination. They are there already. I mean, I would read the Christian Bible in the same way as I read Robert Graves. That is the way I approach things; I take something from each different myth. Now of course if you were a fundamentalist you would say: 'That's terrible, it's a post-modern view.' But I don't think that is so at all. If you go back to pre-modern times people were very eclectic; they took from this and that. This is certainly the case once you get out of the Western tradition.

You have described yourself as a 'naturalist' and this is a term that someone like A. C. Grayling would also use to describe himself.

A naturalist view, as I understand it, would inescapably be friendly to traditional religions (though not obviously on every aspect of everything they do) because they are natural. They are natural things for humans to have. A naturalist is one who accepts the basic structure of humanity as it is. And it is a feature of humans, not that they all have supernatural beliefs, but that they all have myths. A few individuals might not have them, but on the whole, all human cultures have myths. And there are different species of naturalism. In Europe, it has normally been associated with liberalism, the Enlightenment, anti-clericalism and so on. But it needn't be like that. Lucretius, for instance, was quite wary about religions, but he didn't deny the existence of gods, and he didn't want to propose a new cult. He thought that if religion weighed on the mind and produced needless anxieties then you should rid yourself of that. But the idea of having a kind of secular creed instead or even that belief is terribly important are all residues of Christianity. Naturalism, as I understand it, means that we have got to be friendly to religion. To say, 'I'm a naturalist but I am against religion', is like saying, 'I am a naturalist but I'm against sex.' If you repress sex it will still emerge in very odd ways – just look at the Victorians. And if you repress religion you get Scientology, or you get weird cults of all sorts. To get back to Grayling, modern naturalism is almost always associated with a belief in progress. Grayling's naturalism believes that things can get better, that if we would get rid of all the superstitions, traditional religion would fade away and vanish and be replaced by science and so on. I don't believe that.

How did you come to these beliefs?

Well, I've always thought along these lines. In the Cold War I was very anti-Communist, and one of the reasons for that was that I thought it was a very destructive secular religion. I don't regret any of that; it was absolutely necessary to try and get rid of it. But when it happened, when Communism collapsed, then you can see the difference between my views and those of others. I immediately switched to focusing on the risks and the dangers the post-Communist period. By contrast, a classic progressive like Francis Fukuyama thought history had ended! Only a post-Christian could think this. It is why people in non-Western countries cannot understand what the hell he is talking about. But to me, when this great evil of Communism collapsed, I thought 'Good, but there will be new evils.' And if politicians had been really wise they would have antici-pated that there would be great difficulties after such a long period of repression with so many underlying ethnic and religious conflicts frozen or repressed by Communism, but they didn't.

Do you have what could be described as a spirituality or a sense of the numinous?

I think the numinous is everywhere. The numinous is a way of perceiving the world, not that which is perceived. And so if you go around the world looking for little signs of miracles, then you might miss what is already there. If you think that the numinous is occurring in some other world than this one, then you might just miss the numinous experiences that occur to all human beings in everyday life. I think the people who are best on this are definitely not philosophers, though I speak as a lapsed philoso-pher if you like! They are poets like Keats or writers or musicians or dramatists. Film, for instance, has very powerful imagery. Think of the work of Tarkovsky; I don't mean the more explicitly crypto-religious ones, but films like *Mirror* are full of these images. You can ask: 'What do they mean?' But they're numinous, aren't they.

9

Alister McGrath

Do you have a working definition of the term religion?

There isn't one. I mean everyone argues about this, but whatever definition you give, there will be an obvious exception. In Daniel Dennett's recent book *Breaking the Spell* I think he defines religion as 'having a belief in God'; so you can see immediately that that's very bad news for Buddhists! I am resistant to definitions, because very often a definition is polemical; it is constructed with an agenda in mind. So I think all you can really say is that religion is about what really matters to people. You can talk about a quest for a transcendent, but again, you have got to be very careful there because some religions don't actually have a transcendent dimension. Some things that *we* call religions, like Confucianism, are seen by *them* as philosophies of life. So it is a real problem. If you want to limit it to a UK context, then it's probably easier, and you can say, probably, that religion is about a belief in God, and the adjustments to lifestyle that occur because of that.

Can you define faith?

Well, we all have some kind of faith, whether we like it or not. If you are an atheist you have one faith, and if you are a Christian you have a different faith. Basically, it is a willingness to accept a bigger view of reality than the evidence forces you to accept. In other words, it is saying: 'Well I can't prove that something is right, but I think it is right and that makes a very big difference to everything.' And that is a very significant definition because it really is trying to say that all of us tend to go way beyond the evidence in reaching judgements about what really matters, and therefore about the way we behave. So from my viewpoint, the best definition of faith is simply a passionate belief that something is right and makes a difference. Something that you do believe to be true, but when the chips are down you can't actually prove it to be so.

From a Christian perspective, the word faith has a double dimension. I believe that things are a certain way, and if they are that way then it makes a significant difference to life. So in effect it is about a transformative dimension to thought and to life which ensues from the belief that certain things are true. So it has both a cognitive and a sort of transformational dimension. And again, it's difficult to give you a neat definition that will embrace that, but that is the key thing to try and get across. Faith is not simply about saying: 'I believe *that* the capital of Albania is Tirana.' That will make no difference to me at all; it might make a difference to Albanians, but not to me! But if there is a God, then that actually does change the way that you live. So from a Christian perspective, faith is not simply a disinterested form of knowledge, it is something that if it is true, is transformative.

You have a very interesting personal journey, because you have gone from committed atheism . . .

Aggressive atheism.

Ok, aggressive atheism to aggressive Christianity?

Well, I wouldn't say it is aggressive; confident perhaps. I hope I am fairly gracious! I grew up in Belfast and initially I just thought that God and religion pitted people against each other and bred violence. Back in the 1960s I was a Marxist and I really believed that a brighter future lay round the corner and it would be a Godless world and a much better world for that reason. So I took the view that religion was demonstrably wrong, and I was a scientist, so it was obvious to me that religion could be disproved. As I read Richard Dawkins, I see some of the ideas I used to have. And therefore I believed religion ought to be eliminated not just ignored; it was actually wrong and evil, so I was very aggressive. And then I changed my mind.

I think one of the things that changed my mind was discovering more about science and beginning to realize that actually the sciences are much more modest in their aspirations than people like, well nowadays, Richard Dawkins might argue. And actually, I realized that faith plays quite a significant role in science. I realized that you had to make quite a lot of intuitive judgements that evidence doesn't always bear out, but you have this sense that actually this does make more sense than other things, so it is based on evidence but it always goes slightly beyond that, but you're aware that you are doing that.

And so when I came to Oxford, I think that one of the things I thought I would do would be just to rethink things. I was beginning to have doubts about atheism as it just seemed too neat. One of the questions that really shaped up in my mind was: 'If religion really is just bullshit, why do so many people believe it?' And it is a very hard question to answer. I mean you can always say, 'They're mad, they're bad, they're deluded', but as an explanation it's not actually deeply persuasive.

I think I had bought into a whole range of atheist stereotypes of what Christianity was. My view of Christianity as a young boy was of being forced to do things that were unspeakably tedious, and not being allowed to do a whole series of things that I thought were possibly quite interesting. And I thought: 'Why? Why the hell would anyone want to do that?' I couldn't see any reason for it at all, and that was because I hadn't understood, really, that if this was true, then it had this transformative dimension; it had an inner motivation. These elements I didn't like were not the point, they were simply a manifestation of something much, much deeper and that is what really matters.

Can you expand upon this idea of Christianity having a transformative dimension?

I think it is a simple idea; it is some sort of a relationship with God. This can be difficult for an academic philosopher to accept, because they have a rather dry, dusty, cerebral idea of what God has to be like. But actually, it is much more than that and I think this is extremely important to recognize. It is a driving animus, and once you appreciate that it is there, it does actually make an awful lot of sense, so for me that is quite an important discovery.

Can you say something about God?

We talk about 'knowing' God, not just having some sort of idea about what God is like. There is a feeling that there is something there which, although words are not good enough to describe it, you can nonetheless grope around and try and express what it's about, and whatever it is, it is meaningful and transformative, and that is one of the key things to try and get across. Though there is a difficulty in that language lets you down if you try to describe it.

What is meaningful to you about your relationship with God?

I think there are several things. One is that it clearly gives you a prism or a framework for making sense of your experiences and of the world. So in one sense, faith is a 'sense-making' exercise. It says that this interpretative grid, if you like, that I cast, or this Kantian net that I throw over experience, actually makes a lot of sense. C. S. Lewis said: 'I believe that the sun has risen not just because I see it, but because by it, I see everything else.' So it kind of gives you a way of seeing things. But it is more than that; it is much more about a sense of purpose, a sense of location and a sense of meaning. That word 'meaning' is so important because when I talk to university students now the question of meaning is the big thing on the agenda – the question: 'What's it all about?'

What role does scripture or doctrine play in how you understand God?

Well, I think most Christians would relate to scripture as, in effect, talking about somebody we know. There is history, ethics and doctrine there but it is really about connecting me with something bigger than me, and helping me try to work out how I actualize this in my own personal existence.

What is your understanding of the role of mythology in religion?

Well, I think we'd need to discuss what the word 'myth' means, because it is used in different ways by a lot of people. The Greek word *mythos* in the third century BC just came to mean something like an invented fable. And of course, in the English the word has a number of different senses. I mean I think nowadays we would not talk of 'myths', but rather of 'controlling narratives'. In other words, here is a story which actually shapes the identity of a community, and gives a sense of its historical location. The word 'myth' is just very old fashioned. If you look at Alistair MacIntyre, who is much better on this, the point he would make is that actually, whether we like it or not, we are all controlled by these narratives; we just buy into different ones. And therefore the questions are: (a) How do you validate these narratives? and (b) How do you make a judgement between them, this one rather than that one?

Why are you a Christian and not, say, a Buddhist?

Well, I guess the simple answer is because I have looked at the alternatives and believe this one to be better and right. Now that is a difficult judgement to make, but you have to try and set out some criteria, or some understanding of how you make a judgement here. And obviously it will be a complex interaction of history and ideas and so on. The idea of a myth – at least as it was understood back in the 1960s, and I parody a little here – is that it was a nice fanciful story that would make a lot of sense of things, but we have moved way beyond that now. Actually, we should be speaking of 'foundational narratives', which are based on historical events that have been extended in a way that makes sense, not simply for the community's sense of identity and historical location, but also for the individual within that community. That is why 'controlling narrative' is a much better phrase. Also, the word 'myth' does imply falsity to many people. Christians do believe that the stories are true.

Do you not think that had you been a young Egyptian atheist and had had a similar awakening to religion you would have probably gone towards Islam?

Yes, I see the point you're making. I think all of us are limited by the set of options that are presented to us. Jean Paul Sartre once said famously 'I am what I am because of history.' History does limit what your options are. Atheism, for example, is actually a culturally conditioned movement if you think about it. It is not a political thing; it is much more of a cultural one. So all of us are shaped in some way by social and cultural forces; it applies to religion, and it applies to most things actually.

Given your scientific background, how do you relate to the idea of miracles?

The simplest way of defining a miracle I suppose is 'a highly improbable event'.

But with something like the resurrection or the virgin birth, surely, you would have to say they are impossible events?

Well, says who?

Impossible in terms of our understanding of biology.

We've got to be very careful about this because you can very easily end up with a very positivist view of science, which in a sense simply locks you into an Enlightenment worldview, and that is the problem I think. But to look at something specific, let's talk about the resurrection, because that is the big one. For Christians the resurrection is unique and decisive. In other words, if it really did happen then it makes a huge difference to everything. And that's one of the reasons why the New Testament is so excited about it. And I think there are two things that interlock really. One is saying, 'This is how it happened', and number two is saying, 'This is what it means'. And you can see this process of reflecting on what it actually means beginning to unfold in the New Testament itself. So it is extremely important; for example it has a lot to say about human identity, and it also has a lot to say about who Jesus actually is. And again, that would be an extremely important point because it goes against the Enlightenment point which says that all religions are the same, they all have their gurus, they all have their teachings, they all have their adherents. But actually Christianity doesn't think that. Because the language used about Jesus is not simply that of a teacher, it's a much more elevated language. And the distinctively Christian idea that Jesus is in some way divine stands completely in contrast to, for example, Islam, which talks about Muhammad being a prophet. So there is a difference in patterns of revelation in the two religions. Muhammad is told by Gabriel that this is what God is like; for Christians, Jesus actually discloses not just in word, but in deed, what God is like. So there is a very different understanding of how revelation takes place and indeed what revelation is, so it's a very significant part of what the Christian faith is all about.

Do you see there being a difference in the way that the resurrection will be viewed by Christians and non-Christians? You have criticized Daniel Dennett's arguments as being circular, that they start from the position which they seek to prove: there is no God, so the world must be governed by natural laws, and so therefore there is no room for God. Do you not think that the same criticism could be applied to a Christian approach to the resurrection: there is a divine, the resurrection is proof of the divine, therefore the resurrection actually happened?

Oh, well it is the same with everyone. If you're an atheist you find exactly the same situation. It's a hermeneutical circle, and you can enter it at various points, but actually it is very difficult to get out of it. And certainly, you can construct without any difficulty an entirely consistent set of ideas predicated upon the idea that there is no God, just as I can construct an entirely consistent set of ideas focused on the idea that there is, and they don't interact at all; they are circular, that is the whole point about them. The key question then is: 'Which of them actually has the greatest contact with reality?' In other words, we are not simply looking at internal consistency. I mean, all of these things are internally consistent. The key question is how well do they interlock with what the real world is like? And that for me is one of the reasons why I began to look away from atheism.

Lewis Wolpert, unlike Richard Dawkins, does not feel any anger against religion per se, but argues that he is simply looking at what happens and trying to draw conclusions from that. And from this he would say that he just doesn't see any evidence for God. And one of the examples that he has used in this regard is the Bertrand Russell story that an atheist cannot prove that God does not exist any more than a theist can prove that he does. But the atheist would add that he also cannot prove that there isn't a giant teapot circling Jupiter . . .

OK, how many people do you know who believe that there is a teapot circling Jupiter? The point is that this is a rhetorically exaggerated analogy designed to discredit a viewpoint; it is driven by rhetoric. I can't prove that there is a God and he can't prove that there isn't, so in that sense we are all in the same boat. So where do we go from there? Well, if all things are open we could just say: 'Well we can't reach a firm conclusion so let's leave it there.' But actually, no one does that; people then say, 'But' and then they bring in an additional argument and say, 'Well on balance, it's more like this or that.' And the key point, I think, is that actually, for most natural scientists, there are two things that are observably and demonstrably true. Number one is that most of them are neither atheists nor Christians because of their science. They get these ideas from somewhere else and they bring them to their science. And number two – again, a very interesting point – is that most scientists, when pressed, will say: 'Well, what we're doing as scientists actually has no bearing on whether there is a God or not.'

How do you adjudicate on the issue of faith?

Well, I think there are two important things: One is the question: 'What makes the most sense?' And the other is the existential impact – does it give meaning? And I know it sounds trite, but it really is quite important. There are things that may well be right, but they will make no difference to the way that I live, to my sense of identity, to my sense of purpose. For example, when I was doing research in natural sciences, and doing my D.Phil in molecular biophysics, I was looking at a number of very interesting hypotheses, but in the end it didn't matter to me one whit which of them was right. The core thing for me was to try and sort out which of them *was* right. But there was no emotional investment in it of any kind. So it is trying to say that, fundamentally, it is not simply about an intellectual discrimination between this and that, but it is about something which actually, if it *is* right, will have this massive implication for the way we think and the way we live.

Do you think that what you believe as a Christian is right? And if you do, what impact does that have on your ability to interact with another religious standpoint?

Do you know what 'epistemic justification' means? Well, back in the heyday of rationalism 'right' was thought to be consonant with 'reason'. But nowadays, people realize that, first of all, there is a multiplicity of rationalities and, second, there are all kinds of problems about what criteria you use. But what 'epistemic justification' basically means is that what you propose can be shown to be true, or shown to be justified on the basis of the criteria that are appropriate to a system, and it recognizes that there are many such ways of doing this. This is a post-modern idea, which basically says that there is no one way but there are lots of ways. But if you ask: 'Do I believe I'm right?' Well, without wishing to sound arrogant I believe I am, but then I am sure that you believe that you are right in what you believe too. The key question is: 'Does that make you a complete pain in the ass so that we can't actually have an intelligent conversation?!' And so my position, simply, is that I do believe I am right, but I am quite happy to be shown otherwise. Therefore for me, conversation is immensely important because it helps me understand those who disagree with me. But also, for all of us, it is important to keep that option open; if a person's mind is closed then I think that is a real problem. Therefore I am always reading, rethinking, talking and debating. I believe we should have these dialogues in public so that not only will I benefit from the argument, but the audience can then make up their minds about which of us are right.

Everything that you are saying at the moment is very tolerant of different viewpoints. But from a Christian point of view, in eschatological terms, what are your conceptions of heaven and hell, and how does God relate to people of other religions and no religion?

Well, the standard Christian answer, which I would be very happy to endorse, is simply that those who believe and trust in God will go to heaven, and as for those who don't, well that is up to God really. I mean I'm not one of those medievalists who would say that you will go to hell if you don't believe in God, because I have read the Bible rather carefully and see that it is not that simple. The key point is that basically you are judged on what you have available to you, and sometimes that is what you believe to be right, and some of my most interesting conversations with people reveal that there is this quite deep spirituality, or a sense of there being more to life than what we see, and wondering where this takes us. So I basically take the view that Christians will go to heaven. I do *not* take the Islamic view that those who disagree with Islam in any way are condemned to hell. I think that is not the Christian viewpoint at all. I think there is a much bigger shadow land, if you like, or area of vagueness or opaqueness here, and I would not want to go beyond that.

But presumably you would accept that there are Christians who do believe that some people go to hell simply because they don't believe.

Oh, certainly there are; there are quite a lot of those around, but I am not one of them.

What is your view of both the contemporary Christian world and the contemporary religious world?

Well, in Britain I think we are seeing two things happening: one is that a quite significant distance has opened up between what one might call 'institutional religion' and what you might call 'personal faith'. And again, I know from my own work in the field that it is a general trend within the British population as a whole for the younger generation to disengage with institutions and we are certainly seeing that in a religious context. A typical Anglican congregation – not necessarily others, but certainly in the Anglican context – tends to be older. The institutional commitment is an older viewpoint, and it is not there in the young. And you'll see that in membership of political parties and a whole range of things: where there is a choice between an institutional and a more personal way of doing things, younger people will choose the personal way of doing things.

The second thing that is happening, and again this is a recent thing, is a burgeoning interest in 'spirituality'. Now I am using the word 'spirituality', not the word 'religion'. 'Spirituality' would be something like this: a privatized worldview, in which I realize that quite a few things are significant. And it is not materialist. There is a belief that there is more to life than we can see. These people are very impatient with atheism. They would say that it closes down a very important discussion; they would argue that there is clearly more to life than what we actually observe or what we actually encounter, but they would also say that we are not quite sure what it is. And they would say they are getting in touch with their spiritual side. And I suppose that is a recognition that there is a complexity to life that goes beyond what you actually encounter in day-to-day business. And that could end up becoming a religious movement, but it isn't a religious movement at the moment.

So if you ask me what the situation is today, then I would say that we are in uncharted waters, we haven't been here before. Because in the past institutions tended to dominate things. If you look at the nineteenth-century atheist critiques of Christianity, they are predominantly institutional, because the Church behaved abominably. I mean, certainly in older atheist critiques you will often find them engaging with the ideas, but in the late nineteenth century, it was more a critique of the institution. And so I personally think that the future of Christianity requires an institutional link-up with the personal, and also a religious development from the spiritual. And those are two quite different things, but they both need to be done.

Why is the institution important?

There is that saying: 'Without people, nothing happens; without institutions, nothing survives', and there is an element of truth in that. And I think you do need an institution to sustain a vision, and certainly what you invariably notice throughout the history of Christianity is that things that begin outside of the Church, as separate meetings, actually end up being churches in their own right. So I personally think that there is a role for institutions, but my concern is that I see a disconnection between the institution and the individual at the moment.

Do you have a definition of religious fundamentalism?

Well, again, the problem really is that the word fundamentalist is a polemical term. If you say to me 'You're a fundamentalist' it means broadly: (a) you're unthinking; and (b) you're very aggressive.

In America, people like the late Jerry Falwell would describe themselves as fundamentalists.

Well, OK, if you look at it in that sense, you can get a very good definition; fundamentalism is a religion that is reacting strongly and adversely to something. In other words it is oppositional. It's not like a Christian orthodoxy which is just sitting there being Christian orthodoxy. It is Christian orthodoxy which has been frightened by something and it is overreacting, and it's doing so by both bringing down the shutters on any discussions in order to isolate itself, and also by quite aggressively resisting what are seen as secular trends. So it is a particular mindset. Paradoxically, it is not really about a set of ideas, though there are some ideas that are given a particular emphasis by fundamentalists; it's much more about a reactive mentality which primarily is a form of defensive withdrawal. And there is a lot of that around. You know, the word was originally used by American Protestants in about 1925 after the Scopes trial, but actually it has come to be applied to other religions, and actually quite reasonably so because the same traits you saw in American fundamentalism at around that time are there in Islam as it reacts against America, it's there in forms of Judaism, and it certainly there in forms of Hinduism. So it is actually reasonable to describe it as a global phenomenon.

So you see fundamentalism as being a kind of psychological response which manifests itself as a political project?

Well, that is not the totality of it, but it is certainly part of it. And it does help you understand, for example, some trends but not all trends. I mean, the trend it doesn't help you explain is why fundamentalism has become so politically involved *of late*. If you look at the 1960s they were disengaging completely. Again the answer seems to be that they feel now that it's a way of getting things done, and therefore putting on social and political pressure is a major issue and Jerry Falwell was a very important pioneer of that And actually, most of my American fundamentalist friends at the moment would say that political engagement is essential. If I had talked to them or their forebears 40 years ago they wouldn't see it like that at all. So I think the politicization of it is quite recent. And again, my friends who are Islamic fundamentalists would say something similar, that their initial reaction was to walk away, and now they are saying: 'If you walk away, you don't change things; you've got to find a way to get involved.'

Do you think that if you have an exclusive worldview, it is likely to lead to conflict?

It doesn't necessarily do so, but it could do so. I mean, it is certainly true of Christianity at times, and it is certainly true of atheism at times, just look at the Soviet Union. One of the great paradoxes is that some of the most intolerant outrages in the twentieth century were committed by those who believed that by eliminating religion, the world would be a nicer place. Certainly, any worldview that says, 'This is the way it is folks and everyone else is wrong,' is potentially intolerant. And actually this is true of political violence as well, so it is a real problem.

Do you think religions need to find a way of policing themselves?

I do, and that is one of the points I try to make. But the real difficulty is that, not so much with Christianity, but certainly with Islam, what you are seeing are traditional authority structures being bypassed. Why is Osama Bin Laden so attractive? Because he is propounding a vision of Islam which is consistent with the Qur'an, although it emphasizes different aspects from what others will do; it is radical, and he is a charismatic leader. And that is displacing traditional authority; there's no Vatican, there is no centralized authority in Islam at all. And the question is: 'Who can stop this happening?' And the answer is that nobody can. There is no authority in Islam to stop that happening. So it sort of surges with the trends and the way in which Islam thinks.

In terms of Christianity, the biggest challenge is Pentecostalism. Now that is a movement that currently has half a billion members; it's astonishing. And what it means for me as a former Marxist is that the heart of Pentecostalism is where the Marxists used to be, and these Pentecostalists are doing what the Marxists used to do in terms of social programmes and so on. But it is a question of all these things springing up and they are not centralized; in Catholicism there is a centralized authority, in Protestant denominations there isn't really. I mean, the Archbishop would be the first to tell you, he doesn't have very much authority. He has personal authority because of who he is; he has a kind of *ex officio* authority, but actually, if he says something then it doesn't mean people actually have to do it. And so I think there is a real need for a nation to take steps to limit religious aggression.

Would you describe yourself as a conservative evangelical?

Well, I'm not such a conservative. I think conservative means who you define yourself as being over and against. But I would certainly self-define as an evangelical, I would certainly self-define as a Christian, and I would certainly self-define as a Protestant.

How do you read the Bible?

Well, I expect to find things to ponder on. It is a bit like reading love letters: it reminds you of things, but it also reconnects you with something important; it is about deepening your relationship with your faith. But I suppose I also look to it for guidance; you know, for what to do, what ideas I should be trying to express. For Christians, the simplest moral guidance has always been in the person of Christ. You probably know Gilbert Sheldon's famous maxim: 'What would Jesus do?' Well, although you might say it is very naive, it is actually extremely effective. A good criterion for moral judgements is: 'What would Jesus do?' It works very, very well in terms of personal ethics, though it is much more difficult in terms of social ethics. But certainly for how to behave personally it is very effective.

Does your faith give you self-confidence?

Well, I would want to make a distinction between two different types of self-confidence. There is a certain arrogance – which I don't have really – but then there is a sense of stability and inner peace with yourself and thinking, 'Well actually, I've got things pretty well sorted out' and that is where I am at the moment. So, yes, in that sense I do.

Do you have an ambition for your faith or for religion?

Well, because I believe that Christianity is right, I am very happy to present it as such to anyone who will listen, in the hope that they will either argue with me, or accept that they think it's right, So in that sense I have no problems in commending my faith. So do I have an ambition for it? Well, I want people to believe it because I think it's right. But I wouldn't want that to be a passive unthinking acceptance, I would want it to be an informed one. But I think most people would take that view of their own way of thinking; they wish that other people thought the same way. And this is not because they are arrogant, or aggressive, but because they think: 'I have thought about this and think it is right and so I want to share that.'

Can you imagine a situation where you might ever lose or change your faith?

Well, I was an atheist who lost my faith some years ago, and so I have to keep that possibility open, don't I? I think it is true that people change their religious views. I think my experience has been much more about developing within Christianity. Christianity is a very big tent, it has different forms, and you very quickly discover that it is actually very rich, but again, at one point I thought I was a very convinced atheist. I can see that I was young then, and maybe didn't know quite as much as I thought I did, but certainly I would not want to be over-confident. That is what my interest in debate is for, because if somebody gets the better of me I will have to rethink.

10

Abdelwahab El Affendi

Do you have a working definition of the term religion?

The short answer is no. But there is a sociological definition which is that it is 'what a person holds most valuable'. And that is a problematic definition because there might be people who wouldn't hold their religion as the most valuable thing. I would call these people liberals. A definition of a liberal is someone who doesn't take religion seriously.

So you don't think there can be such a thing as liberal religion?

Possibly. But I think liberalism consists of not being too attached, so you are tolerant in the sense that you are open to other influences, but you don't take them that seriously, though you don't abandon them either. It is not that you are an atheist or are opposed to religion, but you are somebody who looks at religion in a broader context. You don't live by religion; it is just part of your life.

A liberal might take principles like rationality and the primacy of the individual very seriously. You are saying that that is not a religion in itself.

Well it could be if you are a militant liberal! Then it would be your religion.

Would you say that Richard Dawkins is a militant liberal?

I think so, yes. And this is interesting because it creates this contradiction: A liberal is supposed to be tolerant, but usually he is not tolerant of people who take their religion too seriously. So there are limits. So in this sense you could say he is intolerant because his religion is liberalism. When somebody becomes so attached to liberalism that they are willing to sacrifice other values for it, then you could say that it is a religion. You might say a similar thing about Communism. Though, of course, some people have a problem with that. They say that if you broaden the definition of religion to take account of all these tendencies then, by definition, you are not following our definition of religion.

Traditional definitions of religion usually include some kind of supernatural or supra-natural aspect. Would your definition also include Communism and militant secular humanism?

Yes. Something could be a religion if it becomes dogmatic. Most religion has a dogmatic core. There is something there that is not questioned. And if a secular ideology develops a core like this, then it becomes a religion. If it becomes militant and dogmatic about its position, then it becomes a religion. And then, of course, when dogma conflicts with reality – as in the case of Communism – then you have to rationalize it in order for it to keep making sense. That is what religion is about. Theology is the process by which we rationalize things.

How do you define faith?

I think I would say it is kind of the belief aspect of religion. It is the way that you perceive the dogma and also it is your attachment to it. When you speak about religion, usually you are speaking about the practice of it, the social aspect of it, the institutions and so on. But when you speak about faith, you are speaking about the individuals' attachment to, and their receptiveness to, the dogma and even their enthusiasm for it. But if you call a religion a faith, you relegate it from the area of social compliance to just a spiritual level. So, for example, when you call the Queen the defender of the faith rather than defender of religion, her status has been relegated to a more spiritual level.

What do you mean by spiritual or spirituality?

Spirituality, I think, refers to the inner dimension of the faith. It is un-coerced, and positive. When people say, 'I get strength from my faith', or 'I have faith in this', it is about something that comes from within. It is usually un-coerced. It is usually something positive and enriching. Religion doesn't necessarily have this quality, because it can be forced. For example, one of the admonishments of Christ to his followers was: 'You people lack spirituality, you comply in appearance and you say you believe and you do what you are told but you don't have that inner strength which is the faith and the belief.' You know; the thing that makes you walk on water!

What about the idea of God?

Well, it depends on what religion you are talking about. Usually in the monotheistic religions God is an individual, a person or a subject. He is the highest authority, the creator and the originator. Of course, if you are looking at other religions, God can be a multiplicity of spiritual beings who have certain powers. But in the monotheistic religions he is the locus of authority, the origin of the universe, a judge and so on. Of course, one of the things about religion is that they start with the presence of God but they end up going through a process of reification. People talk of Christianity or Islam as if *it* was God. For example, in the modern discourse of Muslims people will say 'what Islam supposes' or 'Islam thinks that'. It becomes a kind of entity like an objective thing. If you read either the Bible or the Qur'an you find that it says 'God orders you to do this' or 'God orders you to do that'. It's not 'Islam orders you' or 'Christianity orders you'. But when it comes to polemics, then people start speaking of tradition. You know 'Islam is good' or 'Islam is bad' or 'Islam is evil' or whatever. This is where the problems like the one we had with the cartoons, come from. Religion becomes a kind of identity. So Islam is 'what we are'; it is our identity. So the attitude is 'when you speak about Islam, you are not speaking about God, you are speaking about me. So if you insult Islam, you insult me.' Originally of course, God was the focus, and it was not Islam or Christianity. So if somebody said that Islam has done evil things, then it was seen as if they were saying that God had done evil things, and this was not seen as an insult. But this is not the way it is seen nowadays. God has become distant from the religion, and religion has just become a source of identity. Look, for example, at the way that insulting the prophet of Islam becomes more of a problem than insulting God. So if you deny God, or if you say evil things against God, that is not seen as an attack on Islam because you could be seen as attacking Christianity, or attacking Judaism; because all of them speak about and worship the same God. But when you attack Muhammad, it is seen that you are attacking the Muslim identity, because this is what differentiates Muslims from Christians and Jews – because they follow Muhammad. And this explains some of the social implications of these remarks. There was a writer called Wilfred Cantwell Smith who wrote a book in the 1940s called *Modern Islam and India*, and he noticed that in India as far as Muslim Indians were concerned, you could say whatever you liked about God, you could deny God, but an insult against Muhammad could, from the most moderate Muslim, incite a response of blazing proportions.

I remember in the mid-1980s I was editing a magazine, and we had a correspondent in India. And there was this local newspaper which published a small story about an idiot in a small village, and the title of the story was 'Muhammad the Idiot'. And of course, the people in that town said 'Well, whoever wrote this must be a Hindu, otherwise, why would he choose a title like this?' And immediately there was a riot, and they went to the newspaper's building and they burned it down.

This kind of response does not seem to occur if an insult is made against Christ. The contrast might be particularly surprising given that in the Christian tradition Christ is God incarnate and in the Muslim tradition Muhammad certainly isn't God incarnate.

Well I think, particularly in the Indian subcontinent, it has to do with the communal taunts, the struggle between communities or identities. For example, the Hindus are upset because the Muslims deny their Gods, and the whole of the Qur'an, of course, is anti-polytheism. So they see this as an insult, and so they try to reciprocate and they know that they can do this by insulting the Prophet. And there are already communal tensions anyway over power and all sorts of things, and so this is a part of that. We don't, for example, find a lot of this in other areas. If you go to countries where there are Muslims and Christians, there is nothing like this. This is because the Muslims do not insult Christ; they recognize him so there is common ground. But there are also other problems apart from the religious difference. If you look at the conflict in Iraq there are sectarian and ethnic problems that are not really religious problems. Often, I think, the problem stems from community tensions. For example, I spent about half an hour once listening to a Turkish Cypriot diplomat speaking about how the Greeks have dared steal dishes which are Turkish and called them Greek dishes. And he tried to explain that *souvlaki* and *dolma* were Turkish dishes, and that it was an insult to hear them described as Greek, and that it could be a matter that could lead to a war or fighting as part of the tension between these two communities. But this is obviously not really the issue. The issue is that for a long time these two countries have vied for supremacy in the region, The Turks regard themselves as the Ottomans were when they ruled the Greeks, and the Greeks regard themselves as an ancient civilization which couldn't be ruled by these barbarians. So these kinds of tensions are where the problems arise. And I think in the Indian context it is the same thing. The Indians regard themselves as an ancient civilization and the Muslims are newcomers who have ruled them in the past and they are unhappy about this. And the Muslims feel that they are the ones that should be ruling, because they had been the rulers of the land but the British didn't allow it and so on.

So in these contexts, religion is just another communal identifier in the same way that race or tribe might be?

Yes. Look at Northern Ireland for example. Catholicism in Ireland is part of a communal identity: it is no longer a matter of faith or religion; it is a matter of tribal identity.

Richard Dawkins believes that if people let go of their religion, there wouldn't be a conflict in Northern Ireland. Would your response to that be that in that case they would just find something else to fight over?

Yes. I mean Arabs and Kurds in Iraq have the same religion and they fight. And you find that a lot, that people with the same religion still fight. Of course religion and scripture are involved. For example, a lot of people talk about suicide terrorism these days. And they say of course that religion plays a big part in this. There is this idea that if you die you will go to heaven, and for a lot of people their life is miserable and they are humiliated and so this seems like a short cut to heaven. And you might ask why this idea does not occur in all religions. Well some have argued that in Christianity, especially in Protestantism, you cannot be saved by your works, and so you don't believe that if you do something you will be saved. But, they argue, in Islam, you can be saved by your works. But this is not actually true. Some Sunnis also don't believe that you can be saved by works; you can only be saved by grace. They believe that nobody will be saved by his works because whatever you do is a favour from God. And because they are God's favour, they can never be paid for, so you are always in debt to him. It is up to him to save you if he decides, and doing good deeds may be part of being saved, but it is not necessary. And it is possible that you can do good deeds, but if you do one bad deed it will spoil everything for you. For example, if you steal, or if you have debts, then even if you are a martyr, unless your debts are repaid you cannot be saved. Because if you injure another human being you cannot be saved by just doing good works, you have to repay that person for the injury.

But the point I wanted to make is that although most Muslims do believe that if you are a martyr you go to heaven immediately, not every person would want to do that. So you have to ask why the Palestinians, or some Palestinians and not others, want to become suicide bombers. And there can be people who can be very fanatical, but who don't seem to have gone this way. So there must be complex motives, both at the level of organization – you have organizations which approach potential martyrs and train and motivate them. But also you have a kind of general atmosphere which is created by the occupation and which leads people to use suicide terrorism. So it has to be a complex problem. And Western governments talk a lot about extremism and so on, but this is only part of the problem. If there are British troops in Iraq, or Israeli troops in Palestine, then it is likely that the fanatical groups will find more recruits. But if you look at the history of this issue, for a long time the anti-Israel struggle in Palestine was led by groups that were very secular; they were Marxists or whatever. The Islamists actually stayed out of it for a long time on religious grounds. Hamas refused to join the PLO on the grounds that it was a Marxist-inspired secular organization and the fight was not a fight for Islam, but rather, a fight between secular Arabs and secular Israel and they wanted no part of it. They could only join the fight if there was a legitimate Islamic government. This is because in traditional Islamic thought, only an Islamic government can declare *jihad*. It's not right for Osama Bin Laden to just declare *jihad*, there has first to be a legitimate authority. And initially, the Israeli government encouraged Hamas because they thought they would be a good rival to Arafat and the PLO.

Do you think that human beings have a religious impulse?

Yes, I think that impulse is strong. It is a reality, in a sense, that for many people religion is how they see and relate to the world. But it is not, in itself, a determinant of everything people do. Religious militancy is usually a political thing: militants are more concerned with what other people do. But I would see most religious people as being primarily concerned with their own soul, their own salvation. They are not worried about what the Pope says, or what Salman Rushdie says or whatever. They might be upset by it, but it is not the main issue for him or her. The main issue is how you conduct yourself in an ethical way. So I think it is an abiding reality that there is a religious impulse. But it is also a part of your cosmology. If you believe in an afterlife then it would certainly be an abiding concern. It has been said: 'If you believe for example that if you do certain things such as having illicit sex then you are going to burn in hell for ever, then it wouldn't sound worth it. If you are going to burn for ever, then it is hardly a good bargain!' But that is common sense. I mean, if you are about to smoke a joint and you believe that there are police outside who will arrest you and put you in jail for ten years then you are not going to do it. So that is part of religion, but you can have people who are ethical but are not religious. There are people, like Kant for example, or other people who are pacifists, who want to do things because they feel it is good. And that is a spiritual feeling. If you want, for example, to help the environment, or to help the poor, or to abstain from doing things that do damage to other people, then you can do that as a matter of ethics. But a religious attitude will include God, and a person will say 'I want to do this, or I want to believe in this, because it will please God'; and I think that is what you call the religious element. There is a cosmic reality that means you relate to a supreme being and you are looking toward another life and this could affect people's behaviour. So Muslims will not do certain things because they think it will not be pleasing to God. If you think for example about putting money in the bank in order to earn interest, it may not seem that problematic. But then because God says you can't do it, we don't do it. So it does have this kind of influence. For example, one of the things that defines both Muslims and Jews is not eating pork. But in Islamic law, there is no punishment for eating pork – there is punishment for drinking and doing other things, but not for eating pork. Yet you will find that the last thing Muslims would do is eat pork; they will drink, they will do other things, but they still won't eat pork!

Why is that?

I don't know! A friend of mine was in China during the 1980s and he found that there was an indigenous Muslim community there which had existed long before Communism. And they had forgotten almost everything about Islam, and there was a small Jewish community there too, and the two communities had merged together into one defined solely by the fact that they don't eat pork. They don't read the Qur'an, they don't pray, they don't do anything except that they don't eat pork. So this has become a kind of ethnic identity: they are a community of people who don't eat pork!

Tariq Ramadan could be seen as a conservative reformer who still believes that inspiration or guidance for Muslims comes from a reassessed version of the Shariah. You have been described as a liberal reformer – i.e. someone who doesn't believe that the Shariah should play this role.

Well, I have said that there is a problem with Shariah because anything religious has to be a personal thing. So anything that wants to impose a religion, the countries or groups or movements that want to impose Shariah, have a problem. But if people want, by their own will, to abide by the Shariah then that is acceptable to the liberal tradition, because people should be allowed to do what they like. But you shouldn't impose things. I have written that fundamentalists want to 'drag people kicking and screaming into paradise'. But that is not possible: you cannot be pushed into paradise, you have to believe. So if you conform with everything, like in Saudi Arabia, just because it is law then you are not really a religious person, though you may be a hypocrite or a coward or whatever. I look at faith as the outcome of our values, and I do think it should be encouraged but we should not impose it on others.

Can you say something about your own personal relationship with Islam?

Well, like Tariq Ramadan I want to reinterpret Islam. I work from within the tradition, I don't work against it. I try to reformulate it in a way which conforms to my liberal tendencies, my own personal preferences. That is how I see it.

And has your relationship with your faith changed throughout your life?

I think it has been fairly consistent. I keep saying the same things – it is boring sometimes; but then not many people are listening to me!

11

Richard Dawkins

Do you have a working definition of the term religion?
I wouldn't call it one working definition, I'm aware that there are many different implicit definitions. So, for example, there are people who believe that there is a god, who is a person, who listens to your thoughts, listens to your prayers, forgives your sins, knows what you're thinking, knows what you're doing, punishes you if you do wrong, all that kind of thing. At the other extreme there are people like Einstein who don't believe in God at all in that sense but who sometimes use what sounds like religious language for their sense of reverence for the complexity and the grandeur of the universe, for the scale of geological time and the feel of that uplifting sensation in the chest which they call religion. I think that's a misuse of words, because what most people mean by religion is something closer to the first definition that I mentioned: the deliberate, intelligent, conscious being who listens to your prayers and so on. But you will certainly find people who, in my view, muddy the waters by using religious language for Einsteinian religion, which is not religion at all.

Do you have a working definition of the word faith?
Yes I do: belief in the absence of supporting evidence. There are people who will tell you, 'Oh, but, you have faith that your wife loves you', or something of that sort. But that's not faith because that is based on evidence, subtle evidence, but it is evidence of a lifetime of living with her, listening to catches in the voice, looks in the eye; that's evidence – it's not faith. Faith is believing in something when there literally isn't a scrap of evidence. If there were a scrap of evidence, then it wouldn't be faith. It would be a proper evidence-based belief.

Is it true to say that you think that adherence to a religion or a faith is a bad thing?

Yes. I mean I'm not saying that there hasn't been good done in the name of religion and in the name of faith. There are clearly some very good clergymen, and there are clearly people who do good in the name of faith. But there are plenty of people who do good in the name of other things too. I think they're not really strongly correlated. There are plenty of people who do very bad things in the name of faith, and that really is in the name of faith – faith is vital to that. If you *know* that you are right and the other person is wrong, and if the other person *knows* that she is right and you are wrong, and neither of you has any evidence so it is not possible to argue your way out of your quarrel, then the only thing left is physical violence, which is what it comes down to. You see this in the Crusades, in Northern Ireland, in the Middle East. And by the way, when I say things like Northern Ireland and the Middle East I'm fully aware that when somebody in those troubled places kills somebody else, it's not actually for theological reasons. They're not sort of saying: 'Take that, transubstantiationalist!' It is a tribal vendetta that goes back sometimes many generations. But without religious faith and all that goes with it there would be no label by which to know who is on your side and who is on the other side. It's as if people are saying, 'We know that we are Protestants and we kill Catholics', or 'We know that we're Catholics and we kill Protestants – we don't actually know what the difference between a Catholic and a Protestant is, but nevertheless it was a Catholic that killed my father or a Protestant that killed my grandfather so I have a tribal vendetta going.' If you abolished faith-based education then you would get rid of those sorts of troubles because there would no longer be that tribal identity. It's the fact that this Catholic's father and grandfather went to Catholic schools and therefore were segregated from a very early age from the Protestant children going to Protestant schools that makes for these terrible tribal divisions. So I think that faith is very dangerous; it is not the only thing that causes tribal divisions, but it is a very potent and powerful label for tribal divisions.

There are many examples of places where religion is not the prime factor in tribal divisions – in Rwanda, for instance, or in the Middle East before the rise of Islamism when Arab nationalism was the dominant factor. Why do you think faith-based tribal divisions are so uniquely important?

Well as I said, faith is not the only basis for tribal labels. So in parts of Africa it is literally tribes; these could be defined by different languages, different backgrounds and so on – in South Africa it's different races. So there are other factors. But in a place like Northern Ireland there isn't anything else. People in Northern Ireland tell me that they can tell whether someone is a Protestant or a Catholic. But that's got to be some sort of cultural concomitant of the fundamental religious divide, which wouldn't be there if you didn't have segregated education and segregated areas where people live. And so religious faith is being used as a label in a place where there aren't any other labels.

Could you explain the difference between what could be called a religious project and the scientific project?

A scientific project attempts to discover the truth about the world on the basis of evidence in a very specific way. A religious project knows what is true about the world because it was written in a holy book, or was handed down by a tradition or was revealed by some kind of inner communication with God. I think that religion is actively hostile to the scientific project in the sense that it teaches you to be content with a lack of evidence. It teaches you to be happy with saying: 'I just know that's true, because my people, my tribe, my tradition has always said that's true; I know that's true because my priest says its true; I know that's true because my holy book says its true; I know that's true because a small voice inside me tells me it's true.' That is all anti-scientific. It discourages people from saying: 'Let's go and look at the evidence and find out what actually is true.'

Do you see religion as being in conflict with science because it is trying to do the same thing as science but from a completely different basis?

I do think that, but in that respect I differ from some sophisticated theologians who say there is absolutely no conflict because they are looking at different things, they have no connections. So there is a realm which is science's realm, and religion is not interested in trespassing in that domain. So the realm of the real world, the realm of the universe, the realm of physics and biology, all that is scientific territory and religion has nothing to do with it. Religion has a different territory. It's never been made clear to me what that territory is. It's sometimes said to be a question of morality, it's sometimes said to be questions of what you might call 'ultimate questions'. There's a very naive way of putting it which is that science is concerned with the 'How?' and religion is concerned with the 'Why?' But what is this 'Why?' that they talk about? So I don't take that view; I think that religion is in one sense in the same business as science in that it is making an attempt to answer the same questions as science: What is the universe? Why are we here? What is life? How did the universe start? How did life start? Do miracles happen? These are all scientific questions. Let's take the more profound ones first.

A universe that had a creator God in it would be a totally different kind of universe – scientifically speaking – than a universe that didn't. So you cannot just say, 'Oh well, religion's questions are quite different from science's questions; you can't say that, because the universe, if religious statements were true, would be, scientifically speaking, a very different universe. And coming down to more trivial realms – for instance miracles – well, your sophisticated theologian will say, 'Oh we don't believe in miracles any more, that's a different domain, this is science's territory . . .' But if you imagine a thought experiment in which archaeologists discovered DNA evidence that Jesus never had a father, Jesus was born of a virgin, and that evidence was published in a scientific journal, can you imagine those theologians saying: 'Oh that has nothing to do with us, science is a different area.' Of course they wouldn't. They would immediately embrace that scientific evidence in support of their religious faith. So this claim that science and religion have nothing to do with each other is only made as long as there is no scientific evidence for it. If somebody did produce scientific evidence for a religious claim, then immediately science would be embraced.

So is religion based on ignorance of science?

Well, I would probably have said that about creationism, which is a bit different.

So how do you respond to the many scientists who profess some kind of religious faith – whether it is Robert Winston, who is a practising Jew, or Francis S. Collins, who is the director of the human genome project?

Well when you say many, you've named two. There are about five others of any distinction. I don't think there are that many actually. If you cross-question them carefully, I think you'll find that an enormous number of those that call themselves religious are religious either in the Einsteinian sense which I mentioned earlier, or in the sense of loyalty to a cultural tradition – this is particularly the case if you are a Jew, and my private suspicion is that this applies to Robert Winston. I've tried to get it out of him several times. I don't think Robert Winston believes in God. I think he believes in Judaism; I think he has an immense loyalty to his cultural tradition – as well one would if one had been through what the Jews have been through. It's an ancient tradition, and he is incredibly learned in Hebrew scriptures and a pillar of the Orthodox Jewish community. But if you actually look at what the orthodox Jewish community are supposed to believe, Robert couldn't possibly believe that. You know, they believe Genesis is literally true, they believe the world is only 10,000 years old. So my private suspicion is that Robert does not believe in God, but puts up a front out of loyalty to his cultural heritage. I know Anglicans and Catholics, so called, who do the same. And they're usually more willing to talk about it. Martin Reese, the president of the Royal Society goes to church but is an unbeliever, and the college chapels in Oxford where they have a great musical tradition – like New College, my own College – every Sunday they're full, but they are full of people who love the music and love the tradition.

Why is it important for you to be a passionate advocate against faith-based religion?

Well, I don't feel passionate about the Norse gods, and the ancient Greek gods, but I probably would if I was surrounded by people who believed in them and who were killing each other in the name of Thor and Wotan or Poseidon. So beliefs in non-existent entities are almost infinite in number and are mostly harmless because they don't exist, and nobody believes in them any more. But belief in Yahweh is rife in the world, belief in Allah is rife in the world, and I think enough evil is done in the name of faiths that people really do hold that one is right to be worried and passionate about them. The United States now is run by a born-again Christian who believes that God talks to him, who believes that God told him to invade Iraq, but didn't tell him that there weren't any weapons of mass destruction of course. Whether he believes in the rapture and Armageddon and the tribulation I don't know, but an awful lot of his support comes from people who do. There are a very substantial number of people in the United States – it may even be the majority – who believe that the end of the world will be a good thing because it will be the prelude to the second coming of Christ; they believe the end of the world is most likely to come from nuclear war. In America, there are a substantial number of people who want nuclear war because they think that Jesus won't come again until after Armageddon. Sam Harris says that the fact that a substantial number of people in America believe in something like that is a crisis. It is a crisis when getting on for a majority of people in the most powerful country in the world, with by far the most powerful weapon systems in the world, they are so detached from reality. And not only are they detached from reality but are facing in the direction of those who think that the end of the world will be glorious.

And perhaps less immediately dangerous, but nevertheless extremely unsettling to any scientist, is the fact that about 50 per cent of the American people believe that the world is less than 10,000 years old. That is a huge disconnect from reality. It's not just slightly wrong; it's massively, massively wrong. There are various ways that you can express how wrong it is. I calculated the other day that the error for thinking that the world is

6,000 years old, is equivalent to believing that the distance between New York and San Francisco is 700 yards. That's the magnitude of the error which 50 per cent of the American people believe. Now these are not in general unrealistic people: they are capable of running their lives; they can drive a car; they can dig their garden; they can hold down a job; they can pay their income tax; they can write cheques; they're not incompetent. In most respects they lead a life which is grounded and rooted in reality; until it comes to religion. Then suddenly, they believe things which are equivalent to believing that there is only 700 yards from New York to San Francisco. And I think that's a subversion of the human mind; it amounts to a deceit. It's an infectious disease, which passes down the generations and which travels sideways from preachers who are immensely well financed. I don't know whether you've ever turned on a television and seen their shows, but in America you get bombarded with this all the time. And there is an unbelievable naivety and crudeness to how they con people, get their confidence, and then take their money which they then spend on yet more television stations and television broadcasts to con yet more people to give more money and to persuade people of these extraordinary and fallacious ideas.

Someone like Bishop Richard Harries would probably respond to that by saying that he shares all your criticisms of that kind of religion, but what you are doing is critiquing a whole religious practice on the basis of its worst adherents.

It's a fair point. With respect to the television programme that I made about this, it was a little unfortunate because we did invite the Archbishop of Canterbury, the Archbishop of Westminster and the Chief Rabbi to take part, and none of them agreed to be interviewed. Richard Harries however did, and he did very well, and I know him quite well anyway. But when you say it is picking on extremists, in America they're not extremists. Fifty per cent of the population think the entire universe began after the domestication of the dog. It's not extreme; its mainstream. Pastor Ted Haggard whom I had that altercation with has a weekly telephone conversation with George Bush. He is one of George Bush's chief spiritual advisers. So it is certainly looking pretty bad at the moment, in more or less the whole of Islam and in America. It's OK in Europe at the moment, although Britain has a tendency to take after America. I think one of the interesting points Sam Harris makes about Islam is that there isn't such a separation between the sensible moderate ones like Bishop Harries and the lunatics, because they all are committed to the belief that the Qur'an is the literal word of God, unlike Bishop Harries who doesn't believe the Bible is the literal word of God.

So what would you say was going on with an individual like Tariq Ramadan who is a reformist and wants to vanquish the Osama Bin Laden tendencies in Islam.

Does he come out and say that the Qur'an is not the literal word of God?

He says it should be read in its historical context.

Well good for him, I wish him luck, but there aren't many like that.

You say that religion is an affront to the human capacity and to human knowledge. Why is that so important to you?

Well, setting aside all the suicide bombings and all that, I suppose you could say it doesn't really matter. I mean, people like watching Big Brother, and they're welcome to it. It just seems such a shame that people should go to their grave having got nothing out of their life but falsehood.

Religion may not be true in an empirical, scientific sense, but that doesn't mean that it's not meaningful for those who are religious, and that it's not valuable to them. There is even evidence to suggest that being religious can make people happier.

Well, it may be true that people who are religious are happier than people who are not religious. But I suppose that, being a scientist and being an academic, I care passionately about what's true. And so, if somebody were to say to me, 'Would you like yourself, and your family, and other people to be born, grow up and die believing falsehoods just because it makes them happy', well, I can see why somebody might like that, but I think it's tragic. If you want happiness of that sort, take drugs. There are plenty of ways of making someone happy and evading the truth. Though with taking drugs you don't even have to evade the truth, you could probably find a drug formula that could give you that same happiness whilst still being able to see the truth. I think it's understandable, but I can't sympathize with any view that says religion can be justified by the fact that it's making people happy.

Imagine one of your students came to you, a student who was highly intelligent, and they said to you: 'I'm having a problem, I'm having a crisis of faith, and that crisis of faith is that I'm starting to have a religious belief. It's not something I can argue rationally, it's not something that came to me rationally, but it's within me and I am trying very hard to shake it off but it's growing. I can see that there is no empirical evidence for this and yet it still seems to be true and I cannot negate or ignore my own experience.' How would you respond to that?

I think I would say: 'How fascinating, how interesting, let's talk about this. Where do you think that comes from? I mean you know about the brain, you know that in extreme cases there are people who totally believe they're Napoleon, and where does that come from? If somebody believes they're Napoleon, is there something that you could identify in his nervous system which gives him this delusion? And what makes you think that it's not the same with you?' But I think I would try to talk it through in a dispassionate way, and get him or her to try to analyse it.

You talk about religious ideas being infectious, and you've written about the spread of ideas, and coined the word 'meme' to describe a self-replicating idea. Why do you think religious beliefs are so infectious?

Well, I think, in general, it is not that difficult to understand why certain psychological predispositions are likely to be present in people, especially children. Psychologists have discovered that there is a pronounced tendency for children to believe what they are told by their parents, adults and teachers. And there are perfectly good Darwinian reasons for that. It would be very bad survival strategy for children to come into the world programmed by their genes to experiment and to look for evidence for everything – we'd die! You've got to believe what you're told: 'Don't go near the cliff's edge, don't experiment with it, never mind the evidence; just don't go there.' So there are very good Darwinian reasons for children's brains to be programmed with a rule like: 'Believe what your parents tell you.' And I think there are probably lots of other such psychological dispositions which lead the human mind to be vulnerable to infection by beliefs which are not well substantiated. The analogy with computer viruses is perhaps better than the analogy with human viruses, in the sense that in order for a computer to do useful work – word processing and that sort of thing – it is necessary that a computer should be programmable, and that it should follow instructions to the letter when they're given in the correct language. Given that computers are built in that way, they are automatically vulnerable to virus programs which at best say: 'Copy me, pass me on' and at worst say 'and by the way, while you're about it, do something malevolent to the data on this computer'. So vulnerability to a virus is an inevitable byproduct of the fact that computers work at all. And similarly, vulnerability to mind viruses such as religions is perhaps an inevitable product of both child and adult brains being well set up to survive and obey rules such as believe what you're told. So when I talk about religions as viruses, probably the clearest analogy would be to a computer virus.

Alister McGrath has engaged with that point by saying that it's a powerful rhetorical argument because viruses are nasty things. But then he asks whether you *literally* mean that religion is a virus of the mind? Because if so, he says there is no evidence for that. And if you just mean it in a metaphorical or analogical sense, then he asks: well, aren't all ideas? Why single out religion?

In a sense that's obvious. Because the whole point I'm making is that there is a similarity between legitimate computer programs like Microsoft Word, and viruses. I mean, as far as the computer is concerned, they're no different. A computer just gets its instructions; you know: 'Jump to location A, then jump to location B, pick up a number here, put it there and so on.' A computer just does it; it has no way of distinguishing between the viral programs and the legitimate programs like Microsoft Word. Now, another aspect of what a virus does is self-copying; it has built into it the rule: 'Copy me'. A program like Microsoft Word doesn't have that, there is nothing in the Microsoft Word code that says: 'Copy me and pass me on to the next person.' But there is in computer viruses. And if either a scientific idea, or a good computer program, or a good poem or something, appeals to people's minds, then people will pass it on. So there's a kind of sliding scale between ideas that spread just because they say, 'Spread me', which is the most naive kind of computer virus, and computer viruses called Trojan Horses, which are not technically viruses, but work by appealing to computer users, and they will worm their way in for instance by being pornographic, and so people will want to open it, and then the computer gets infected. So that's using the human mind as the copying mechanism. It's similar to the chain letters that people get in the post. The most naive kind of chain letter will just say: 'Make six copies of this letter and send it to six friends.' The slightly more sophisticated ones will use a bit of cajoling; they will say something like: 'If you don't send this letter on to six friends then some terrible misfortune will befall you, but if you do, you'll win a million pounds.' There are enough idiots out there who believe that. And, of course, often there's a great baggage of anecdotes which support the warnings in the chain letter. And as long as some people are fool enough to believe it, they will pass it on. Hence the idea that both computers and the human mind are devices which are to a greater or lesser extent vulnerable to 'copy me' instructions of various types, which can be very naive instructions, or slightly more sophisticated instructions like 'Copy me or else'. Or, not really saying copy me at all, but just a very funny joke that somebody has told you so you automatically pass it on, or a very good tune so you automatically pass that on and it infects somebody else. So I don't want to stand on a tremendous distinction between ideas that are spreadable because they have a sort of low-end viral quality of just saying 'Copy me' or a high-end quality of being copied because they're good. There's probably a sliding scale between them. But something which is good because it's a good tune or a good joke, call it a virus if you like but I don't care, I'm glad it spreads. If somebody tells me a joke I'll tell somebody else, I think that's fine. I think that religious ideas, in many cases, spread just because people are very naive. When I'm asked to explain the evolutionary origins of religion, I find the viral analogy quite convincing.

So do we have a proclivity for religious belief?

Yes. As I've said, we have psychological predispositions which manifest themselves as religious beliefs in some circumstances. And we all have a proclivity to obey authoritative commands, whether it's parents or police-men, or politicians or whatever. And that proclivity, under the right cul-tural conditions, will manifest itself as religion. We all have a tendency to believe what we're told if we see it written down, more than if we just hear it as gossip. For instance, once gossip becomes enshrined in the pages of the *Sun*, people somehow are more likely to believe it than they would have done if they had just taken it for what it is; which is just stuff that has been made up.

Do you think these proclivities could be taken in any way as inherited myths?

I think that they give rise to inherited myths, and inherited myths are another of the manifestations of such proclivities. There is certainly a ten-dency for people to believe gossip in the *Sun* because it is written down. Another thing that will lead people to take something seriously is if it is very old. And so a rumour that was invented yesterday will be less impres-sive than a rumour that was invented 2,000 years ago and that has been handed down over generations.

Do we have an urge as human beings towards something that can be called the transcendent?

Well, we probably do, and if by transcendent you mean what I was trying to convey when I talked about Einsteinian religion then I'm all for it, I've written books about it myself. But let's be clear about it, it's one thing to feel a sense of awe at the world, and it's quite another thing to believe all sorts of other things. I remember having an extraordinary argument with that woman that did *Desert Island Discs*, Sue Lawley, because one of my choices on *Desert Island Discs* was Bach's *St Matthew Passion*. And she asked me how I could possibly choose the *St Matthew Passion*? And what I didn't say, though I probably should have done, is that I can enjoy

Wuthering Heights without believing that Heathcliff and Cathy really ever existed. It is fiction, and obviously one can be moved by fiction, that's why we read novels.

One of your major concerns about religion is the violence that people are prepared to do in the name of God, and that idea seems to rest on the belief that an atheistic world would be an inherently less violent and divisive one that a theistic world. John Gray points out that in the twentieth century, the great destructive ideologies were Communism, Maoism, Nazism and fascism and that they were all actually non-theistic, or atheistic. One conclusion might be that human beings have a natural propensity towards violence and a belief in God or otherwise is incidental to that.

The argument about Hitler and Stalin and such people is sometimes expressed as though Hitler and Stalin were actually motivated by atheism rather than it being incidental. Actually, I don't think Hitler was an atheist, but Stalin certainly was. But I don't think anybody could seriously maintain that Stalin did the terrible things that he did in the defence of atheism or something like that. I mean, he was an atheist, but it was more important that he was a Marxist, and his attitude to Marxism had many of the worst features of religion. It was dogmatic, he strongly believed in the end justifying the means and so on. So I often get a bit impatient with people who bring up Hitler and Stalin in that context. But the case of Hitler is complicated by the fact that he probably was a religious man, in a funny sort of way. He certainly believed in providence, and he claimed to be a Catholic.

Julia Neuberger has said that 'religion is neither good nor bad – it just is', and the moral way in which it manifests itself is too complex to judge it in one way or another.

Well OK, I mean I think that's probably right. I certainly don't think we should go through history picking examples and just tallying everything up. I think she's right about that. I do think, however, that whenever you've got disputes, whether its war, or just plain arguments between people which are threatening to become violent, if reasoning your opponent round to your way of thinking isn't an option (because your opponent isn't interested in reason, they're interested in faith), that seems to me to be an unpromising start. We are likely to get less violent if at least there's common ground in the following sense – that each of us knows what it would take to persuade us that we're wrong. And if you listen to scientists arguing, it is true that scientists get egotistical, and can get very committed to their long held beliefs, but all scientists at least as an ideal pay lip service to the idea that they know what it will take to change their minds; whereas if you talk to a religious person, they are proud of the fact that they won't change their minds. They would say: 'I know this is right because I have faith, because it's revealed to me; nothing will talk me out of this.'

Look at the case of Kurt Wise. He is an American geologist who read geology at Harvard under Steven Jay Gould. I've written about him in my book, *The God Delusion*:

He obtained a degree in geology at the University of Chicago, followed by two higher degrees in geology and palaeontology at Harvard. He was a highly qualified and genuinely promising young scientist, well on his way to achieving his dream of teaching science and doing research at a proper university. Then tragedy struck. It came, not from outside but from within his own mind, a mind fatally subverted and weakened by a fundamentalist religious upbringing that required him to believe that the earth – the subject of his Chicago and Harvard geological education – was less than 10,000 years old. He was too intelligent not to recognize the head-on collision between his religion and his science, and the conflict in his mind made him increasingly uneasy. One day, he could hear the strain no more, and he clinched the matter with a pair of scissors. He took a Bible and went right through it, literally cutting out every verse that would have to go if the scientific worldview were true. He wrote at the end of this ruthlessly honest labour-intensive exercise, there was so little left of his Bible that:

[T]ry as I might, and even with the benefit of intact margins throughout the pages of Scripture, I found it impossible to pick up the Bible without it being rent in two. I had to make a decision between evolution and Scripture. Either the Scripture was true and evolution was wrong or evolution was true and I must toss out the Bible . . . It was there that night that I accepted the Word of God and rejected all that would ever counter it, including evolution. With that, in great sorrow, I tossed into the fire all my dreams and hopes in science.

I find that terribly sad; whereas the Golgi Apparatus story moved me to tears of admiration and exultation, the Kurt Wise story is just plain pathetic – pathetic and contemptible. The wound, to his career and his life's happiness, was self-inflicted, so unnecessarily; so easy to escape. All he had to do was toss out the Bible. Or interpret it symbolically, or allegorically, as the theologians do. Instead, he did the fundamentalist thing and tossed out evidence and reason, along with all his dreams and hopes.

Perhaps uniquely among fundamentalists, Kurt Wise is honest – devastatingly, painfully, shockingly honest. Give him the Templeton Prize; he might be the first really sincere recipient. Wise brings to the surface what is secretly going on underneath, in the minds of fundamentalists generally, when they encounter scientific evidence that contradicts their beliefs. Listen to this peroration from Wise: 'Although there are scientific reasons for accepting a young earth, I am a young earth creationist, because that is my understanding of the Scripture. As I said to my professor when I was in college, if all the evidence in the universe turns against creationism, I would be the first to admit it, but I would still be a creationist, because that is what the Word of God means to me.'

Well, I think that's dreadfully sad. This is a mind that has been absolutely ruined by infection; a perfectly good mind, ruined by infection. Now that's evil. And he's only the tip of the iceberg; we know about him because he's honest, but there are millions out there like him.

What is the Golgi Apparatus story?

My belief in evolution is not fundamentalism, and it is not faith, because I know what it would take to change my mind, and I would gladly do so if the necessary evidence were forthcoming. And it does happen, and the Golgi Apparatus story is a wonderful example. It's the story of a respected elder statesman of the Zoology Department at Oxford when I was an undergraduate who for years had passionately believed, and taught, that the Golgi Apparatus (a microscopic feature of the interior of cells) was not real: an artefact, an illusion. Every Monday afternoon it was the custom for the whole department to listen to a research talk by a visiting lecturer. One Monday, the visitor was an American cell biologist who presented completely convincing evidence that the Golgi Apparatus was real. At the end of the lecture, the old man strode to the front of the hall, shook the American by the hand and said, with passion: 'My dear fellow, I wish to thank you. I have been wrong these 15 years!' We clapped our hands red. No fundamentalist would ever say that. In practice, not all scientists would. But all scientists pay lip service to it as an ideal.

12

Julia Neuberger

Do you have a working definition of the term religion?
No. It is different for different faiths, different belief systems, different groupings. Being Jewish, it's something about people-hood, something about shared values.

How do you define faith?
I think faith is absolutely about a belief system. It's about entering, sharing, being committed to, and being influenced by a set of beliefs that you share and think are basically right.

And where does God fit into that?
Well for most people God is absolutely central to that, although you'll find amongst quite a lot of Jews more agnosticism than you would necessarily expect. In many congregations, probably less so amongst the orthodox, but even amongst the orthodox, you can find people with a somewhat agnostic position in terms of belief in God as most people would understand it, but who nevertheless carry on the prayers and traditions as if they believed in God. It all gets quite complicated. I mean, I have a very basic belief in God, rather a simplistic belief in God, but that's what I grew up with and curiously it has stayed with me. Not necessarily a God who is a great being sitting on a cloud or anything like that, I don't have a sense of God's gender or of God being particularly like any being we would recognize. Rather, God is just there and both has a care for us and in some sense created us. I'm quite sure.

You are a Reform Jew. What does that mean?
The key difference is that if you're orthodox, you regard the Torah, the five books of Moses, and the rabbinic law as coming direct from God in one

single revelation on Mount Sinai. And people who aren't orthodox – and that's quite a wide gamut of opinion from what we call conservative, right through to liberal – take the view that revelation is not a one-off thing, that God reveals Him, Her, Itself to us continually, and you have to keep this informed sense of an ongoing revelation constantly in your mind and any knowledge you receive from any source, as well as the law that was revealed whenever. So we believe in what's called progressive revelation.

And so we believe that anybody can hear the voice of God, that sometimes the voice of God is your conscience within you. And so, for instance, in the book of Leviticus there is very strong condemnation of male homosexuality and we think that you have to say to yourself, is this really the word of God or is it really the attitudes of the men who were writing things down, who may have thought that it was the word of God – but were they right or were they merely revealing the views of their time? And if you say that everybody is shaped by the period they live in, and don't believe it's all solidly one-off revelation but believe that there is also a lot of human stuff in there, then you measure the texts by your conscience. And that's one of the reasons, for instance, that non-orthodox Judaism has been very accepting of gays.

How do you distinguish what is the word of God and what is the commentary of the time?

Well that's one of the difficult things. And that's always been difficult. All you can do is think and pray and listen to your conscience and argue things through, and in the end come to a decision in the light of the general thrust of what is right to do. And nobody is suggesting that we always get it right.

As the second woman ever to run your own synagogue you were a pioneer of sorts. Did that bring up ideas of faith or tradition that you had to challenge?

Not really. I was in a non-orthodox Jewish community, a liberal community, who were very keen to have a woman rabbi. I'm sure that my presence and my outspokenness were challenging to many other people, but did I feel I was challenging lots of things? Not really, no.

Can you draw parallels between your experience and with the issues involving the position of women in Christianity and Islam?

Much less with Islam, which tends to be pretty negative about women; it tends to regard them negatively so far as leadership is concerned. Orthodox Judaism does that. Non-orthodox Judaism has proclaimed woman's equality. And Reform Judaism in Britain was one of the many, many organizations that pushed for proper women's and girls' education. So it's bound up in all of that. So, as a parallel it is more like the position in the Church of England before they had women clergy. I often found myself preaching in cathedrals up and down the country because they wanted to show the liberal argument in favour of women clergy – but I wasn't a threat, as I was not Christian.

Would you say something about Judaism's relationship to Christianity and Islam?

The three are interconnected. I often think that Judaism and Islam are in many ways much closer together than either is to Christianity. Christianity is much more, in that sense, faith based. And the idea of doctrine and dogma is much stronger in Christianity than in either Islam or Judaism. Both Islam and Judaism have things like basic faith principles which you adhere to, or that you're expected to adhere to, but Islam and Judaism are much more likely to understand a thing like a common law or whatever it is by *doing*, by religious duty and carrying out prayers at a particular time of the day.

Also, I don't think Judaism is related to myth. I think Christianity may be related to myth. For example, I don't believe in the idea that there can be a human son of God – I believe that to be impossible and I don't believe in divinity being made human. Jesus, to me, is someone who was originally a teacher of Judaism, who was a human being, a prophet, a teacher. Judaism is different to Christianity in that regard. The story of the binding of Isaac in the book of Genesis is, I believe, designed to tell people not to sacrifice human beings. And if you don't believe these stories are true, that they actually happened, which is the non-orthodox approach, then you read them as having a particular purpose.

So what principles do you use when approaching biblical stories?

Reform Judaism still regards the rule of law, the Torah, as very important but we look at the stories and ask: 'How do we interpret them?' And we interpret them in the light of modern scientific knowledge, in the light of ideas and attitudes and legends current at the time of their writing – for instance the Noah's flood story and how that relates to the Epic of Gilgamesh and the ancient flood stories.

You consider yourself to be a religious person.

Yes. I do. I consider myself very religious but not very observant. That is to say I don't observe all the sorts of things that an orthodox rabbi would observe. But let's unpack that a little. So in terms of practice, which for so many people is what religion actually means – and this is something that

Richard Dawkins absolutely doesn't understand because he's so coloured by the particular type of Anglican upbringing he had – religion is how cultures mark birth, maturity, marriage, death. If you ask people on the Indian subcontinent, religion is not always about what you believe, it's about how you mark or how you celebrate or mourn or how as a community you treat certain issues. And that's really important and part of what it means to be part of a religious faith group. So, for example, I really hate it when we have to delay a burial following a death, because my religious community believes in quick burials. In Northern Ireland it's similar and people become uncomfortable if the person can't be buried quickly. And that's part of what being religious means: how we mark things. And I think those things are important and we should think about these things as part of our anchors. So that's one thing.

The second thing is to do with the faith bit. Now, for many Christians, what I'm going to say just will not make much sense, because many Jews, for quite a lot of the time, are not sure whether they believe or not. But they continue to practise as if they believed even though some of the time they're not sure. So they are not certain but are giving God the benefit of the doubt. Just imagine Richard Dawkins trying to understand that. He'd think we're all bonkers!

And then there's the thing about the awareness of spirituality. And you sometimes hear people talking about this in relation to nature and great works of art, great paintings for example. And all of that has been widely recognized. But I'm talking about something slightly different, the sense of the holy; for instance when we are gathered together for a ceremony and then there is a sense of solemnity and the sense of calm and still which descends over the community and not just you as an individual but over the community which you are with. And this is the sense of spirituality and being away from ordinary life which I think is very important.

So you think religion is a good thing?
It's neither good nor bad – it just is. I think it is good, and it can be used for good and it can be used for evil. People prey on religion in order to justify and do terrible things and they prey on religion to so some very good things. But it is a fact that human beings are faith seekers and our religions are neither good nor bad. For me it is important because it governs how I live my life and it helps me think that it is important to think of those who are disadvantaged, and it makes me feel that it's worth doing difficult things. For instance, I feel that the attitude that our society has towards refugees and asylum seekers is shameful. And part of that is because my mother was a refugee but part of it is shaped by the strong awareness that you find in the Bible and which is then shaped by one's

informed conscience that we do have a duty to look after the stranger, the widow and the orphan. In that way religion shapes the way I view the world.

Somebody like Richard Dawkins would argue very strongly that religion is a bad thing.

I think Richard Dawkins is a bad thing.

Why's that?

Because I think he's destructive. I don't think he listens. I think he's completely obsessed by his own views and doesn't listen to anybody else. I think people like Richard Dawkins and A. C. Grayling are very frightened by what they see as the rise of religion. They think religion is the equivalent of believing six impossible things before breakfast and they find that very hard to take. They feel that they are wholly convinced by Enlightenment values and that science gives them all the answers. But of course science only gives you the answers to the type of questions you set. So science is a way of looking at the world as well, which is something that they often forget. Take the way they say: this is a hard fact; if you wanted to challenge it you could. Let's take an example of the way people test drugs: randomized controlled trials. It's a very good method of finding out whether drugs are effective or not. But it excludes so many groups, like older people and women of child-bearing age, that actually it's only a very good method of telling you whether the drugs are effective for middle-aged men. So it's very important that they recognize the limitations of the way they look at the world as well. I'm passionate about science; I'm very pro-science and I don't think that religion and science are irreconcilable, but I think there is there view they've taken, ascribing too much to scientific method and not listening to other ways of thinking about the world.

But the reason they've got into this situation I think is that they are very frightened by the rise of religion. Whether that's Islam (and I think that's particularly what's tipped it off in Britain) or whether it's the fact that they see young people going to evangelical churches (which I also find deeply disturbing, because I don't understand what mean when they talk about speaking in tongues) I'm not sure. But they are so angry with religion and that seems to me to be very ill placed. So I feel that I'm being the rational one and that they're being irrationally angry. I mean Richard Dawkins' book *The God Delusion* is a rant. I don't rant about religion but he rants against it. I mean, if you simply say, religion is nonsense, we don't respect it, how are we going to even begin a conversation with an Islamic country? Surely we have to say that we don't agree with you about everything but we do recognize that you are seriously motivated by what you are talking about. We respect that but we won't always agree. I'm the moderate rational liberal.

Is there anything valid in what he says?

Well it's as I said to you, religion is neither a good thing nor a bad thing. He's created a structure in which it appears a bad thing. I could equally argue that science, or the way that people view science or that particular people in education talk about science could also be a bad thing, but I don't particularly think that science is either a good thing or a bad thing; it's a way of finding out things in the world. There are maybe things that religions do or that specific religious groups do that are absolutely terrible but it doesn't mean that religion itself is either good or bad.

You've written a book called *The Moral State We're In*. Is it your view that morality has to be based on a religious practice?

Absolutely not.

And do you differentiate between a moral code and an ethical one?

Can I just disentangle that a little: first of all, *The Moral State We're In* was not a book about morality in that sense, but about how a society treats its weakest. I think that is both a moral question and an ethical question. Many times I think people use 'morality' and 'ethics' interchangeably. I think that it's ethics inside morality actually. But do I think there is a difference between morality and ethics? I think there are some principles. Some people would say they are ethical principles, I would say they are moral principles and the study of ethics is how to apply those. But anyway, that's the differentiation I would make.

Do you have an ambition for religion? I'm interested because Judaism isn't an evangelical religion.

It's not proselytizing, at all.

And some of the Christians I have met are evangelical and their ambition is to convert people to a 'righter' or a better way of seeing.

I think that they should mind their own business myself. I think that people *may* discover religion, a particular religion, as a good way to live their lives. And may find a faith in God as a way to give a focus for their live. But I don't think that other people ought to try and persuade them to do it.

To look at Islam. Is its connection with power a problem or is the nature of the religion inherently aggressive?

No. It's plainly not the nature of the religion. The nature of the religion is by no means inherently aggressive. There is an Islamist movement within Islam which, within Islamic countries, is growing in influence and which is both quite fundamentalist and aggressive and has a variety of goals, one of which is to reclaim Islamic land for Islam. I think the best parallel really is: it's a bit like the Christians in the medieval period in the Crusades, claiming land for Christendom. And I'm dismayed to hear very good Christians and Jews criticizing Muslims when actually it's not very different from the medieval period and from some of the language used about Christendom. But I don't think it's inherent to Islam. It depends which Islamic writers you read, which part of the Qur'an you read. You can find in everybody's religious texts, things, particularly when taken out of context, which suggest land-grabbing or whatever. But I don't think Islam is by its nature violent or aggressive. I think there are elements within Islam at the moment which are.

Can you account for the current rise of religious fundamentalism?

I can't account for it because I don't understand it. But in a funny kind of way Grayling and Dawkins are part of it because I think there is in the world today a desire for certainty. And I think what people mean when they use the word fundamentalism is actually extremism. And the thing about extremism is that it doesn't allow for doubt. I think we live in a very uncertain world and that's frightening, and when people are frightened they tend to look for certainty. And in this sense, fundamentalism could be defined as a deliberate search for certainty. It's not about literalism you see – it's about certainty. People may use literalism to establish certainty but actually fundamentalism is about deliberately looking for certainty. That's the motive.

In terms of religion as it is taught or communicated in the UK, is it your view that it should be kept as a personal or a private matter?

Well we have an established church and although I think in principle I would prefer to not have an established church I actually think it works quite well; and I don't think I'd try to fiddle with it at the moment. I think the real issue for Britain is that increasingly we're a really secular society. And certain bodies, like the liberal press, are very anti-religious. And they caricature it because they don't understand it: they don't try and get in there; they don't try and get into doubt and diversity and faith and how the different religious traditions work. They don't understand the nature of religious authority other than when they see an Imam laying down the law or a Catholic priest laying down the law. They don't see what else happens across the churches or in liberal Jewish reformed circles. They don't see. It all comes out as monochrome and rather extreme. So I don't think it's about making it personal; it's about saying: look it doesn't matter if you're religious or not, that's a personal matter, but try to understand what it's all about.

Are you involved with interfaith dialogue?

Yes. Though the problem with interfaith dialogue is that it tends to get the people of like minds, the moderates of all faiths, together and the problem is what you really want to do is to have a conversation with people who disagree. I think I have a closer relationship with moderate Muslims and moderate Christians than I do with extremists related to my own faith community. Nevertheless, what you can achieve from it is a certain amount of understanding and you can also encourage children to learn about other faiths and other ways of approaching the world. And I think that this is just as important as children learning about science and learning about the humanistic values of the eighteenth century, because it may help society to respect the rights of people to live different lives from our own. And I suppose that this is the centre of interfaith conversation: that we want to defend the rights of people to live different lives from our own but don't defend the right to practise in such a way that damages members of our own faith group or members of other groups. So in the interfaith conversation we always have to be prepared to say: 'Fine, that's what you believe, but I can't defend that bit.' So I say, you should respect people who believe differently from you but not always agree.

13

Fraser Watts

Do you have a working definition of the term religion?

Well that's a big problem isn't it? That's the short answer to that! There's a big debate about what religion is, and there's a tension between broad and narrow definitions. So religion in one sense could just mean something like belonging to the Christian Church and that kind of thing. There are other people who take a broader definition, describing it as whatever it is that gives you a sense of being connected to the divine. William James, I think, said words to that effect. But, neither of these definitions are quite satisfactory. The narrow definition's a bit too narrow, the broad one's a bit too broad, and really no one, I think, has come up with a good idea of how to steer a path between the two. And now, to complicate things, there's the additional problem of the relationship between religion and spirituality. There are a lot of people in the world who are sympathetic to spirituality, but who don't want religion. And so 'spirituality' is a good word, 'religion' is a bad word for lots of people, and there can be really quite a sharp divergence there.

Do you feel a tension between your role as a psychologist, and your role as a theologian?

Some people assume there must be a tension between my background as a psychologist, and my religious belief and indeed my priesthood. But I don't feel that myself. Rather, I feel there is a convergence. So, for example, when I'm preaching I think I just instinctively have two different questions in my mind: Is this sound theology? And, is this psychologically helpful? I think that at an implicit level I'm constantly asking those two questions, and I find they tend to nudge me in the same direction rather than in opposite directions.

Do you think of religion as psychologically helpful?

It can be. For most people it is. If you look at the empirical evidence then on the whole there tends to be a positive correlation between mental health and religiousness. That's not what Freud would have expected, but actually that's the way it mostly turns out. But not invariably, and religion can do people damage, and it can become part of a sort of vicious circle, in which it sort of keeps people locked in unhealthy positions. So, for example, if you have somebody who has a strong sense of guilt, they can get locked into a form of religion which entrenches that guilt and just reinforces it. So some confessional practices where you go along every week and sort of go through all your sins and misdemeanours for the last week is a form of religion that can keep you entrenched in that sense of guilt, rather than give you the sense of forgiveness which a more balanced form of religion ought to be giving you. So it can work either way, but mostly, I think, religion's good for your mental health.

Is there a psychological explanation as to why that might be?

Not one that we've nailed down in research, but at the level of what's likely to be true, I think there are two things, partly social, partly cognitive. It gives you a network of supportive people, who believe in the value of love and looking after one another, and at its best that can make for a very helpful, supportive community. Not that all Christian churches are characterized by an outpouring of mutual love! But I think that, at its best, that's how it works. And then, perhaps as an extension of that social aspect, there is a sense of a supportive relationship with God. I think that that plays into the support as well. But there's also the cognitive side, in terms of how you look at things. And casting things in the sort of broader framework of religious belief gives you an opportunity to make sense of a lot of experiences that might otherwise be difficult to process. When we have difficult experiences of loss, whether it's losing a job or a loved one and so on, there's always the idea at the back of your mind, that in the broad scale of God's purposes, some kind of blessing may come out of this. So you may lose a job, but you have a sort of underlying belief that this may open up opportunities, and it may lead you in unexpected directions that God wants you to go. And so it gives you a very big framework of meaning.

So is there something psychologically comforting about abdicating responsibility to God?

I think of it as a partnership more than an abdication. I mean, I think there is something psychologically reassuring about that partnership. But

I think it would be to portray religious belief in an unbalanced way to talk about it as abdication. It's you and God together, sharing the responsibility for things.

How does the theologian in you respond to the argument that as a species we invented God to make ourselves feel better?

Yes, well, I mean, it's a good point. And I think it's illustrated by the kind of switch round in attitudes there's been to religion in psychoanalysis. I mean, Freud was very hostile to religion, and thought it was damaging to people and a sign of immaturity and so on. And I think, for the most part, he was simply wrong about that. Religion is actually helpful to people, psychologically, in the majority of cases. Even though for some people it can switch round. But I think you're absolutely right to pick up the point. That's only saying that religion is helpful; whether at a metaphysical level it's true is a completely different thing.

There is no conclusive argument for the existence of God, but there is a broad range of considerations that makes it a hypothesis that that is more likely or not. I mean, it gives you a framework that makes sense of a broad range of things that don't otherwise make any sense. So, for example, the remarkable fruitfulness of creation, the anthropic principle, the idea that the universe is remarkably fine tuned to be fruitful. You know, you would just not have expected it to be like this. All life depends on carbon, and carbon is a very unlikely element to form. There are a whole series of these apparent coincidences, such as the fact that there are some nuclear resonances which are exactly right to facilitate the formation of carbon and other things like that which make the universe fruitful where you wouldn't expect it to be. Even Francis Crick said: 'It looks as though someone's been monkeying with the physics.'

And there is the fact of religious experience, which is surprisingly widespread amongst people, and there are the teachings of the important religious leaders, like Jesus, the Buddha and so on. I mean, all that makes sense within the framework of theism. And I could give you some more things in that kind of list. But that's the sort of argument, a cumulative case argument which says that there is quite a broad range of things which make sense in the light of the hypothesis that there is a God.

What evidence of religious experiences are you referring to?

There have been a number of surveys of religious experience, mostly in the United States, but the main one in the UK has been conducted by David Hay and is detailed in a book called *Exploring Inner Space*. Hay found that if you ask a fairly broad question about spiritual experience, you find about a third of the population have had quite a powerful

religious experience at some stage of their lives. It can be quite emotionally transformative. In the short term these things tend to happen when
people are tense, and they tend to leave them happy and peaceful. They
are, for most people, some of the most important experiences they've had
in their lives. And people tend to be rather private about them, and of
course they're not sure if others would understand them if they talked
about them. I think this is why most people would probably under-
estimate how many individuals have had these experiences.

**As a Christian, how do you see the psychological relationship between
Christianity and the individual differing from that between, say, Islam
and the individual, or Buddhism and the individual?**

Well, Christianity is quite diverse I think, and I guess the other religions
are as well, but Christianity perhaps more than most. And it's also unlike
many other religious traditions in that it is elective. It isn't just a cultural
fact that you belong to it. I mean if you ask a Hindu or a Jew what his
religion is, that's a slightly odd question, I mean the Jew says: 'I am a Jew,
it's not simply that Judaism is my religion.' But Christianity, and Western
Buddhism I think, have become unusual kinds of religion that people can,
and do, opt in, and opt out of. And that gives them a different kind of
psychological impact. I mean, I think people approach them with more
freedom, more as a matter of choice. That seems to me to be quite healthy,
rather than just sort of being born into it as a fact of life.

Do you have a working definition of faith?

Well faith, I think, has got two sides. It's partly a relationship, and it's
partly what propositions you sign up to. I think the relationship side of it
is the more important. It is about the fact that there is a spiritual being
who you call God, in whom you believe and trust and have some sense of
personal relationship with. And then there are also the things that you
believe about that spiritual being and what he's done – the kind of things
that are recited with the creed. But the relationship of belief and trust, I
think, is the heart of faith. In the baptismal service these days, the question is: 'Do you believe and trust in God the Father who made the world
himself?' I think that's the right question.

**As a psychologist and as a theologian, how do you account for the
current rise in religious fundamentalism?**

For me, as for most people, that's a puzzle. I think the rise of fundamentalism has been a puzzle to most secularists, like Richard Dawkins, and it's
been a puzzle to most liberal Christians, like me. We wouldn't have expected
it, I think either of us, and don't quite know what to make of it. I suppose

it's partly that it provides convictions of complete certainty in a world where things are becoming more relative and confusing, and a lot of people are feeling: 'I just don't know what to think about anything.' I guess that religion of certainty has got to be part of it. It also gives a very sharp division between 'insiders' and 'outsiders', and I think that's also reassuring. I mean it believes that there are the kinds of elect who believe the right things and there are the rest. It's a bit like Margaret Thatcher asking: 'Is he one of us?' And I think that's the kind of question fundamentalists also ask. And in a period of uncertainty I think there is something reassuring about that. But I'd be a bit cautious about going the extra step and saying that there is something sort of mentally unstable about particular fundamentalists.

Do you have a psychological profile of yourself, as to why you might believe, or draw confidence from your own liberal Christianity?

Well I have a story about why I got involved in it in the first place. Though I guess that after several decades the reasons for staying with it become sort of complex and multifaceted. But I first got involved in the Church as a choir boy when I was about 10 or 11, and several things drew me to that. But the most powerful, I think, was that I just sensed that this was a community of people who believed in treating each other well, and that it was the best example of that that I had come across in my life so far. It chimed in very well with my instinctive attitudes to life, and I just felt that this was the kind of community I wanted to be part of. There were also some other things about the sense of mystery and openness to the transcendent. But I think it was more the sense that this was a place where people treat other each other decently. I think I hadn't found my childhood until that point particularly easy – I hadn't had an easy relationship with my father – and I think it was out of that context that this was particularly appealing.

One of the things, in the broader relationship between science and religion as opposed to psychology and religion, that has been a sticking point is the idea of miracles.

Miracle, I think, is a concept that's been distorted by the rise of science over the last few hundred years. So I think it's come to mean something that it didn't quite mean before, which is something that is sort of scientifically inexplicable. But it's only when you have a sort of rigorous concept of scientifically grounded laws of nature that you get to thinking of something that is outside that. I don't want to make that move, and I don't want either to have a narrow concept of laws of nature or to set up miracles as something outside it. I would want to have a kind of broad naturalism, within which it's possible to have extraordinary events of religious significance that we call miracles.

I think that unusual things can happen under extreme conditions. Now science has an idea of boundary conditions: laws of nature operate within a certain domain, and there are things which are predictable. But once you get into unusual circumstances, what you thought were laws of nature may no longer operate. So I want a kind of expanded empiricism that can, at least under unusual conditions, handle a variety of phenomena that we can call miraculous. And I think that there are various ways in which the scientific paradigm is expanding at the moment. Physics, I think, has produced a number of examples of this during the twentieth century: quantum mechanics and chaos theory and so on. But also, I think parapsychology is an interesting development. It seems to me that the evidence for various parapsychological phenomena is quite strong, and it's rejected by the sceptics because they, so far, just can't make sense of it, they can't assimilate it into an expanded scientific paradigm.

Could you give some examples of parapsychological phenomena?

Well, I think the most interesting work at the moment is that of Rupert Sheldrake. He's written a couple of interesting books recently; the last one was on the sense of being stared at. It seems that people can, better than chance, guess whether they're being stared at by someone whose outside of their field of vision. And, as he likes to say, private detectives are actually trained not to stare at people, because people will know if they're being stared at. There's a sort of practical wisdom in the world of private detectives that this happens and so you need to take it into account and not stare at people because of this. I mean, people in intellectual circles may scoff at this, but people who sort of need to know this for the effectiveness of their daily work, just assume it happens.

So, if we became more aware, and more able to understand those kinds of things, how would that relate to religious belief?

Well, it may give you a way of understanding intercessory prayer. I mean, if you pray for the healing of someone, then that may be understandable within a broader kind of naturalism in which you allow for the effects of mind on body. It's what you might call Biopsychokenisis. That's not to leave God out of it, but it's to present how prayers for healing work in a way that's not completely disconnected with an expanded scientific point of view.

You have been very critical of Francis Crick's *Astonishing Hypothesis*: that conscious experience is not caused by the behaviour of neurons, it is the behaviour of neurons.

That's right. And because he wants to give a physical explanation of consciousness, he then wants to make the extra move, so saying that somehow consciousness is not real, the soul is not real, and that we are really just a bundle of neurones. He argues that the other things that emerge from our physical state are somehow not real, so if you talk about what we really are, then you can just home in on the physical things; you can't home in on the higher mental and spiritual things that arise from it. That seems to me to be quite an illogical position. I mean I do think that all of our properties and abilities do emerge from our physical nature, but I still think that mind and soul do emerge, and that then they're part of us. I don't think you can say with Crick that we are just a bundle of neurones; actually, we are a combination of brain and mind and soul and we have all those aspects.

How would you distinguish between mind and soul?

Well, it's a good question. I mean, I don't think there's any very clear consensus about terminology here. But as far as mind goes: it is the various mental properties and powers, and the ability to perform a variety of intellectual tasks, is, I think, what we're talking about here. But as for soul qualities, I think they largely come down to the things that are relatively distinctive about human beings. So: spirituality; a sense of the transcendent; a moral sense; a capacity for relationships; those sorts of things.

What is the language you use to talk about God?

It's difficult to find any adequate language to talk about God, which, I think, is the first thing to say. Any language you use is going to be inadequate. And to talk about God, I think you need at least two discourses. There's nothing unusual about this, I mean you often need more than one discourse to talk about things adequately. I used to do some research on going to sleep; to describe going to sleep adequately, you need to talk about the changes in the electrical rhythms in the brain, but you also need to talk about what happens to people's experience of losing sense of time and place and so on. So these are two different but complimentary descriptions of the same thing. And so, for God, you need both an impersonal and a personal language, I think. You need an impersonal language that talks about God as the kind of totality of all things, and as a particular kind of powerful energy in the world, an energy that is moral, that is on the side of love rather than hate, that kind of thing. But also, you need to express the loving totality of all things that is experienced in personal terms. You need to talk about the fact that, in some sort of strange way, you can actually have a sense of relationship with this loving God of all things. So you need both of those languages.

The language you are using about God being on the side of love and not on the side of hate seems like a binary or polar understanding of how these two emotions exist. From a psychological point of view, can't the emotions of love and hate sometimes seem indistinguishable? As a psychologist, how does your psychological understanding of feelings inform your theological or Christian understanding of those concepts?

Well, I agree about the psychology, and I think it is an everyday experience, and some psychoanalysts have been good on this. Jung was particularly interested in extrapolating from psychology to theology. And he is very emphatic about the importance of the shadow side of the personality, and the importance of recognizing it. But then, he wants to extrapolate from that to how we think about God and he talks about some kind of shadow side of God which is incorporate in the Godhead. So in a rather wacky kind of way, and I wouldn't entirely follow him in this, he sometimes wants to expand the Trinity into a quaternity and to put the devil or evil in the fourth quadrant, as a part of the totality of God. Personally, I don't think that's quite the right way of doing it, but nonetheless he is actually recovering an important strand in the Hebrew Bible, which has a strong sense of the wrath of God, as an aspect of God's nature. And Jung would say that we tend to go for a too nice, or anodyne view of God, and that we need to recover some of the sense of the wrath of God as part of his majesty.

You spoke earlier about God having a moral dimension. Doesn't a tension arise when we use a human, natural discourse to speak of the supernatural?

Yes. It's something anthropologists of religion are quite interested in at the moment. And a lot of anthropologists would certainly tell you that it's a category mistake to talk about this impersonal thing in personal terms. And so the argument is that at some point in the evolution of religion, there was just a kind of mistake, when we started to talk about something impersonal in personal terms. I do see that as a possible line to take. But then, as I say, I do think a lot of things need converging discourses to describe them adequately. And God may be one of these things or beings. God does seem to be experienced by a very large number of people as some kind of personal being. *Some* kind of personal being; I mean, obviously not a person exactly like us. But he can be experienced as a kind of force with whom we have a personal relationship. So my inclination is to hold those two kinds of languages together, rather than just say, as with most anthropologists, that personal language is a mistake.

In your working life, as a Christian psychologist, do you have much contact with say Muslim psychologists, or Buddhist psychologists?

Not a lot. But there is an interest in Buddhist psychology. I think of all the other faith traditions, Buddhist psychology is by far the most interesting. Buddhism is interested in the phenomenology of meditation, and it's had to develop quite a rich psychology to handle that. There are some aspects of the psychology of the contemplative mind that you could find in rudimentary ways in the Christian tradition, but they are much better elaborated in the Buddhist tradition. And elements of this seem to have some scientific value. Some of my former psychologist colleagues have made use of a form of 'mindfulness' in the treatment of depression and it seems to significantly enhance the benefits of cognitive therapy for depression if you bring 'mindfulness' into it.

Currently, there is a major political debate in America over creationism. Some suggest that the creationists are boxing clever, by trying to present intelligent design as a scientific rather than philosophical or theological argument. Do you think that they have a legitimate case or do you agree that it's just a mask for a form of creationism which Rowan Williams has described as a 'category mistake'?

Well I think it can be different things in different people's hands. I mean, I think it was developed as a kind of an acceptable way of repackaging creationism in a scientific culture. And it's interesting that creationism in the 1920s started off by being disparaging about science. But there's been a switch round, and I think creationism now recognizes that we live in a scientific culture, and if you're going to win the argument for creationism, it's a matter of having to join them rather than beat them. You have to make out that creationism is scientific. So, in part, I think that's just a sort of PR ploy, but actually there may be a bit more to it than that. And I want to have a broad scientific theory of evolution in which natural selection certainly plays a major part, but may not be the only factor. I mean, I think there are a variety of puzzles about evolution that aren't adequately described by natural selection, like the fits and starts it goes in, as Stephen Jay Gould used to draw attention to. And in Cambridge at the moment, Simon Conway Morris is very interested in multiple convergences in evolution, like the eye. The eye is an evolutionary development that's remarkably good for survival. And it seems to have developed independently at quite a number of points in evolution. Now that's surprising because it's a rather unlikely development really. So what is it that gives rise to these sorts of converging evolutionary developments that are remarkably useful for survival? It's not a million miles between that kind of interest in convergences, and some of the saner parts of the intelligent design movement.

You see the argument, then, as one that is suggestive of a God, rather than a proof.
Yes.

Doesn't it run the risk of being just a sort of sophisticated 'God of the gaps' idea, where God or the divine plugs the holes in our scientific understanding?
It could be that, but it's more likely to be so if you operate from the sort of stark division between scientific naturalism and God that I want to get away from. But also, if scientific naturalism runs aground then you should be careful not to just flip and say, OK, it must be God. If you operate with the kind of expanded naturalism I want to, then there's more middle ground.

Do you feel in your Christian faith that you are right? That you have a truth that is more right than another belief?
Well, I suppose I do basically think that. But I wouldn't want to go round expressing that in a way that sounded arrogant and dismissive.

Finally, we've talked about the psychology of religious belief. What do you think the psychological motivation is, or how would you describe the psychology, of the vehement, radical atheism of people like Dawkins and Crick? What do you think is going on there psychologically?
It's an interesting thing, and there has been much less work on the psychology of atheism than on the psychology of religious belief. I mean, we need more case studies. There's been some quite good work now on the psychological origins of Freud's atheism, and I think there is a story to be told there in terms of his relationship with his father. So I think it partly comes out of those background personal relationships that exist. Also I think the kind of religious environment that people are brought up with is very relevant. And some people who become vehement atheists – I think this may be true of Richard Dawkins, but I'm not categorically sure – are brought up in a very fundamentalist form of religion. I think I read an old interview somewhere where he talks about this, but I also know that he sometimes denies it, and I don't know what the complete truth is. But people like Dawkins, I think, may be brought up with the idea that religious belief and evolution are incompatible. I seem to remember hearing him saying that until he was about 13, he just believed that evolution was

wrong, and then he switched sides and decided that evolution was right and religious belief was wrong, but he then continued with what he'd been brought up to believe which is that they're fundamentally incompatible. And Dawkins is as passionately committed about his atheism as any Christian. I mean, Dawkins pretends to be against religion, but he is religious, and doesn't seem able to see that.

14

Azzam Tamimi

Do you have a working definition of the term religion?

The word religion is English of course, but in the case of Islam, most Muslims don't feel happy with it because it is not the exact equivalent of what is considered to be its counterpart in Arabic: *din*. Because this word, which is usually translated as 'religion', relates more to accountability, to reckoning, or to the idea of a contract. I don't know if the English word gives the same meaning. It is mostly associated with reckoning and accountability because the 'day of *din*' is the day when we are brought back from death to be called to account. So as for the term 'religion' itself, I really have no definition for it. But if you ask me what 'Islam' means that is easier, because we tend to differentiate between Islam and other religions. And so it is easier to talk about Islam specifically than religion in general.

Is it more appropriate then to ask you if you have a working definition of the term faith?

If I were to think of a definition, well it would be something that you take for granted, something that you don't question.

Could you compare it with the notion of belief?

It's probably the same thing, I'm not sure. But these are semantics, aren't they.

What are the better questions to ask in order to understand the point of view of Islam?

Well, from the point of view of Islam, God is the creator to whom we submit ourselves; hence the word Islam, which means submission, or submitting oneself in peace, willingly, to God. And therefore because He created us, He tells us how to live, how to do things, what not to do, what to avoid. And so He defines for us the area of freedom where He doesn't necessarily expect a certain mode of action from us, so it is up to us. But He does all of this, not by coercing us, but rather, by expecting us, through knowing Him, to submit ourselves to Him willingly. So there is no human authority within Islam to present God; there is no pope, no church, nothing. A mosque is a place of worship, but it doesn't represent authority. The only authority is knowledge, and so we refer to our scholars as *ulema*, as someone who has knowledge. So the more knowledge you have, the more authority you have, but that authority is acquired through people's recognition of your knowledge, and not through your claim of authority. In other religions, people claim to have authority and they appoint themselves, or someone appoints them, whereas in Islam people give you credit or discredit you depending on how they see you behave. And whether they recognize your authority and knowledge is to do with your mode of behaviour. So if there is a contradiction between my mode of behaviour and my knowledge then I will be called a hypocrite and I will no longer be an authority.

What is the relationship between God and the prophets?

A prophet is a human being who is selected by God for certain qualities in order to remind people of God and to convey to them His message, which in some cases is in the form of a book like the Torah or the Gospels or the Qur'an. We Muslims believe in all of these books, although we don't consider them to be as authentic as the day they were revealed. We accept Moses as a prophet of God; Jesus too was a prophet of God. We believe that God revealed to them His message through a book which regrettably afterwards was adulterated, manipulated and distorted. Whereas, we believe that the Qur'an, which is the final message to humanity, is still as intact as on the day it was revealed.

Would you say a little bit about Muhammad specifically?

Well, Muhammad is a descendant of Abraham from Ishmael's side, and he was born into a well-known but poor family – he was an orphan, his father died whilst his mother was still pregnant with him, and his mother died when he was six years old. His grandfather took care of him, and after the death of his grandfather, his uncle took care of him. He grew up as an illiterate, because most Arabs were illiterate. The Arabs had one innovative quality, which was poetry, but despite having lived in that environment, he was never able to speak poetry. And this, for us, is a manifestation of his miracle which is the Qur'an, because the Qur'an is neither poetry nor prose. It is a completely different style of literature, and it was a challenge to the Arabs. So this is a man who was illiterate – he had never read a book, he never went anywhere to learn – but in the book, which is God's final message to humanity, miracles are manifest. In modern terminology, the Qur'an talks about embryology, botany, the mountains and geology; it talks about history and what happened to the previous prophets. The book also talks about a mode of conduct for human beings to adopt in pursuit of perfection. Although humans can never be perfect, they can still strive to approach perfection, for the objective of dealing with others around us in peace and harmony. This book, the Qur'an, sets forth a noble code of morality.

Can you explain why criticism of Muhammad seems to be so painful for Muslims?

Muslims' frame of reference derives from two sources. First, the Qur'an – the text that Muhammad brought to us from God through the angel Gabriel; and second, the documented sayings and actions of the Prophet himself – how he lived and behaved. So if somebody tries to undermine the Prophet, this undermines the edifice of Islam. In our way of life, we are supposed as Muslims to try to the best of our ability to follow the model of the Prophet. Obviously we often fail; nevertheless we do try to follow his model as a husband, as a father, as a neighbour, as a head of state or head of the community, as a young man or an old man or whatever. In all stages of life he is our model. And his actions are documented in books called the *Sunnah*. The word *sunnah* means literally 'way'; here it means the way of the Prophet. We, Muslims, believe that all prophets are infallible; it would defeat the purpose of their prophethood for them to be sinners or wrong-doers. They have to be perfect because they are the models, and this includes all prophets – Jesus, Moses, Abraham and Isaac, all of them. The life of our prophet has been well documented and preserved. All these people who say things about the Prophet that we believe to be wrong were not part of that documentation of history. And in our opinion they abuse him for political or ideological reasons. To us, our prophet is someone that any sane human being would love to emulate and follow. Additionally, all the negative things that people can say about the Prophet are wrong. They cannot prove any of it. When they portray him as a terrorist, where does this come from? Was he a violent man? Go and read the history and you will see how compassionate he was and how merciful. The Qur'an describes him as someone who was a source of kindness to humanity. Was he a womanizer? Was he this, was he that? All of these accusations are totally unfounded and totally wrong. Muslims have no right to be offended if someone were to come to them and say, for instance, 'There's something I don't like about your religion' or 'There's something I don't understand about your religion', or 'It doesn't make sense to me.' Then we can enter into a debate and there is no harm in this. But for someone to come up with cartoons depicting our prophet as an evil man, that is what we cannot accept. Not to mention that our prophet cannot be depicted in any form of drawing or sculpture, whether negative or positive.

Why is that?
Any picture depicting him will be less than what he is and so will demean him. The Prophet, any prophet, including Jesus cannot be drawn or pictured. That's why we Muslims feel offended by images of Jesus.

That's very unlike the Christian tradition.
Well that's where, we believe, the Christians have gone wrong. The Christians stayed away from perfect, pure and pristine monotheism. And the reason why they depict Christ is because they worship Christ. We don't worship the Prophet; we worship the God of the Prophet, the creator of the Prophet, who created us all, that is the difference.

Ziauddin Sardar in an article in the *New Statesman* argued that one of the problems with contemporary Islam is 'the fetishisation of the prophet'. He suggests that, in popular, though not necessarily scholarly or theological thought, the Prophet has replaced God as being the core of Islam. And that this focus on the material world through the life of the Prophet has distorted Islam.
Some Muslims might have adopted such an extreme position, but this is not the way it is supposed to be. The Prophet is a human being, but he is a human being selected by God for his special qualities, to be a messenger. If you are going to choose a messenger, he has to be the best, and Muhammad was the best of his community. But to exaggerate his position to the extent where people seek help from him although he is dead – I mean, he is helpless now, he can't help anybody – is wrong. We only believe that he can help us on the day of judgement where intercession might be allowed by God – sinners will approach God and say: 'Oh God, forgive us our sins; how can we do this?' And He will say: 'Go to Muhammad and ask him to ask for forgiveness for you.' So he will ask for forgiveness for people on the day of judgement, but that is all he can do; now that Muhammad is dead, you can't say: 'Oh Muhammad, help me'. You have to say: 'God help me'. That's what monotheism is about. Some Muslims, especially within some extreme mystic traditions, do see the Prophet as more than this, but this is not a general phenomenon. However, the angry response of Muslims around the world to what the Danish did was, in my opinion, fully justified. I would disagree with the violence that occurred in some places;

expressing anger through the use of violence was not a legitimate response, but the anger is legitimate. Anger should have been manifested through peaceful forms of protest only, including boycotts.

You are talking about the cartoons depicting the Prophet published in the Danish newspaper *Jyllands Posten*. Is it the mere act of depicting the Prophet which is seen as so offensive, or is it the fact that there was considered to be an ulterior motive to the publication of the pictures?

I think most Muslims reacted without much consideration for the motives. Some of us in intellectual circles talk about the motives; we seek to understand what the most likely reason was. But for the general masses there was not much discussion about why they were doing it. The mere fact that the act was perpetrated is offensive in itself. Every action has behind it a motive of some sort, but the action itself can be very offensive. If you search for the motive behind it, then it might become more offensive, it depends on what people think. In the case of the Danish issue, I read an article which claimed that the editor who commissioned the cartoons had been in the United States meeting with some prominent figures within the Neo-Cons and the Zionist lobby in America. It would seem, from that article, that it wasn't a coincidence that upon arriving back in Copenhagen he decided to embark upon this. Whether the allegation is right or not, I think there is another element to the affair. Here in the West, modernity has been a revolution against religious restrictions, against despots as well as clerics who claim to speak in the name of the divine; people therefore champion the act of demeaning religion. It's seen to be a heroic act to speak against Jesus or God or religion. And I think that certain people within the intellectual elite feel challenged by Islam. They ask 'Why do Muslims treasure their religion so much? We have done away with our religion; nobody cares if we speak against God.' So I think that some of them are trying to challenge the idea that Muslims cannot accept the process of secularization that has happened to the West. But they do not pay sufficient attention to the differences between the history of Islam and Christianity.

How do you relate to the Qur'an and the *Sunnah*? How should they be read?

In Islam there is no restriction on anybody reading anything. So people can come to the Qur'an and read it and interpret. But if one wants to do things the right way, then one should learn from scholars. Because if you open up the Qur'an and read it without sufficient knowledge, then there is a very high chance that you will misinterpret it. Let me give you an example: the Qur'an is compiled in an order that has nothing to do with the chronological order in which it was revealed. So what do you do when there appears to be a contradiction between what two different verses are saying? There is an entire science called 'The Causes of Revelation' which seeks to establish the order in which verses were revealed. So, people who pick and choose from the Qur'an on both sides, Muslim and non-Muslim alike, can portray the Qur'an in the most vicious way if they want to, because you can choose a verse which talks about slavery so that you might think: 'Oh you can have slaves in Islam.' Or: 'You can sleep with a slave girl.' Or you can go to a verse which says: 'Kill them wherever you find them and drive them out of wherever you find them.' And you can just take it out of context, without going back to the history of *why* it was revealed and what happened afterwards. And there are certain verses that came later in time which repealed an earlier verse but which don't appear chronologically in the Qur'an. For instance in the Qur'an it says: 'Don't perform prayers when you are drunk.' Well, from that you might think that we are allowed to drink alcohol. But the prohibition of alcoholic drinks came in stages, because that Arab community to which the Prophet was sent with the Divine Message relied heavily on slavery, on wine and alcohol, and on usury and gambling. These were the pillars of their economic and social structures. And they were not banned immediately in one go. The community was prepared over a period of 23 years to get rid of all of this and to make a fresh start while ensuring that the social and political structures that brought the community together did not suffer and were not undermined. So the knowledge of the reason for each revelation is vital, as is the knowledge of the Arabic language. The Arabic of the Qur'an is the language of the tribe of *Quraysh*; it is a language that was spoken 1,400 years ago and very few Arabs speak it today. Sometimes we use vocabulary today in a manner that is different to the way such vocabulary was used at the time. The invention of Arabic grammar was necessitated by that fact that when millions of people were coming into Islam of Persian, Roman or Abyssinian origin they had no knowledge of Arabic and so they started reading the Qur'an wrongly. In Arabic, if you change the inflection on a word the whole meaning can be changed, so specific punctuation marks had to be created in order to prevent people from misreading the Qur'an. So if you want to read or study the Qur'an, first you must realize that there is a difference between reading it and studying it. Reading the Qur'an is encouraged; it is recommended that you recite a certain part of the Qur'an every day as we believe that we get both blessings and rewards for reciting it. But studying the Qur'an is something else. You have to be guided by a scholar and you have to know the basics. And this is where disagreement comes from, this is where extremism comes from and this also is where it's opposite comes from, when people want to relinquish the fundamentals of Islam because they want to interpret it however they wish.

Would you talk about what Islam says about non-believers? How would I be seen in relation to Islam? Am I an infidel?
Well, that's a very interesting question because it is the one question where different Muslims may give you different answers. My own study and my own work in this field show that the Qur'an and the *Sunnah* talk of 'others' in very different ways. My own conclusion is that it all depends on the position that the other takes. For example, for the first 13 years in Mecca the Prophet spoke to the people about *thinking* about what you are doing. 'Can't you think?' he asked. 'You are burying your daughters alive, you are worshipping an idol made of stone, you are worshipping an idol made of timber, you are killing each other and abusing each other; can't you think that this is bad for you?' So he appealed to their minds. When the elders of the community in Mecca started opposing the Prophet, and hindering the passage of his message to the rest of the community, he challenged them by saying: 'Let the people listen and decide' because he was confident about what he had to say. But, of course, they were not so sure, because they said to him: 'You have come to change everything we have inherited from our forefathers.' And the Qur'an responds by saying: 'What if your forefathers were insane? What if they were wrong? Why don't you think for yourselves about what you are doing?' But what happened after 13 years of a debate centring on this area was that they expelled the Prophet and those who believed with him from their town. So he and his followers migrated to another town further north called Medina, and the people of Medina accepted him. They said: 'Come to us, we will recognize you as a prophet, and we will recognize you as a leader of our community.' So here is an important watershed or turning point in the history of his mission. Because from being an oppressed, persecuted minority in Mecca, the believers had become the majority in Medina. And then, the style of the Qur'an changed here. We say there are two types of Qur'an discourse, a Meccan discourse and a Medinan one. The Meccan Qur'an emphasizes thinking about the world, travelling the earth and seeing the mountains and the seas, thinking about what happened to the people who existed before and what will happen to them on the day of judgement; and it describes in detail hell and heaven. In Medina, the Qur'an talks about human relations, setting up a community, how to govern, what do to with those who commit crime. So it establishes a social and political order.

Now the people of the Quraysh tribe, who threw the Prophet out of town, started to see him as a threat, because neighbouring tribes started coming to him; his message was very appealing. So they started to wage war against him. This is when *jihad* changed from being a concept about striving in order to self-preserve through restraining oneself from responding to violence with violence. When the Qur'an talked about *jihad* in Mecca it meant to say: 'Yes, we understand, you are in pain, you are suffering, but be patient, don't use violence.' And that is why it was called *jihad*, because it was about striving to refrain from responding to violence with violence; even though someone might be doing something to you, you keep quiet. But in Medina, a change occurred and *jihad* came to be associated with *qital* – combat or fighting. The Qur'an, as in Chapter 2, tells the believers: 'Fight in the cause of God those who fought you, but you do not initiate aggression.' So if they come to you to fight, then fight them; if they come to kill you, kill them; if they come to drive you out of town, then drive them out of town. By then, as you see, there had been a completely different situation. So, the attitude of Islam towards the 'other', who is not a Muslim, very much depends on how this 'other' treats the Muslim community. This is not about the perception of the 'other' of the Islamic faith because the rule in Islam as it is stated in Chapter Two of the Qur'an is that there is no compulsion in religion. In other words, for a person's conversion to Islam to be legitimate, it has to happen out of absolute free will. It cannot be bought with money, it cannot be under duress or threat, because faith is between a person and his God; it is not between the person and some human authority. And that is why, in Islam, the people of the book are recognized; Christians and Jews have a place in Islamic society, and their churches, crosses, synagogues or whatever symbols or shrines have to be protected and preserved, and they have the right to apply their own rules and norms to themselves. In the old days people lived as faith communities; the notion of citizenship did not exist at the time. So there was the Christian quarter and the Jewish quarter, and within its own quarter a community had autonomy so long as it did not show hostility to the Muslim community.

But hostility was shown in the early stages of Islam, namely during the last ten years of the Prophet's life. In the town to which he migrated, Medina, there were three Jewish tribes. These Jewish tribes entered into a deal with the community that embraced Islam according to which they became part of the new collective community – the *ummah*. Incidentally, the word *ummah* has different imports: at one level it refers to those who belong to Islam, at another level it refers to those who belong to humanity. Yet, at a political level, it may refer to those who belong to the entity that is governed by Islam whether they happen to be Muslims or non-Muslims. It was agreed, as stated in the Medina Document (constitution), that the Jewish tribes would be part of the *ummah* providing they participated in the protection of the whole community on the side of the town on which they lived. When the war intensified between the people of Mecca – the *Quraysh* – and the Muslim community in Medina, some of these Jewish tribes collaborated with the *Quraysh*. And that's when the Muslims had no choice but to punish those who betrayed the trust put in them by the entire community. Apart from that initial period, the rest of the history of Islam, until the beginning of the twentieth century, was a history of perfect harmony between the Muslims and the Jews. The reason why we have a problem today between the Muslims and the Jews is because of Zionism, because of Israel; the conflict in Palestine is not a religious one but a purely political conflict. Unfortunately this political conflict is perceived by some people as a dispute between Islam and Judaism or between Muslims and Jews.

It's interesting that you say it is a political rather than religious conflict. After several decades since the beginning of the occupation, the conflict from the Palestinian point of view is being led by religious organizations, mainly Hamas, who you work with. You argue that it is legitimate to use violence to resist the occupation in terms of settlement building and the presence of Israeli troops in the West Bank and Gaza. But, when that changes into using violence against individuals in Israel proper – whether it is Tel Aviv or Haifa or wherever – and you have a situation whereby civilians are being attacked, do you not think that, in the context of the passages in the Qur'an which strictly forbid the targeting of civilians, that behaviour is in contradiction to Islamic tradition?

Hamas is not a religious group but a political organization that derives its guidance from Islam. In contrast, Fatah derives its worldview from secular nationalism. Though actually, when Fatah was born, it was born out of the same womb: that of the Muslim Brotherhood. The founders of Fatah were members of the Muslim Brotherhood, an Islamic socio-political organization. But what happened as a result of regional and international pressure is that they became increasingly pragmatic until they ended up agreeing to recognize the legitimacy of the state of Israel. The problem the Palestinians have with the state of Israel is not confined to what we call the West Bank and Gaza – the areas occupied in 1967. Fatah was created in 1957, long before the West Bank and Gaza were occupied. The very existence of the Israeli state itself is an act of injustice as seen from the Palestinian or Arab point of view. The Jews of Europe, or the Jews of America, or the Jews of South Africa have no right to come and take our homes and our land and build a state for themselves, a safe haven. The Europeans persecuted them. It is nothing to do with us. Why should we be made to pay for somebody else's crime? So this definition of 'Israel Proper' is nonsensical, it means nothing really, the whole area is Palestine.

But nonetheless, the people who are caught up in these attacks are surely innocent? If you were born in Tel Aviv in 1983, you have nowhere else to call home and you are not responsible for the creation of the state of Israel.

True.

And if that person is innocent isn't the violence being done to them in violation of a very strict Qur'anic injunction against attacking the innocent?

Well, in Israel, every single adult, apart from the Ultra Orthodox, serves in the Israeli army. And where do they serve the Israeli army? They go to Gaza and the West Bank to persecute the Palestinians and oppress them as occupiers. Of course there is an innocent category within Israel. The children are innocent; people who don't agree with Israeli policy are innocent. Martyrdom operations, when adopted as a tactic by Hamas, were a result of long deliberations. There was a debate about whether this was suicide or sacrifice. Suicide is forbidden under Islam; you are not allowed to kill yourself. However, self-sacrifice is not only permitted but is encouraged in defence of a noble cause. What about the targets? Which target is legitimate and which is illegitimate? The general rule is that these are not preferable operations – if one could avoid them, that would be best – but they were resorted to out of an extreme necessity, because the Israelis were killing the Palestinians without discrimination. At the time that these operations were first resorted to – in April 1994 – it was a couple of months after Baruch Goldstein entered the Ibrahimi Mosque in Hebron and sprayed the Muslim worshippers with bullets. The Palestinians felt exposed and vulnerable; anything could happen to them as there was nobody to defend them. So the idea of the martyrdom operation is to deter the Israelis from doing what they are doing. And that is why, from day number one, they were always accompanied with an offer of a truce. The offer was first made by Sheikh Ahmed Yassin in his prison cell when he was approached by Israeli intelligence officers. It was then made by the head of the Hamas political bureau in Amman, Moussa Abu Marzouk, at the time. Hamas said: 'OK, if you want this to stop, stop killing us and we will stop killing you.'

And how does that idea of truce sit with a belief that the very existence of the state of Israel is a violation of Palestine?

A truce is a contract to stop the killing for a given period of time, but it does not entail recognition of the legitimacy of the status quo. You recognize the status quo, by saying: 'It is there, I cannot change it now, and I am willing to agree not to try to change it for 20 or 30 years or whatever.' This is an Islamic principle. And if the other side agrees, then you have to abide by it; it becomes a religious commitment because it is based on Islamic values. The difference between this and recognizing the legitimacy of the state of Israel is that in the latter case you ask that all Palestinians should forget about the land that was occupied in 1948 and accept that none of it will ever come back and that the refugees cannot return to their homes which happen to be in the entity that is today called Israel. The majority of the Palestinians, whether Islamists or secular nationalists, would, deep within them, say that they would never recognize the existence of the state of Israel as legitimate, because it is not legitimate.

Other Muslim scholars argue that *jihad* can only be declared by a legitimate Islamic government, and that the scholars who are arguing about sacrifice or martyrdom are not necessarily doing it within a context that is actually connected with their own tradition?

Because we don't have a religious authority – we don't have a church or a pope – it is inevitable that there will be different opinions and different people saying different things. But eventually, what determines who is right and who is wrong is the degree of acceptance of any given idea by the people. That is why certain schools of jurisprudence became predominant in certain areas but not in others. Some of the schools of jurisprudence exist only in books; they don't exist in reality because nobody adopted them. You might call this a democratic process. And the only way that you can find out for yourself who, for certain, is right and who is wrong is to study thoroughly what each of them says. Alternatively, you just follow your own instincts by saying simply 'I trust this person but I do not trust the other person.' Where I come from, the person who argues that *jihad* can only be declared by a legitimate Islamic government is totally wrong. I would describe him as someone who lacks knowledge of Islam. This is because there are two types of *jihad*: one that we call *fard kifaya* and one that we call *fard 'ayn*. Now *fard kifaya* means an act of *jihad* in which only a small number of people will suffice in order to carry it out. This kind is not a *jihad*, which is undertaken under immediate threat. Here, it has to go through the proper institutions – a head of state, the caliph, or what-ever, or at least this is what jurists in the old times said. This rule was aimed at denying just anybody the right to declare *jihad* at any time, because obviously you need, under normal circumstances, to keep peace with neighbouring countries. And the confusion in the minds of some people is that they apply certain jurisprudential opinions that existed in the old days to a modern situation that is completely different. Today you have nation states, in the old days you didn't have nation states; today you have international law, in the old days there was no recognition of such international instruments. So this is what *fard kifaya* is about; for instance, if a thousand people are sufficient for the job to be done, then the rest of the people are exempt from the duty of *jihad*. Whereas *fard 'ayn* means that every single person has a responsibility, and that you have to come and join in. This applies when a Muslim land is invaded by a foreign power. When a Muslim land is occupied by a foreign power like in Palestine or in Iraq or in Afghanistan, you do not require permission from anybody to go and fight, you just go and fight. This is because the immediate threat is so great.

But at a wider theological level, the injunctions in the Qur'an against killing civilians are very clear. Would you say that there are times when the need for *jihad* negates the importance of those injunctions?

Well, people can easily justify what they are doing depending on the context. When Palestinian children are cut into pieces by American weapons used by the Israelis in Gaza and the West Bank, when Jenin or Rafah is torn apart, it is very easy for the Palestinians to sanction the killing of any Israeli, let's not fool ourselves. The question that should be asked is not whether it is right or wrong, but whether it is understandable. If you killed somebody's children, how can you be sure that your children will be safe? It is best not to ask whether it is morally good or religiously acceptable, but rather to ask how we can stop it. And there is a formula for stopping it. In Islam, the rule is as in the Torah: an eye for an eye and a tooth for a tooth. Islam is not a pacifist religion, it is very clear. Yes children are innocent, yes those who disagree with Israeli policies are innocent, but in exactly the same way as an F16 bomber does not distinguish between fighters and civilians in Gaza, a human bomb cannot distinguish on a bus between an innocent and a non-innocent. So drowning ourselves in this argument leads to nowhere really.

Recently in Britain there was a court case over a Muslim school teacher who insisted on wearing the veil while teaching. Would you say that it is just the responsibility of the other, the non-Muslim, to accept that as legitimate, or is there room within Islam to accept the other's nervousness about something like that? Is there a responsibility that Islam has to take in understanding the other?

Personally, I am opposed to the *niqab*, the veil. I have never liked it; I don't think it is part of Islam. There are others who disagree with me, who think that Islam requires it. Of course, I am talking here specifically about covering the face. There is no disagreement about the need for the head to be covered.

We have a concept in Islam called '*awra*, which means the private parts of the body. The private part of the body for a man is the area between the navel and the knee; a male should not show this part of the body to anybody but his wife. For a woman it is all the body apart from the face and the hands. So a woman cannot show any part of her body apart from the face and the hands to men – except of course her husband – who are not immediate blood relatives. This is an accepted Islamic principle; it is an injunction and it has to be respected. The debate is about the covering of the face. There is no disagreement among the scholars that covering the face was compulsory for the wives of the Prophet because they had a special status, and because following his death they were not allowed to marry anybody else, since there was a purpose in their marriage to the Prophet – each of them became a school that told us about aspects of the Prophet's life: that is how we document his life. Each of them came from a different background, and so they emphasized different things about his life: the youngest one Aa'ishah had a brilliant memory; she reported to us a significant number of his sayings. So his wives had a very special status, and they were unlike any other women in this regard so the strictures on them were tighter.

The majority of Muslims don't see the veil as compulsory. However, some Muslims, and in my belief it is mostly because of traditional and cultural influences, see the veil as a basic requirement for women. Now, how this young woman behaves or other women behave in terms of insisting on the veil has to do with their own attitude rather than the dictates of Islam. For instance, sometimes when it is time for prayer, and we pray five times a day, if I am in a public place I won't want to offend anybody; I make a personal choice out of courtesy, and it is not something I would enforce on others, not to pray in public. This is because I make the assumption that perhaps someone will not understand what I am doing and it will cause problems. And there is this rule in Islam that says 'necessities remove prohibitions'. If I were in the place of that woman, I would not have created the problem in the first place. I would think: 'OK, if they don't want the veil, they don't want the veil, it's no big deal.' If I was to insist on the veil then I would say: 'OK, I don't want to work, I resign.' It was unnecessary in my opinion to take the school to court and to make an issue out of something that the majority of Muslims don't consider important.

But I think what that woman was doing was exercising her right as a citizen of this country, and this is what people should see. Rather than see her as behaving as a Muslim fundamentalist, as some people might call her, see her as a British woman who is trying to exercise her rights as a British citizen through the court of law, and anyone and everyone should be entitled to that. It is up to the court to decide what is right and what is wrong. So in this sense there should be nothing wrong with it, but as a personal choice I would have preferred none of this to have happened, because this is not the issue, this is not what Islam is about.

What is your ambition for Islam?

Well, my ambition for Islam is to live in peace with everybody else. The problem is that we are not left in peace. We do behave wrongly sometimes as Muslims, but I think that the greatest tragedy in our history is that, for the last 300 years, we have lived constantly under the onslaught of colonialism. And in some circumstances we don't have the luxury of thinking freely, thinking rightly, or of rebuilding ourselves, and that is why we have all these tensions within the Muslim body and between it and others.

15

Ann Widdecombe

Do you have a working definition of the term religion?

I don't think I have ever thought about it in those terms. To me, religion means that you have a faith in God, that you follow that through actively, and that it is not just a cultural thing. 67 per cent of people in this country claim to be Christians, but the church-going population is just a fraction of that. So I think you have to distinguish between a cultural claim to a religion and religion itself which is actually founded on faith and belief.

How do you define faith?

Well, consider the Christian Creed. Some people might call that a statement of belief. After all, it begins with the word 'credo' or 'I believe'. However, I would say that it is not a statement of belief; rather it is a statement of fact.

Lewis Wolpert argues that there is a clearly defined scientific process to establish facts which involves double blind testing, repeatable observations and so on.

Well, whatever else he might be he is not a biblical scholar. If you are going to say that you only accept as fact that which you can repeat by observation, then Napoleon didn't exist and Caesar didn't exist because we cannot repeat those observations. What we do is rely on historic testimony: we examine it and we match it and we adjust our understanding in the light of it from time to time. And if you read books like *Who Moved the Stone?* by Frank Morrison, which actually examines the evidence, you will come to the view, as he did, that it did happen. Now Morrison set out to prove that the resurrection did not happen, but he decided in the end that it did. So you arrive at these views as a result of a process of historical exploration. Why, for instance, do you suppose that some very, very clever men believe it? People in academia who have spent their life studying it and being challenged on it – why do you suppose they believe it if it doesn't stand up to pretty rigorous tests?

There are some very clever men who don't believe it and some who believe wholly different things, be they Islamic, Buddhist or even fascist.
No, you have gone off the precise point that I was making. If it is not academically rigorous and didn't stand up, then why would very intelligent men believe it? That is my question.

What does 'God' mean to you?
The supreme being and the supreme first cause.

I notice that you have a copy of Richard Dawkins' book *The God Delusion* on your shelf.
No, Richard is off the end of the scale. I didn't buy that book, it was sent to me, and I don't wish any comparison to be made between what I'm saying and what that man says. I mean, the most hilarious book I ever read by him was called *The Selfish Gene* in which effectively he explained Original Sin. His whole thesis in *The Selfish Gene* is that man is intrinsically selfish. If it had been presented by somebody with faith, it would have been called Original Sin.

Do you see a parallel between scientific and theological understandings of the world?
Well has it ever occurred to you that the order of creation in Genesis has never been disputed by science?

What do you mean?
Well, the order of creation in terms of which came first, animals or man.

But the order of creation as described in Genesis is said to happen over six days.
I'm not talking about that, I am talking about the order of creation – come on, you're intelligent, you can understand the difference! The *order* of creation has never been disputed by science. It is just worth making that point.

When there is any sort of discussion about evolution and Genesis then the idea of creationism seems to appear. How do you understand something like that?
Well, I think that there has always been a completely false conflict postulated between what you call creationism and what you would call

evolution, which is often set up as the opposing view. And indeed, the Pope himself has said that there is not actually a conflict. If you look at the order of creation then it is perfectly possible to match the two. You only have a problem matching them if you are utterly literal. Instead we should see creation simply as an order of events that is clearly set out, and that happened in seven phases, which science does not dispute. If you see it like that, then there is no difference. Everybody should just calm down!

Would you talk a little about your own personal religious journey?

Yes. I was brought up with very deep Anglican roots. My uncle was a vicar, my brother is a vicar and my little nephew has just become a vicar. I sometimes think the Widdecombes exist to keep the C of E in vicars! But I say all of that to show that my roots were very deep indeed. I was a practising Anglican. It was not just something on a bit of paper. We went to church every week without fail, I went to Sunday school regularly, and of course at that time we were taught straightforward Christianity at school – the scriptures and all the rest of it. There was no comparative work or anything like that, everybody spoke with one voice. But when the time came for me to go to boarding school I went to a Catholic school. So although it was different, there was still a very strong Christian ethos.

As an Anglican were you in a minority?

I was in a minority, yes, but it was a large minority. It was one of those schools where the Catholics went free if they had passed their eleven plus, and the Protestants paid if they hadn't passed it. That was the set-up. And there was a very strong Christian ethos. We would go to chapel four times a week, we studied scripture, and we prayed three times a day. So I would say that from the age of nought to the age of 18 I never queried for one moment the central role of religion and Christianity in my life. Now the religiously active elements of my family tended to be very evangelical. My father was middle-of-the-road Anglican, but my mother and my brother were very evangelical. And of course one of the tenets of the evangelicals is that there is a precise moment of conversion, a precise moment when you come to know that the Lord is your saviour, and you can actually pinpoint it. And I was taken through that allegedly precise moment when I went to an evangelical meeting with my brother at the age of nine. But I later came to the view that actually there does not have to be one precise moment, but that faith can grow. And this becomes relevant in terms of what happened to me later.

I left school at 18 and went to Birmingham University where I joined the evangelical Christian union and took part in the mission to the university – I remained unquestioningly an evangelical. But I began slowly to get very disenchanted with the Church of England.

Why?

Well, they appeared to be very willing to compromise: to sacrifice creed to compromise; faith to fashion; doctrine to doubt. I was quite good on my alliterations! And at that stage we hadn't yet heard the Bishop of Durham, Jenkins, make statements in which he actually queried the articles of the creed. Now I didn't mind that, but what I did mind was that he could then remain the fourth most senior bishop in the Church of England. It was considered to be quite compatible to disseminate doubt while holding bishophood. But at that time we did have Hugh Montefiore, who had said that Christ might have been a homosexual. In other words there was the beginning of a departure from orthodoxy in the Church of England. All of this was going on in the 1960s as I was coming to maturity. But it never occurred to me then that I would ever be anything other than an Anglican albeit a slightly disgruntled one. I then went to Oxford and again I joined the Christian Union and took part in the mission and so on. And that was fairly straightforward. The reason why I reject this idea of there being a precise point of conversion is because very gradually, almost impercept-ibly, I became an agnostic. Now people often ask me what made me do this, and I say that it was nothing. There wasn't a flash or a reversal of Damascus. I always describe the passage into agnosticism as a gradual erosion of belief, and the passage back as a gradual erosion of unbelief.

Would you elaborate on the term agnostic?

I want to, I am coming to that. During that period between those two things I was an agnostic, but I was what I regard as a real agnostic. Usually today when people say that they are an agnostic they just mean that they haven't got a clue, they haven't made their minds up. But an agnostic actu-ally means that you believe you can have no knowledge beyond material phenomena. And that was the line that I held to. I wasn't an atheist. It wasn't that I just didn't know. I actually adopted the agnostic position.

So if an agnostic says that we can only know things through material phenomenon, would you say that the scientific approach is by definition agnostic because it is studying material processes?

An exclusively scientific approach which says, 'I can't explain this, there-fore there must be something else', is very different from a very rigid approach which says that, 'unless I can hear it, and see it, and touch it, and taste it, then it didn't happen'. But then, as I say, that means Napoleon didn't happen. So my answer to that is partly yes but also partly no. There are many very devoutly believing scientists, largely because they know their limitations. Anyway, my period of agnosticism slowly passed; it took about ten years. But when I came back I was even more disillusioned with the Church of England because I had seen it from the outside. When you look at something from that point of view, you can be much more dispassionate about it. And so I had got very much more critical by then. At that point we had had the Bishop of Durham making the remarks I mentioned earlier, and I thought, 'Well what does this Church stand for? It doesn't know what it stands for any more.' But nevertheless, because of my roots, which is probably quite a lazy way of looking at it, but it is true, I came back as an Anglican rather than a Catholic.

Years passed, I came into Parliament, and I joined David Alton's campaign to reduce the time limit for abortions. And for the first time since I was 18 and had left the Convent, I was brought into regular daily contact with Catholicism. The major supporters of that bill were at opposite ends; they were either Catholics or Evangelicals. The people in the middle were very woolly. I had known the Evangelicals for years and was very familiar with them, whereas I had once had been familiar with the Catholics but wasn't any longer. So I was going through a process of being disillusioned and was therefore carrying quite a large bundle of straw but not quite the last straw. And a lot of people have asked me: 'If there had been no Anglican decision to ordain women, would I have still been an Anglican?' To which my answer is: 'Probably not now, but for a long time afterwards, yes, but carrying a larger bundle of straw.'

So something else would have been the last straw?

Yes, and I can tell you exactly what it would have been. It would have been the publication by the last Pope of *Veritatis Splendor* – The Shining of Truth – the central contention of which is that you cannot decide what is right by what is popular. Something can be very popular and be deeply wrong. And something can be very unpopular and be absolutely right. In other words you can't blow about on the winds of fashion; you either believe something or you don't. And indeed the Church has maintained some very unpopular positions on things like contraception and divorce, etc. I think that would have been it, but as it happened that was not it and I left after the ordination of women. Now the main thing that irritated me about that was not so much the decision, but the debate that surrounded it. I followed the synod debate and it was scarcely at all about theology, about whether this decision was right and compatible with Christian teaching. Rather, the debate, led by the then Archbishop George Carey, was all about, 'If we don't do this then we won't appeal to the modern world.' And I said to myself, 'hang on, wrong way; the Church is supposed to lead, not follow'. He then wrote me a letter asking, 'How could I, a woman MP, not agree with women priests?' And my reaction was a polite version of, 'I don't stand *in persona Christi* at the point of consecration; what are you blathering about Archbishop?' You couldn't just look at the Church as a career, and if this was really what we had ended up as I didn't want anything to do with it.

I did not, as most people think, become a Catholic there and then. I left the Church of England in November when we had had this wretched debate and this exchange of correspondence, and I then asked 'What?' There was a big question mark. I didn't really know. I wanted an apostolic church, I wanted something that could trace its roots back to the early Christian Church.

Where were you worshipping at this point?
I had, up to that point, been going to a mixture of churches depending on where I was. In Westminster I would go to St Margaret's. In my constituency I would go to churches there. If I was speaking somewhere I would go to church there. From this moment on I began going to Westminster Cathedral, but I had not actually converted yet. I went because I had to worship somewhere. And for four months I did not take the decision to become a Catholic, because I had certain doctrinal reservations.

Such as?
Such as purgatory.

Why was that a reservation?
It was a reservation because my belief was that Christ's sacrifice was enough. You can't improve on it. It took me some time to be persuaded that that was a misinterpretation of what purgatory was about. Now, but for one other thing, I would have converted. And that one thing is that when you are received into the Catholic Church, you have to say what no cradle Catholic ever has to say, which is that 'I believe all the Church teaches to be revealed truth.' Now if you are born a Catholic, at a later stage you can develop a doubt about this, or a worry about that, or a reservation about whatever, and nobody bothers, you can still turn up at the communion rail. But if you are being received you have to make that completely unambiguous statement. And I actually said that to the Cardinal; I said: 'The threshold that you erect for people coming over is actually very high.' And it is probably one of the reasons why they say that converts are the most devout of all. But for that I probably would have crossed in November, but I didn't because I had to say it and couldn't say it truthfully with regard to one or two things: purgatory, and also the alleged sacrificial nature of the Mass, which is a massive Protestant misunderstanding.

In terms of the issue of transubstantiation?

Transubstantiation is a part of that issue. But the major thing is that Protestants think that what Catholics do is repeat the sacrifice at Calvary every week at the Mass.

And that was your misunderstanding?

Oh yes. But it was a very strong one because that was what we were all taught in the days that these things mattered. But be that as it may, four months later I did become a Catholic and I have been a Catholic ever since. So that is a potted history of Widdecombe's religious journey.

How do you see the role of women in relation to faith?

I take my example from Christ himself. Now it is very obvious that he valued women highly. A woman was the first witness to his resurrection; a woman caused him to do his first miracle. There is no doubt at all that He valued women highly. But He didn't appoint a single woman apostle. And that is why I don't believe in women priests. But I think that to say a woman can't be a priest is not to say that women can't play major roles. Look at Mother Teresa. Is someone going to tell me that she was crushed by the Church? And Saints down the ages have shown that women can have a very major impact. Indeed, as I have pointed out, we used to have in the Catholic Church mitred abbesses and any mere priest would have quailed before a mitred abbess! So I think that women can play a full role in the Church.

But a woman has a particular role to play. And I still believe that, however unpopular it may be, a woman should still take the central role in raising children, and the Church has always blessed and encouraged that. And I don't care what anybody says, that is worth it all. In terms of the wider question of, 'Is faith good for women?', well, the Jews of course have rabbis. And then one looks, of course, at the problem of Muslim women. Now most Muslims who've integrated in this country look at their women quite normally. But when it comes to putting women in a burqa, making them look out of a one-inch slit, if she is not willing, that is horrendous. If she is willing, that is her business.

Would say something about your understanding of the afterlife? Whether you believe that there is a heaven and hell and how that relates to ideas of justice and mercy?

I believe absolutely that there is a personal account to be rendered at the end of your life. Theologians dispute whether you are asleep before you are judged or whether you have two judgements, but whichever, eventually you answer. And whether that is immediate, or whether you are in oblivion for a thousand years first, is irrelevant. Ultimately, you answer. Therefore I live very aware of the judgement to come. And I can't help observing that it is a major loss to us, now that religion has lost its authority and that we have lost the general understanding that people used to have because of it. I think it is a major loss because even when you are alone you are still accountable, and the idea of resisting temptation was very strong. And so I do believe that there is accountability at the end. And I do believe that as a result of that judgement you will either be admitted to the presence of God, which is heaven, or you won't. Now, when people ask me what heaven is like I say I haven't a clue. I do have a picture language of it, which is the standard Christian one: angels floating around with harps and people with halos on clouds; but that is rot. I don't think it is like that at all. It is being in the presence of God. And hell is being completely divorced from God. And so that is what I expect to happen at the end of my life.

And is the judgement which God makes made on the basis of your moral behaviour or your personal beliefs? Is it possible for an atheist, an agnostic or a Muslim to get into heaven?

You must ask that question of almighty God. I do not know whom he admits through his gates and whom he does not. But I think it would very much depend on whether you had ever come into contact with Christ and rejected him or whether you had never known about him. I mean, if you were brought up in the Soviet Union and you spent years being told that religion was a bad thing and the Church had been pushed underground then you probably would have never had any information on which to make a judgement. And that is very different from somebody like Richard Dawkins who has got as much information as he could possibly want. So I don't know. All I know is that the judgement will be made. But I don't think you can earn your way in there just on your own moral behaviour. I think that what was done on Calvary is fundamental. And it is that which has opened up heaven to us, not just our own moral behaviour. But God makes these judgements and he is infinitely wise and I am not. And nobody knows the population of heaven or hell. We may think we do, but we don't know such things and we shouldn't believe that we do.

So if hell is a real place in some sense do you have an idea of what or who the devil is?

Oh yes. And if that is a disguised way of asking me if I believe in the devil then yes I do.

As a self-conscious being?

Yes. I mean he is not a chap with horns and a tail and waving a trident. But the devil is the opposing force to good – evil. So what is the devil? He is the embodiment of evil. And what does he do? He fights what is good. And in what sort of way does he fight? Well, on two levels. First for individual souls, and second in the world: death, disease, wars. These things are certainly not made by God. And he is the source of temptation. But as I say, he doesn't run around with horns, a tail and a trident.

One of the fundamental distinctions in Christian moral philosophy is between natural evil and moral or human evil. Human evil is often explained in this regard by an appeal to the notion of free will. But how do you understand natural evil? Take something like the tsunami of 2004. How can that event be reconciled with the idea of a just order of things?

Well if you look at the history in both the Old Testament and the New Testament there is nothing there to suggest that God's job is to make it a cushy life for you on this earth. I always say, look at the saints: Peter was crucified upside down; Paul was beheaded; Stephen was stoned to death. Later martyrs suffered even more horrific things as human evil got more ingenious. But what is the worst that people have to face today? Well, I face a grilling from Jeremy Paxman and that is about it. On that level, things are probably easier. But the things that mankind has to face, those haven't changed. The children of Israel who wandered through the wilderness for 40 years went through famine and all manner of hardships. And in a way it is a very fleeting test. It seems to us a very long time, but not in God's eyes, where a day is like a thousand years and a thousand years is like a day. So there is no suggestion that this earth is meant to be perfect. Heaven is where things are perfect. Where there is no sadness, no pain, no tsunami. But that is not here.

So are you saying that in terms of the world as we experience it, there are manifest injustices that are beyond human control? Someone can be born into privilege and someone else can be born into poverty in Sri Lanka and lose their whole family. Should you respect a God that allows that to happen?

Well it is something of a challenge to the rest of us. Why is somebody who is born into poverty left there? There is plenty in this world to go round you know. But we don't do it, do we? So it is very easy to yell at God and say to him: 'Why have you done that?' But there is a great deal of supposedly unavoidable wrong in this world which actually is very avoidable.

In your Archbishop Worlock Memorial Lecture you spoke about how there are moral absolutes in Catholicism but that as a politician you are engaged in what you describe as 'the art of the possible'. And despite your opposition to abortion, you supported a bill that would not abolish abortion outright, but that would reduce the time limit to 18 weeks.

An awful lot of us supporting that original bill didn't actually believe in abortion at all.

In 2002 you said that the death penalty would be acceptable if it prevented further loss of life. As I understand it, the Catholic Church teaches that the death penalty is not acceptable.

No, the Catholic catechism allows the death penalty in very restricted circumstances, and it also allows conscience. So it doesn't say, as it does with abortion for example, that it is a grave sin and that if you do it you are at risk of damnation. But there are two issues to raise here. The first is about moral absolutes. The big decision in the abortion bill which we had to take was not so much about reducing it to 18 weeks, but about children who had handicaps. And it became very obvious to us at the second reading of the bill that we were not going to save the kids between 18 and 24 weeks unless we made the concession about the ones with handicaps. Now it was an anathema to us, but we looked at the figures: 92 per cent of all children who were aborted from 18 weeks onwards were not handicapped, and 8 per cent were. And there were some people who argued the moral absolute and said we should not concede that. And I said that if I was standing on shore and there was a shipwreck with 100 people on board and I could only get 92 off, then I wouldn't refuse those 92 for the sake of the eight. And I said that was the position we were in. And you either save as many lives as you can or you stand on a principle and thereby sacrifice lives that you could have saved. And if you do sacrifice lives that you could have saved then you have got a moral responsibility for that. That was and remains my position. So similarly, when you look at the death penalty – I have no interest in it, nor is it defensible as a form of retribution. But supposing you can show that it saves lives. Then, a moral responsibility comes into it. If someone is dying and you walk past them without helping then you are morally responsible for their death, because you could have prevented it. And if it can be shown that the death penalty is a deterrent and you do nothing, then you are morally responsible for the innocent lives that are lost. So the question for me always is: 'Is it a deterrent?' I looked at the figures. And in the five years following abolition in this country when we still, as we don't do now, collected figures based on capital and non-capital murder, the capital rate went up by 125 per cent. And I said: 'OK, that's it. There's very, very clearly a link and one has to accept the moral responsibility.' So that is why I support the death penalty. Not that it is ever coming back of course.

Contraception is forbidden by the Catholic Church. Yet it seems that all the studies that have been done in Africa argue that contraception could significantly help to reduce the risk and spread of HIV, and that it could help to control a population that is expanding extremely fast.

Well there are three big things there. Firstly, the Catholic Church does not ban contraception, it bans artificial contraception. It does not oppose natural contraception, indeed, it advocates that method. The second thing is, I dispute utterly the argument that contraception could significantly help to reduce the risk and spread of HIV. Because where has the biggest drop in HIV been? It's been in Uganda, massively big. What did Uganda do differently from everybody else? It didn't just rely on the condom campaign, it relied on an abstinence campaign, and it had a massive effect. The same thing is true if you look at certain American states where they have had abstinence campaigns, which have had a dramatic effect on teenage pregnancy. So the idea that the only answer to the spread of the disease is contraception is wrong. Third, let's get right back to basics. The Church says you should be faithful within marriage and chaste before it. And if the whole world had stuck to that we wouldn't have AIDS or any of these other problems. Having rejected the Church's teachings and having got these problems, you're now saying to the Church: 'So sorry that we've done this, but now you have got to reverse all your teachings just to meet our failures.'

Is it fair to say that people in Africa have consciously rejected the Church's teachings? Surely the things that govern our sexual behaviour are more complicated than that?

Mr and Mrs Individual may not have rejected the teachings, but society as a whole has moved away from following the teachings of the Church. And what I am saying is that the Church clearly said that the safest word in contraception is the word 'No', and the safest way not to spread disease is fidelity; chastity before and fidelity within. That is your answer to disease. The world having rejected that cannot then turn round and say that because we have rejected it, therefore the Church must amend its teaching on everything else that flows from that. I just don't find that remotely logical.

As a Catholic, how do you perceive people of other Christian denominations and beyond that, people of other religions or no religion? How do you think they should be interacted with politically, personally and morally?

First of all we are all God's children, even Dawkins although he doesn't admit it. And therefore everyone starts at that basis. Now the Muslims call that God Allah, and the Jews call him Jehovah, and I call him God the Father. But we are all God's children. I also start from the idea that you only really get to know about things if you explore and talk about them. It is significant what I said earlier about the fact that when I first came to Parliament I came into my first regular contact with Catholicism since I was 18. I would never have understood Catholicism if I had not had that contact. And so therefore it is very crucial indeed that Christians have contact amongst other faiths and are open to them – not open to their beliefs but open to them. And politically it is essential. You can't run a country on the basis of one group. You run a country on the basis of all its citizens. And so, of course, politically, you must deal with everybody, and I do.

So are you a supporter of secularism in a public space where the word secular is defined as being 'a place of no faith but for all faiths'?

No. I am more anti-secular than I am anti any other faith, but I would not use your definition of the term. I simply say that if you are running a society you must talk to everybody who is in it. And when I say everybody I mean everybody. When I was prisons minister I visited prisons and spoke to prisoners, I didn't just look at bits of paper from the Home Office. I think that is crucial as otherwise you end up with a situation like Northern Ireland where people frown at each other over gun barrels. And indeed with the horrendous spread of Islamic fundamentalism and the damage that does, it is utterly crucial for Christians and Muslims to be talking so that we understand each other. The worst thing is not understanding. I understand the Labour Party very well and I don't find that incompatible with being a Conservative. And so understanding the Muslim faith is not incompatible with being a Christian. To understand does not mean that you surrender your own beliefs. And that is something that I have often stressed. In this country we have started to confuse the act of respecting other people's faith, which we should do because God has given us free will, and the act of surrendering our own faith, which we should not do, but seem to be quite busy trying to do.

Do you think that your faith is right, or more right than another faith?
Every religion I know, or at least all the major ones, claims absolute truth, and the Catholic Church is most certainly no exception to that.

But why should I be a Catholic rather than, say, a Muslim?
I think it very important that you should accept Christ.

The Catholic Church believes that miracles still occur today.
So do pretty much all Christians.

There doesn't seem to be any scientific evidence for them. Why are they so rare or intangible?
Well, I don't think they are that rare actually. I think to a certain extent the Catholic Church is its own worst enemy on this one. Because it is so afraid of being taken for a ride and sanctioning something that actually turns out not to be a miracle that it has put in place the most incredibly bureaucratic procedures to identify them. For example, on the day of the Cardinal's funeral, a blind man rushed into Westminster Cathedral and said he could see. Now my line would be that we should immediately ask: 'Where is the evidence?' But forget it. That's still going through the Vatican. So we become in many ways our own worst enemy because we are afraid to celebrate immediately. But if you consider the miracles that Christ did, he didn't do them for everybody. He gave this man his sight, he gave that man freedom from leprosy, and he raised Lazarus from the dead – but he didn't do it for everybody. So it is not going to happen to everyone, but its going to happen to some. Let's take the case of my own mother. She was an evangelical who believed in miraculous healing and she had arthritis in her right hip at a time when hip replacements were not as they are now, which is two a penny. And she went to a healing service at Guildford cathedral and she prayed and then thought nothing more of it. But at the end she ran down the cathedral steps and she stopped and said, 'Hello, what's happened?' Now she never had any more pain in that hip. And those of us around her can testify because we know. Years later the other hip went and by then it was the age of hip replacement operations so she went not to a healing service but to see a surgeon and they took x-rays and the surgeon said, 'Well of course I'll do the operation but I should do the other one first because its much worse.' And she said that she had no pain in that one and the surgeon said, 'You're joking?!' But she said there was no pain in that one and there hadn't been – I am a direct witness to that and I can't explain it and nobody can tell me that it didn't happen. And that's not chronicled anywhere and there are lots of instances like that. Now I've

used healing but in a different way, not as a miracle. The Church has very strict definitions of miracle. It has to be immediate, and it has to be medically inexplicable. But I went to see one of the great healers of the Catholic Church who has had some very extraordinary results which were again unsung. Mine would not qualify as any sort of miracle because it was not immediate and he said to me that it may be gradual but I went out with an immediate improvement, and the ailment went. So I believe in healing, I believe in miracles, I believe that God works miracles today if only you look. But they are not two a penny, and as I say, I think this is one where the Church actually is its own worst enemy. I mean, the blind man I mentioned, I don't know how old he was; for all I know he could be dead by the time they decide it was actually a miracle, and that is no good. In the Bible people celebrated immediately.

In the Bible miracles seem to happen in a fairly arbitrary way.

Yes they do. If you look at Christ's healings they were very arbitrary.

So how does that fit with an idea of justice?

Your idea of justice is an idea of human justice. It is saying that nobody should be blind – well that's patent nonsense in practical terms. And Christ heals in lots of ways, sometimes as a miracle. He does that as an act of witness, so that one man may glorify him and act as a witness. To another man he will say: 'You'll be healed over time, because I am going to give you something you don't know about at this moment, an improvement in medical knowledge, and that will heal you.' To another he will say: 'You are going to go through life blind, but you will see in heaven and I am going to give you other spiritual gifts.' And we all have to be open to God and when things happen to us, the most human reaction on earth is to say: 'Why me?' But sometimes we should be saying: 'Why not me?' Why is it that you and I are physically fit, active, articulate, educated, had loving parents? We had the works and we should say: 'Why have I had all of that and what can I do with it?'

There are passages in the Bible which say that homosexuality is wrong. There are also passages which say that if you mix two different kinds of seed in a field you should be put to death, and say that slavery is acceptable and so on. Why is homosexuality such a big issue for the Catholic Church when agricultural methods or the idea of reintroducing slavery are not? Is there a double standard in the way the texts are being read?

The Church is very interested in families, the raising of children and marital fidelity. It is into that category that homosexuality and certain heterosexual behaviours, like living together without the blessing of marriage, fall. And the Church has always distinguished – for 2,000 years – between essential doctrine and rules. Now it is a central doctrine that Christ rose from the dead. And it is a rule that the clergy don't marry. And rules can be broken. It was a rule that you had to cover your head when you walked into church; it was not a central doctrine. And so I think that you do have to distinguish between fundamental doctrines and things that are merely rules. But if you look at Leviticus and all those rules about washing and mixing dishes and then you look at the state of modern hygiene then you will realize why. There actually is a danger from raw meat and things like that. We now know that scientifically, but isn't it wonderful that it was all set out in Leviticus long before we even knew what a germ was?

Do you think religion is dangerous?
Religion has always been dangerous when perverted for man's purposes. The Crusades, for example, were thought of as great things to do. But, in fact, no forced conversion is ever worth anything – it doesn't mean a thing. I wish the Muslim fundamentalists would recognize that. You can't force someone to believe something; it doesn't work that way. You can force them to behave in a certain way, but you cannot control what goes on in their heads, as tyrants throughout the ages have found out. So yes, if you pervert religion for man's ends, to promote a particular dynasty for example, or as it has been perverted in Northern Ireland, then it is dangerous. But then as my priest said to me about Northern Ireland: 'It's very interesting, you have Protestant atheists and you have Catholic atheists and they will fight each other in the name of Protestantism or Catholicism and yet they are both atheists!' And this has nothing to do with religion. So the perversion of anything can be dangerous. The perversion of medicine can be dangerous – just look at the concentration camps. There is nothing wrong with medicine, but the use to which it was put there was wrong. But you don't condemn all scientific research because it was perverted on a particular occasion and likewise, you must not condemn faith because it has been perverted on occasions. But the answer to your question is that religion, perverted by man, can be highly dangerous and it is one of the worst forms of danger.

Why do you think that religious fundamentalism, Islamic or otherwise, seems to be resurgent?
I think it has come straight into a vacuum which has been created by secularism and the loss of authority on behalf of the Christian Church. If you open any women's magazine, you will get all sorts of cult things – 'psychic Gordon' or whatever. I don't mean horoscopes, those are bits of

fairly innocent nonsense to be looked at over coffee, but I mean people really writing in, wanting psychic messages and so on. Now where is this coming from? It is coming from man's innate recognition that there is something beyond, and his desire to try and find it. Now the Church fulfilled that need for centuries. But the Church retreated in the second half of the twentieth century and the first decade of this one, and this has left a vacuum into which something has come, which knows what it stands for, is extremely motivated by what it stands for, and which does not like what it has found, and wants to drive out from the vacuum the remnants of what is there. That is what I see has happened. So I think fundamentalism is strong and resurgent because of this vacuum. And it wouldn't be if that vacuum had not been created. If they had come over here and found a 1950s approach to Christianity in the twenty-first century, it would have been different. But they effectively have come into a vacuum. And when I say 'they' I do mean the fundamentalists and not Mr and Mrs Moderate Muslim. I have a dear Muslim friend who came to my mother's evangelical funeral and coped brilliantly – it was a good example of courtesy and everything else. So I am really not having a go at Islam; I am having a go at Islamism, which is different.

Can you conceive of a situation where you might change or even lose your faith?

No. I've been through the loss, and have come back from it stronger because of it. I am now part of a church which is demanding as well as helpful and encouraging, and I am utterly convinced of these things. Now, one should never say, 'I will never', because the flesh can be weak and the devil can be strong, but I do not believe that I will ever lose my faith again. I don't see that happening.

16

Karen Armstrong

Do you have a working definition of the term religion?
It's a difficult term because if you look at it historically, the word religion was only applied to faith systems by people hostile to them. In the Enlightenment period, for example, people started discussing a phenomenon called 'religion' which was quite alien to places such as India. You might ask: 'What is the religion of Hindus?' Well there are ways of being what we might call religious for Hindus, but there is no system. And yet our Western lust for system has imposed a systemization on Hinduism which was not there before. Basically, what I would say is that it is a search for ultimate meaning. We are meaning-seeking creatures – unlike animals that, as far as we know, don't agonize about the canine or feline condition. But *we* do. And if we don't find some kind of significance in our lives we can fall very easily into despair. Human beings started to create what we now call religion at the same time and for much the same purpose as they started creating works of art. The two are closely linked. So despite the dispiriting evidence to the contrary, life could be seen to have some ultimate value. Art also gives one a sense of transcendence. Transcendence is part of the human psyche. It has been interpreted in many ways, it has been called God or Brahman or Nirvana, but the experience of transcendence is part of the human condition. It is a peculiar characteristic of the human mind that we all have experiences or ideas that go beyond our conceptual grasp and this is something that we seek out. If we don't find that sense of 'extasis' – or 'ecstasy' which means 'stepping outside of the mundane' – in a church any longer, then we will look for it in art or music or drama or sex or sport or drugs. These are things that make us feel deeply touched within and which lift us momentarily beyond ourselves. At such times we feel that we inhabit our humanity more fully than usual. And so I think that religion is really an art form, not a science.

Religion has always expressed itself in terms of art, not in terms of propositional statements. It expresses this sense of transcendence and it enables people to experience this transcendence in things like architecture, painting, poetry, dance and music. If you think about it, before the advent of the CD or the printed book or the public art gallery, people could only find art and therefore get the sense of transcendence that came with it, in a religious context. It was the only time that most people saw any painting or heard any music. And people are very pragmatic. If they don't find a sense of transcendence in a religious institution they vote with their feet. And that is what has happened in the UK. The churches are empty because people have got bogged down and the religious quest has got stymied in some way. Since the eighteenth and nineteenth centuries we have started to treat religion as though it were a science. So basically religion is a search for meaning and a search for the transcendence that we need to live fully.

And religion shouldn't be about curtailing our minds or curtailing our behaviour with absurd rules, or encasing us in strange garments. It should be something that makes us live more fully. Buddhists say that the serenity and the ecstasy they achieve in their yoga is entirely natural to humanity. They have no conception of the supernatural at all. Anybody can be a Buddha if they work at it. A Buddha shows the power of the human spirit just as a dancer or an athlete shows the potentials of the human body, which is way beyond most of us who lack either the talent or the training to achieve that. There is a nice story in relation to this about the Buddha. One day the Buddha was sitting in concentration and was serene, when a Brahmin priest walked past and says: 'I've never seen anything like you. Are you a god? 'No,' said the Buddha. 'Are you an angel or a spirit?' 'No,' said the Buddha. 'Well what are you?' And the Buddha said: 'I'm awake'! And that is what the word 'Buddha' means. It is someone who is alive to the full significance of life, to the transcendent element in life. And who also uses part of their humanity that usually lies dormant.

How do you define faith?

Faith, again, is one of those words that have been very much abused over the years. Today, it is usually equated with belief. And that is a development that has only occurred since the Enlightenment. The word '*beleven*' in Middle English actually meant 'to love'. It is the same as '*beleben*' in German. And '*credo*', I believe, comes from '*cordo*', to give your heart. It had nothing to do with believing things. There are no propositions in the early creeds. In the early church you would recite the credo – the creed – as you were being baptized. This represented a real act of commitment because it meant you were likely to be persecuted and so you were accepting the possibility of a violent death. So the questions that are asked in this situation are: 'Do you commit yourself to God the Father?' 'Do you commit yourself to, and love, God the Son?' And so faith – *fides* – means loyalty. It has nothing to do with believing in certain things.

A better example of faith, I think, is that experience I have just described of the Buddha. It is a sense of joy and confidence, a sense that you can exist amidst the suffering and pain of life with serenity and confidence. It is not that you don't feel it – religion is not an anaesthetic – but it means you will feel able to deal with it. There are images which symbolize this in all religions – Jesus on the cross is in charge of his death, forgiving his enemies and his executioners. He speaks kindly to the thieves on either side of him and looks after his mother and in doing so he commits his spirit to God even in his despair. And that is the role of religion – to help us. But that does not mean it helps us run away from suffering – that is bad religion – rather it enables us to feel that sense of serenity and confidence and courage and even joy in the midst of suffering.

What about the idea of God?

Well God is one of the names that we give to transcendence. Our notions of God bear very strong resemblances to the way Nirvana or Brahma is spoken of in other parts of the world. In the monotheistic religions the notion of God has been personal. But, as I showed in my book *A History of God,* Jews, Muslims and Christians have all said: 'Yes, you can start off with the idea of God as a personal being, but you can't go on like that, because God transcends personality.' The best Christian, Jewish and Muslim theologians – and these are major figures like Ibn Sina, Aquinas and the immensely important Greek Orthodox theologian Dennis the Areopagite – all insisted that God is not one of the things that exist. God does not exist like this table, or you or me or the atom which is unseen but can be proved in a laboratory. God is 'other', or as the Muslims say, '*Allahu Akbar*': God is greater.

The trouble is that most of us first hear about God when we are very young – at about the same time as we learn about Santa Claus. And our ideas about Santa Claus become more sophisticated in time, just as our ideas about art do – remember art and religion are related. I remember being very fond of a song called 'The Teddy Bears' Picnic' when I was a little girl, but I moved on! But most people's idea of God stays at this very infantile level of there being this person up there manipulating things. But it is supposed to develop and grow! And while you can think about God as personal as a starting point – and this has value as it helps you to see all human beings as sacred – ultimately, these Jewish, Christian and Muslim theologians say – you cannot call God a supreme being. Because the term 'supreme being' implies that God is just another being like you or me but at the top of the scale, whereas it is other than that.

And the problems with this infantile view of a personalized God is that we end up just seeing God as simply a bigger version of ourselves with likes and dislikes similar to our own. And then, of course, most people assume that this kind of God is always on our side. The crusaders went into battle crying: 'God wills it!' when they slaughtered Muslims and Jews, but God, whatever God is, willed no such thing, But they were simply projecting their own fear and loathing and prejudice on to this imaginary being that they had created in their own image. And you can make God do what you like. You can make him an arch conservative or a member of the Communist Party, an extreme republican or an ardent democrat. And you don't even have to be a crusader or a terrorist to do this. How often do you hear inept people on the radio, or from the pulpit, saying that: 'God wishes this'; 'God hates that'; 'He forbids the other'; 'He loves this'? And it is uncanny how frequently the opinions of the deity are made to coincide with those of the speaker! This is what the Buddha would call 'unskilful religion'. It's idolatry. And all the monotheisms are very much opposed to idolatry. Idolatry is not just about bowing down before a statue. It is about endowing a purely human idea, 'God,' with an ultimate reality. So a lot of theology is idolatrous! Whereas theology should be like a great poem, or a great piece of music, that introduces you to transcendence. And just as when you listen to a great poem you can feel that there is nothing more to be said, you've gone into a sort of silence or peace, or at the end of a symphony sometimes there is often a beat of silence in the hall before the applause begins, so theology should always remind us that when we are speaking of what we call God then we are at the end of what words and thoughts can do.

Would you describe yourself as a religious person?

Yes, I would. But I often don't because I have had a peculiar religious history.

Would you say a little bit about that?

Well, I was a nun for seven years and I limped away from that experience, which was not a good one. And then I went away from religion. I wanted nothing whatever to do with it. I was disgusted by it. And then after a series of career catastrophes I found myself on Channel Four making highly critical Dawkins-esque programmes about religion.

And was this a reaction to the understanding of religion and of God that you had imbibed from being a nun?

Yes, it was an inadequate notion of God. The prayer that we were taught to do didn't suit me; I couldn't pray, I couldn't do it. And I was expecting, you see, in this naive way, that if I prayed, there was someone up there listening who would get in touch. And of course that's not it! You're barking up the wrong tree! Now some people can do it, it works for them. They can start talking to God and get some kind of answer – because human beings are, I think, split worldwide between those who can experience what we call transcendence as coming to them from outside, and those who, like the Buddha, engender it from within. And I think there are a lot of Buddhists trapped in Christian revelatory settings, and probably there are Buddhists yearning for a revelation from outside. Indeed they're developing forms of Buddhism that speak to that need. But I couldn't make that theistic idea of a personalized God work for me. It didn't work for me because it was rather unimaginatively conceived. And I thought that was it – that the idea of God actually corresponded to an ontological reality 'out there'. Whereas what you actually learn is that your ideas are partial. And so I sort of projected all of my anxieties about my own inadequacies on to this God who seemed like a sort of big brother, endlessly peering over my shoulder, and never satisfied with anything that I was doing. So of course it didn't work. But eventually I started studying, as part of my research for TV and for my books, other religious traditions, and gradually I started to learn that I had a very provincial 'Christian' idea of God. In Judaism, for example, there is no orthodoxy. Nobody can tell a Jew what to think about God or the Bible.

There is a great Talmudic story where Rabbi Eleazer, one of the great early rabbis, is having a row about a scriptural ruling. He cannot persuade his colleagues to come round to his opinion and so he asks God to intervene and perform a whole bunch of miracles to prove that he is right – and the house shakes, and a stream starts flowing uphill and a tree moves of its own accord and so on. But the other rabbis look at him and say: 'So?' They're not impressed. And so Rabbi Eleazer asks God to adjudicate directly, and obligingly a voice from heaven booms down: 'Why are you fighting with Rabbi Eleazer? The *halacah* is exactly as he says.' But again the rabbis are not impressed and one of them says: 'No!' And he quotes back to God, God's own scripture, a verse from Deuteronomy: 'It is not in heaven.' In other words: the Torah, when you gave it to Moses, came down to earth. It is not in heaven any more, so it is not yours any more. It is in the hearts of men. And that means nobody can tell me what to think, not even God Himself.' And the story goes that when God heard this, he smiled and said – and this is a myth of course – 'My children have defeated me!' In other words: My children have grown up.

So most religions are not about belief systems – Christianity is peculiar in that respect. The other faiths are concerned not with doctrine or dogma or belief, but with doing things, behaving in a way which changes you at a profound level. They provide rituals which are there to help you. Muslim prayer teaches you through the body about the surrender of the ego that is required. Instead of prancing and posturing around arrogantly, you prostrate yourself and that teaches you what is required, an act of selflessness. And that alone will bring you into contact with the divine. So it is all about doing things. Buddhism has no dogmas. It has certain myths which are supposed to introduce you to a sense of transcendence. But they won't work unless you put them into practice. That is the thing about myths: they are methods, prescriptions for living, but you don't see how they work until you translate them into practical action. That is crucial to Judaism, it is crucial to the Jewish interpretation of the Torah, it is crucial to Islam, and it used to be crucial to Christianity too. You could see this very clearly in St Paul. So it's not good enough just sitting there thinking, 'Do I think that God exists?' or, 'When I have satisfied myself intellectually I will be a Christian.' These theologians would say: 'No. *Do* it first, then you will know.' It's like the instructions for a board game. When you read them they sound complicated and abstract, but when you start playing, it all falls into place. And that's what these religious doctrines are – myths about God, telling you what you must do in order to empty yourself or to be more compassionate. And then you will get intimations of transcendence. And that is all we will get: intimations of God.

How do you achieve such intimations?

For me, it is study that does this. I spend time in my study constantly reading sacred texts, or texts about God, and I will get milliseconds of wonder and awe and delight. And Rabbi Blue – who used to be a colleague of mine when I taught at a Rabbinical college – told me that this is what Jews do when they study the Torah and Talmud. They don't talk to God in the way that Christians do, but they study. And the method of study in a traditional *yeshiva*, through argument, question and answer, is part of the spiritual process that gives you those moments of, as it were, rapture – the sort of thing that you might get in a concert hall or at a night club. But it must be translated into practical action. The Buddha says: 'After receiving enlightenment you must go back to the marketplace and practise compassion for all living beings.'

For me, my study taught me about first: ecstasy, and second: compassion. Because when I was studying a twelfth-century mystic, or a seventh-century prophet like Muhammad – from a sceptical angle initially – I realized that I had to put clever post-Enlightenment Karen on the backburner and enter the minds of these people with a completely different mindset if I was going to understand what they were about. It was no good poncing around from the point of view of the twenty-first century. You have to enter, in a disciplined, scholarly way, into another worldview. It's the same as when you are interpreting a great piece of literature of the medieval period or from ancient Egypt. It is no good saying: 'This is all rot because I don't understand the symbols.' So I had to leave myself and my worldview behind. And that is what ecstasy is. And I had to feel with the other. And that is what compassion is. I had to stop myself making simplistic judgements. And that changed me quite a bit because I used to be a very angry person, I was filled with rage. I'd learnt at my reverend mother's knee and at Oxford how to cut people down to size, how to make cruel quips, etc. And I found I couldn't do that any more. My work, my practice, was rubbing off. The endless discipline of leaving my simplistic judgements behind and entering into something else and learning from it meant that I wasn't able to live in quite the same way in the real world. And I also learnt that right across the board the essence of religion is not about particular beliefs, it is about the golden rule. And every single one of the major world faiths has enunciated the golden rule and all say that it is the bedrock of faith or spirituality. And the golden rule is: Don't do to others what you would not like them to do to you. Look into your heart, discover what it is that gives you pain, and then refuse, under any circumstance whatsoever, to inflict that pain on anybody else. Confucius was the first person to enunciate it as far as we know. Five hundred years before Christ. And he said that it was the thread that pulled all his teaching together. And it was something that his followers should practise all day and every day. Jesus taught a version of the golden rule.

My favourite version of it comes from an early rabbi, Rabbi Hillel, who was an older contemporary of Jesus. One day Rabbi Hillel was approached by a pagan who promised that he would convert to Judaism if the rabbi would recite the whole of Jewish teaching while he stood on one leg. And Rabbi Hillel stood on one leg and said: 'That which is hateful to you, do not do unto your neighbour. That is the Torah, everything else is commentary. Go and study it.' And that is an extraordinary statement. *That* is Judaism. *That* is the Torah. *That* is the whole of Jewish teaching. There is no mention of God, no mention of the creation of the world, no mention of Mount Sinai or the 613 commandments, or the promised land, or the exodus to Egypt; because that is all just commentary on the golden rule. And it is a behavioural thing. Once you start behaving like this, as Confucius said, all day and every day, then you begin to understand. You leave yourself behind, you dethrone yourself from your world and put another there, and you achieve transcendence from selfishness, and that is what God is.

If the major world faiths have such a common core how do you account for, what are at least perceived as, the enormous differences between faiths?

Each religion has its own particular genius, and each its own particular failings. They each have their own particular insights into that compassionate core and their own particular inability to deal with it. Why are there all the quarrels? Well, because most religious people don't want to be compassionate, they want to be right.

So would you argue then that people wanting to be right are not being religious?

I would. This is bad religion, just as you can get bad art and you can get bad sex! Are you going to abolish sex just because some people commit pederasty, incest or rape? No! There is bad sex and bad selfish sex, but there is also inspired sex. And there is bad art, a hell of a lot of it around, and are you going to abolish it all because not everybody is like Michelangelo? No. And the great temptation of religious people, and I have to say some secular people too, is that above all else, they want to be right. This is ego. When people say of religion 'This cannot be that', the Daoists ask: 'Why can't they both be true? We are talking about the ultimate here.' But it has to do with ego. We identify ourselves very strongly with our opinions and that gives us a sense of righteousness. You can hear it in people's voices – pomposity and enchantment with themselves. This is what the Buddhists would call 'unskilful'. I don't like saying it is bad because that implies a sort of self-righteous, lip-smacking thing on my part. But it is unhelpful. It won't get you anywhere. It won't work for you, in the same way that a bad diet will weaken your athletic prowess rather than strengthen it. It is unhealthy. And we are a very opinionated society today. We love opinion and we encourage people to have their opinions even though they might be talking about something about which they know nothing – just listen to phone-ins on the radio! Everyone is sounding off all the time. But religion says get beyond that.

Do you adhere to a particular faith? And how would you respond to someone from another faith saying that yours was illegitimate?

Do I follow a particular path? No. Because I have had my peculiar religious history, I would describe myself as convalescent. And so I would ask people who say that is illegitimate to be kind, to be compassionate. I don't think we should condemn each other. That is ego too. But I can see the point that a critic like that might be making. Ideally I think it is much, much better to stick with the religious background that you were brought up in and use the symbols that it provides you with to go forward. But I can't do that with the Catholic Church to be honest. Partly because Catholics in this country hate my guts! It's not very Christian. Some have even sent me excrement in the mail; though this isn't the case with American Catholics. I have just been given an honorary degree at Georgetown University, which is obviously a great Catholic university. And at Notre Dame, another Catholic University, I told them about my problem with British Catholics and they said 'Oh but why? You're a national treasure!' So if I stayed a Catholic I would be constantly fighting battles, and I am too feeble to be doing that, I would get myself into a twisted knot. And as for Anglicanism, I can't sort of deal with it. I think it is fine if you have been brought up with it, but as a Catholic growing up in the 1950s I never felt quite English. We were all conscious of the fact that we were persecuted. Of course, this is part of the problem that Catholics have with me, because they see me as a traitor who has gone over to the other side. Growing up we were persecuted. We all lived in a kind of ghetto,. We went to Catholic schools and never went to other religious services, so as a result we never really felt quite English. And of course most of us came from Ireland which is a whole other, difficult, ball game. And Anglicanism is largely a religion about being English, you know: 'England's green and pleasant land'; and so I didn't fit in there either. Who knows what may happen in the future, but at the moment I am just studying them all. I see study as my prayer and compassion as my practice. When I am in the United States, where religion is slightly livelier, I spend a great deal of time at Harvard and I always go to the Memorial Church services. They are interfaith. They have beautiful sermons, wonderful music; you can get a real sense of transcendence and fellowship and all the rest of it. Every morning they have a little service in one of the smaller chapels that lasts only about 15 minutes and one of the faculty will give a five-minute talk. There is lovely music by the choir and we sing a couple of hymns. It's a lovely way to start the day. But I also go to Jewish ceremonies and Muslim ceremonies. I can see the point when other people tell me that if you stay with one religion it will still take you to the same place if you work it skilfully. But because of my peculiar religious history, I just can't quite do that at the moment.

Some people think religion is dangerous.

It can be. Like sex! Because it is dealing with very powerful emotions! But I have just been involved in a United Nations commission, looking into the causes of extremism, called The Alliance of Civilizations. And from this you can see that every informed person would say that much of the terrorism that we are experiencing at the moment is politically inspired. It is not inspired by religion, even though it may be articulated in a religious idiom. Look at Hamas for example. It is a resistance movement. And often in Middle Eastern countries, people are trying to get beyond the Western ideologies that were imposed upon them during the colonial period, to what they see as a more authentic way of speaking. But they are perverting the religion that they are professing to espouse. Because once you kill in the name of God you have lost the plot completely. The respect for human life is crucial to all religions.

The Bible, the Torah and the Qur'an are complicated and internally contradictory books, but they all contain passages which seem to condone or encourage violence. In the past you have spoken about this and quoted a passage from the New Testament where Jesus encourages his followers to take up swords.

Yes. Well, first we have to realize that there is far more violence in the Bible, both in the Old Testament and the New Testament, than there is in the Qur'an. And Islam has had a much better record of tolerance over the centuries than Western Christianity. If the Qur'an had indeed inspired the kind of violence we have seen in the last few years then presumably we would have seen similar atrocities all through Islamic history; if that was endemic to the experience of reading the Qur'an. But we haven't seen that. It has come now as a result of despair and bad governments – who, by and large, have been supported by the West in order to get cheap oil, when we promoted people like the Shah in Iran and Saddam Hussein in Iraq. And there is also a sense of hopelessness in many of these countries, and the ongoing conflict with Palestine which never gets any better. And so people lose faith in the political process. And then people lose hope and then you get nihilism and lawlessness and horror and from that mixture you can produce a suicide bomber. Gallup has just done a poll in the Muslim world where they interviewed people in ten Muslim countries including the toughest – Saudi Arabia, Afghanistan, Pakistan – and they found that only 8 per cent of the interviewees agreed with the atrocities of 9/11. Ninety-two per cent said it was not justified. They may not like American foreign policy, but then neither do many British people. And when asked what the West could do to stop the widespread hostility that exists for all sorts of historical reasons, their number one response was: 'Show more respect for Islam.' Number two was: 'Stop interfering with our internal affairs.' Number three was: 'Give us more economic aid.' But way above these last two was respect for Islam and Islamic traditions. And there is a deeply rooted Islamophobia in Western culture – it goes back to the time of the Crusades. And just like anti-Semitism it is part of our Western ethos. The trick is to keep that figure at only 8 per cent. But our continual loose and highly uneducated talk about Islam is embarrassing. If, like me, you know about Islam, and you hear people talking about it, you feel embarrassed. We can look so ignorant – like a bunch of rednecks talking about things we really don't understand, and it is embarrassing. And if we allow this loose talk to go on in our papers, books and on television, then it will feed extremism and play right into extremists' hands. This is not worthy of our culture which prides itself on its tolerance and lack of bigotry.

A. C. Grayling in his book *Against All Gods* argues that religion is not inherently worthy of respect and that to believe something in the face of evidence and against reason is ignoble and ignorant.

That position is not helpful. That kind of remark just sounds arrogant. Some of the people who make these kinds of remarks have an infantile view of religion and God. They have a post-Enlightenment notion of it. They regard Western religion as it exists now as typical. Whereas actually, Western religion as it exists now – since the Enlightenment and the scientific revolution – is extremely untypical of religion.

Grayling argues that anybody who acts because of a leap of faith is behaving unreasonably. He would argue that using faith as a justification for action is irresponsible, dangerous even.

Well it can be. But are we totally rational people? When we fall in love, for example, are we behaving rationally? We might look at somebody and say, 'I want to take a leap of faith and marry this person', even when there might be very good and rational reasons for not doing so. I look around our world and I do have quite an apocalyptic sense that we are heading for some utter catastrophe. We are making matters worse with things like Iraq. I mean, I started writing about Islam because we did not seem to have learnt anything from the experience of the 1930s and 1940s. This slagging people off and perpetually saying that someone is not worthy of respect enabled the death camps. Hitler could not have done what he did without that kind of bigotry. And I think we can't have people wipe out whole swathes of human experience simply because they don't understand them. Unless an ideology increases respect for 'the other' – people who are not in our happy and congenial little catchment area – then I think it is failing us. It is not helpful. Our world is about to implode I think. And even in our private discussions, to encourage a lack of respect for any group of people is illegitimate. It is like saying: 'We should have no more art.' Plato said that. He said there would be no art, no playwrights and no poets in his ideal city. But this is not a good idea. And we should not be stirring up a sense of resentment in parts of the world where we don't want any more resentment stirred up.

I have written a book about the history of fundamentalism in Judaism, Christianity and Islam, and when we attack these movements I have found that they always become more extreme. Because every single one, whether Jewish, Christian or Muslim, is convinced that modern liberal secular society wants to wipe them out. And that is not just paranoia. In Judaism fundamentalism took two major steps forward: first after the Nazi Holocaust when Hitler had tried to wipe out European Jewry, and second after the 1973 Yom Kippur war. Religious Zionism suddenly appeared in Israel where it hadn't been before – Zionism, traditionally, had always been a secular movement. But let's look at creation science, which is what Grayling and Dawkins and others get so het up about. Before the Scopes trial, the monkey trial, Christian fundamentalists in the United States had been on the left of the political spectrum, willing to work alongside socialists and liberal Christians in the newly industrializing cities of the North-eastern United States. And even though they were literal in their interpretation of scripture, creation science, which was in its infancy, was part of the lunatic fringe. After the blitz of criticism and the outpouring of contempt in the media in response to the Scopes trial, they swung from the left to the right of the political spectrum. They became far more militantly literal in their interpretation of scripture and creation science became, and has remained, the flagship of the movement. And so it depends whether you just want to sound off about things and ease your own opinions when you say that something is not worthy of respect or that you have only contempt for this kind of belief. Or do you want to make things better? If you want to make things better, it is better not to attack, because you will make things more extreme.

This approach is not worthy of us. People like Grayling and I have lived lives of utter privilege. We have been to some of the best universities in the world, and though I can't speak for Grayling on this, I know that I have never been seriously hungry, I have never feared that knock on the door. That puts me in a tiny percentage of privilege. Whereas these people in the Middle East whose religion is the bedrock of their lives, quite rightly feel that they have got a raw deal out of us anyway. So when we start pouring this arrogant disdain on their way of life it is just appalling behaviour. We must remember how privileged we are. Now I have nothing against atheism. I think that it is a perfectly respectable position. I think it can be much more, dare I say, spiritual, than a facile or weary 'Santa Claus' type theism. But arrogant atheism that is unkind and lacking in respect for other human beings who are less privileged than us gives atheism a bad name.

So how do we deal with fundamentalism in both an intellectual and a practical sense? I don't just mean this in terms of fundamentalist political movements like al-Qaeda and Hamas, but more generally. You referred earlier to a Gallup poll in the Muslim world which asked what the West could do to stop generating hostility. And the number one reply was that the West should show Islam more respect. But would you agree that many of those Muslims who were polled might have a similarly infantile understanding of God to that which you have criticized in other faiths?

No. That is mostly in Western Christianity. Though they are beginning to get it now as Western modernity and our rationalistic way of looking at the world spreads. But most religious practices in the world are precisely that: *practices.* They are not about beliefs. In fact the Qur'an is very scathing about religious belief and theology; it calls it *zanna* – self-indulgent guesswork about matters which nobody can prove one way or the other but which make people quarrelsome, unkind and sectarian. So they don't have that kind of ludicrous idea of God. And similarly, when you go to some of these countries as opposed to reading about them from a safe Western armchair, you find an entirely different kind of attitude. Take Pakistan, where I have been recently. It is a very complex country and you can't generalize, but in the cities the form of Islam practised is extremely laid back. They would serve alcohol to us, and I hardly saw a veiled woman. Now, of course, it would have been different if I had been in the villages. But there was a very great concern for pluralism, because the Qur'an is a pluralistic scripture. Now of course there are some Muslims who have gone against that because they like to think that they alone are right – like some secularists and atheists. But there are others who say that we must get back to this pluralist attitude that sees all religions as guided by God.

So how do you negotiate a path between showing a genuine respect for Islam and dealing with Islamic cultures which exhibit traits difficult for most modern Western societies – in their attitudes towards women for instance?

Well, none of the world religions has been good for women, not a single one – not even my friend the Buddha. But again, before we point a finger, let's not simply think that things are great for women here – I speak as one! Take veiling for example. Everyone gets on their high horse about that. Now I spent my early girlhood heavily veiled as a nun and nobody ever asked me to take that off – so we need to ask ourselves, why? Second, my veil and my religious habit was far more unhygienic, uncomfortable and inconvenient than any hijab I have seen. For seven years, from the time I was an early teenager to the time I was a young woman, I never once had to think about my make-up, my hairstyle and the rest of the junk that Western culture encourages women to fill their minds with. I never had to wear man-pleasing clothes or give a thought to the idea of whether I was appealing to a male taste – never once. It was a great liberation. One of my neighbours' daughters has just come back from doing an internship at *Vogue* in New York and when she went into the loos there all she could hear was girls throwing up. Now there is something sick, something wrong about this. And we use women's bodies to sell products and things. So before we point the finger at others, which is something we do all the time, we must realize that we do not live in a Nirvana for women.

I'm not saying that.

You are in a way. What you are saying is, 'How do we deal with these people and their attitudes to women?' when actually, they look at us and say, 'You think we've got problems?!'

No, I didn't mean to imply that, and I'm not saying that there are not big problems with how women are treated in the West. I'm trying to give an example where it would be difficult for a modern Western society to show *carte blanche* respect for an Islamic society. Surely there has to be a place for mutual engagement and mutual criticism?

Well yes. But so long as it is respectful criticism. And a lot of our Western criticism is not respectful and it's not informed. And again, history shows that when people in the West have attacked the veil, women have rushed in ever greater numbers to put it on. That is what happens. So it is no good lecturing because it will make matters worse. So again, we need to realize that we have had 300 years to modernize. We did not give power to women out of the goodness of our hearts, but rather it was because women became part of the productive process of the country during the world wars, and so we could no longer be confined to the kitchen. That is why women got the vote, not because people had any respect for women per se. Like democratization as a whole, it is part of a modernizing process. So we have got to realize that we have had a long time to develop in this way. But the basic thing is politics. If we sorted out the Arab–Israeli conflict so that both sides were satisfied then a lot of the heat would go out of all this politically orchestrated extremism. The issue has become sort of symbolic. It is no good just saying, 'You've got to stop being religious in this way.' Whether people like Grayling or Dawkins like it or not there is a religious revival in the world. And in fact Dawkins is very frightened by this because he believes that atheists are being squeezed to the sidelines and it is going to make him really disadvantaged. Though I don't see how that is the case for him given the privileged life that he has as an Oxford Don. I think atheists rule in the United Kingdom to be honest. This country is the worst market in the whole world for my books! And that is OK; I can see how we got to this point and I have respect for atheism as long as it is respectful of others. But in other parts of the world there is a religious revival, and the trick is to make sure that the political context in which this revival takes place is healthy. Not a context like Saudi Arabia, whose inhuman system we have supported through hell and high water, or Saddam Hussein or the Shahs – all of whom we have backed to get cheap oil – or Afghanistan, which we used as a theatre during the Cold War and then deserted.

We have got to stop promoting appalling dictators who feed extremism. Because when you deny people the freedom to speak out, as happened under the Shahs or under Saddam, then the discontent goes to the mosque because it is the only place where people can let off steam. And most dangerous religion has grown and developed not because people read the Qur'an and then rushed out to stick a bomb under an Israeli tank, but because in these regions violence and warfare has become endemic: Afghanistan, the Middle East, Gaza. And when you live in an atmosphere of continual violence and warfare, if you see tanks on the street every day, housing being bulldozed, suicide bombings, soldiers with guns, then this affects everything you do. It affects your fantasies, your dreams, your relationships; and religion gets sucked into it and becomes part of the problem. So if we want religion to be healthy it is no good banning it in a disrespectful way. You can't ban it any more than you can ban sex or art – it is something that people do and they are going to do it whether Dawkins and Grayling like it or not. The thing to do is to make sure that the political context in which it develops is healthy, and that we don't, for short-term political goals, create a situation where a malaise sets in and religion goes bad along with everything else.

17

Shelina Janmohamed

Do you have a working definition of the term religion?
For me it is a system of guidance that helps human beings to live better lives, and that system has to transcend the individual. So the system or the helpful set of principles has to come from outside the person.

People often reject the term 'religion' without really thinking about the fact that it refers to the set of beliefs each person has. I think every single person can have what they describe as their own religion. I could say, define Joe Bloggs, and we could tease out all of his beliefs, and document them and that religion could be called 'Joe Bloggsism', and it would have a following of one. You could say, 'Well according to Bloggsism it is nice to help little old ladies across the street', and he might want to tell other people about this particular goodness and then that would become him trying to impart his religion. But that is a very simplistic first principles approach and doesn't help us to understand the sophistication and complexity of religion.

When we talk about religion we actually mean something that can provide guidance to a lot of people. And so I think it is much more valuable to talk about religion in the sense of Christianity or Islam or Judaism. I think all world religions have truth in them and Islam is the last in the chain, building on what has come before. And so for me, Islam is the epitome of what religion is, not because it tells me that I must do this or I must do that, that I must pray, I must fast, I must be nice to the people who live next to me. But it is about training me so that I live in the most harmonious way with my environment and surroundings.

And to live in harmony, those principles have to come from something outside me; I can't know everything about me because we know as human beings that we keep learning things. So I can't know, at my age now, what wisdom I will have at 65. I will know more about my universe then. So for me religion is a way to be in sync with the system, the matrix, whatever you want to call it. It is a way to live a better life by tapping into knowledge and wisdoms – particularly about God, whom I believe created everyone and everything – about how you can be a better person, live a better life and be happy. And the spiritual aspect is about how you can approach God, how you can become closer to the creator, which, of course, is the ultimate aim.

How do you judge the reliability of that thing that comes from outside you?

I think as human beings we have an instinctive sense of what it means to be good and how one should live the good life. And I think those instincts relate to ideas like the sanctity of life, helping others, not stealing or committing murder, creating justice and things that most human beings would broadly agree with. These have to be the foundation of any religion if the religion is to make sense. So to judge the reliability of what is outside, it needs to be in harmony with the fundamentals that we instinctively know to be right.

If those things can be called our fundamental principles then everything beneath them needs to relate back to those principles, and then it becomes a question for interpretation. If I read a text, whether it is the Qur'an, or the Bible, or even a newspaper, I will assess it on the basis of the fundamental principles that I have. If we come to a point where you and I argue about the specificity of the manifestation of a particular idea, the correct way to address it would be to go back to your principles and ask: 'OK, how did I get from the fact that I think we should be nice to everyone to the fact that in some cases Islam might say something like, "be firm with those who disagree with your opinions"?' And I think the real tensions and arguments come from further down the chain of reasoning and from those who forget to look back at those fundamental principles. The main question to ask should always be: 'What is the core issue we are trying to tackle here? Is it the fundamental belief, or is just a particular manifestation or interpretation of it?'

Would you define faith and belief?

I think faith is something that governs your essence. Belief is something that starts in your head. Faith comes from somewhere deeper, perhaps so deep in your DNA that it will govern what you do. You may not be able to prove faith in something through experimental science or through logic. But even though faith is often easily rejected because it can't be proven in this way, we have examples of similar concepts that we all agree with. Take love. How do we know that somebody loves us? We basically just have faith and trust that they do. So we all have a sense of it, even if we don't like to admit that we do. But from an Islamic point of view faith and belief overlap. There is the Arabic word *iman* which means, 'those who believe', but also, 'those who have faith'. And one of the fundamental principles of how you define a believer according to the Qur'anic rules is, 'those who have *iman* in the unseen'. When you talk in English, saying that you believe in the unseen it sounds a bit kooky; saying that you have faith in the unseen, in a strange way, gives your faith a kind of legitimacy because you have said: 'I am putting myself on the line for that thing and I have chosen to take that step.' Faith takes things one step forward because it institutes trust in the thing you have faith in and a deeper connection to it.

Do you have a definition of God?

Asking for a definition of God is an empty question for a Muslim because God cannot be defined. It is part of God's essence that there are no limits. There was a very famous sermon by the son-in-law of the Prophet – Ali – where he says, 'Don't ask "Why?" of God because when it comes to God, God created "Whyness"; you can't ask "How?" because God created "howness"; you can't ask "What?" because God created "whatness". The creator is not such as I can draw a line around him where I can put a collection of words together and say "That is him or her or it".' So in a very specific sense, I can't answer your question.

I understand your question though; that for the purposes of a conversation about how Muslims approach God, we need to find a way to approach God, so the best way is always to approach Him through the names by which Allah likes to be called.

The 99 names?

That's right. Traditionally the most common are 99 names, but there could be more; some traditions say there are a thousand. The names provide a good way to reflect upon how to know God and relate to Him. And then for me there is another path, which is knowing God through your own heart. And again there is no language to describe those moments when you feel or sense it. You just know. You might see something happen which touches you and brings tears to your eyes and in that moment it is as if there is something else going on which you have opened your heart to, and which makes you feel a little softer and more sensitive. And in those ways you come to know God, and to form a relationship with Him. And the process is all about making your relationship to Him closer. And the closer you get to Him, the less you can describe God because your experience becomes so different from what you can describe in words.

The closest example I can think of is when you are thinking of someone and the phone suddenly rings and it's the person who you were thinking of, and you say, 'I was just thinking of you, isn't that strange?' Everyone has experienced that and you can't really explain what that feeling is like, you just know it. So I think that you can describe in language the names of God and how they relate to you, but we can all have as human beings a soulful or other experience of God which you can't really describe except through analogy and parallel.

Would you describe yourself as a religious person?

I like to try to be a practising person. And for me that means believing in my head but also constantly asking myself, 'How authentic is that in my experience?' For me, that is the essence of being religious. So I ask: 'How authentic am I in my relationship with my creator?' But also: 'How good am I in the world I live in? Am I nice to people around me? Do I help in situations where it is needed?' Those are the two components of religion for me; connection with God and practice. And as a Muslim, there are two dimensions to practise – the first is to obey the creator and the second is to serve the people around me. And if I define religion in this way, as being in sync with the system, and trying to do my part in the way things work; then I would hope that I am being religious.

Often, if you look at people, the more you perceive them to be religious, the less they will say they are religious. And it seems to me that the closer you are to it, the less you will feel it, and the less you will want to describe it because it is just very natural for you to be like that. In Islam, one of the names of God is *al-huq*, which means 'the truth', but it also means things being in their rightful place. So, for example, if you have a flower and it blossoms, it is testifying to its true nature, which is to be a flower that blossoms, and therefore it is testifying to the name of God which is *al-huq*. And so when a human being also testifies to their true nature, to serve those around them, to implement justice, to create social balance, then they are testifying to the name *al-huq*, to the ideas of truth and justice. That to me is being religious – testifying to the truth of the creator and being in harmony with the system and environment.

As I said, God talks about knowing Him through His names, but He also says, 'You should take on the qualities of My names. You should try and imitate Me and the qualities that I have.' And so, you get to know God through His names but you also try to be like Him by testifying to those things. So if God is kind, you learn to be kind, if God is beautiful you learn to be beautiful, and if He is powerful, yes, learn to be powerful, but also remember that God is kind, just, tender, merciful and loving.

Would you talk about how your own relationship with Islam developed?
I was born into a family who had been Muslim for about 150 years. And there was still a sense of conversion of strength and commitment to the new faith. My family is Indian and so we were Hindu in distant previous centuries. My parents came to Britain in the late 1960s and I think they were fairly unusual in that, for them, faith was quite important in comparison to culture. As a young child of four or five years old I didn't really understand what it meant to be Muslim. I would turn up at school and I knew I couldn't eat sausages and beef but I didn't really know why. As I grew older I started to learn the basics and understand it as I matured. When I was about 13 I began to wear the *hijab*. It was an important first step in my outward declaration of being Muslim. I wore it everywhere apart from school, which I suppose highlights some of the internal conflict about my identity and commitment.

This changed when I was 18, and when I went to Oxford I started to wear the *hijab* in all aspects of my life. That was a turning point. I felt much more comfortable there to talk about my faith and to be who I was. And I was learning more about Islam and meeting people who came from different aspects of my faith and in a way it was an intellectual exploration for me because I was testing out my ideas.

The next important moment for me came when I went to work in Bahrain in the Middle East. And because Bahrain is a Muslim country, I had been expecting to experience my faith at a higher level, and I thought I would be able to be much more open about my faith. But actually I found that I had to explain the same things about why I was a practising Muslim in Bahrain as I did in the UK. The fact that it was a Muslim country was actually almost completely irrelevant. It might have been a little easier to find people like me, and the fact that I wore the headscarf might have been a little more socially acceptable, though I still had locals coming up to me saying 'Why do you wear a headscarf?' And you can get that a lot when you travel around the Middle East; people ask: 'Are you Muslim? Do they really have Muslims in Britain?' And the thing that I took away from that experience is that people are people wherever you go. And this idea has stayed with me. We all have the same challenges and issues. People still have the same theological confusions; the same social challenges; the same type of human behaviours. People behave, react, question and challenge in similar ways wherever you are. This simple realization put into perspective the challenges I had been feeling in the UK about being a person of faith and interacting with the people around me. I realized that the internal and external challenges I had faced were not because I was Muslim and people in the UK around me were not. Rather it was because I was a person of faith amongst a society that broadly was not. The Islam part simply added a layer of complexity in the UK.

And something else happened to me at around the same time. I had grown up with this idea that religion was just something that I did because I knew somehow that it was right, although it was never formalistic in the sense that Catholicism might be. But this 'just doing it' is at odds in my mind to a great saying in Islam: 'God created human beings in order that He could be loved'. And this obviously creates a deep conversation about why God needs to be loved. Is God dependent on human beings for validation?

A friend of mine said something to me at the time which had a profound effect on me. He pointed out that 'loving' is a transitive verb, it needs an object and so that is why God created human beings. Love needs an object. And that definition of that connection to God completely changed my world and the quality of my prayer was transformed. Suddenly I had a relationship with God. And it is amazing to think that I had spent all those years being Muslim without that. But it changed the quality of that relationship, and the meaning of it, and it turned into something that was intangible yet somehow so much more real. Now in one sense the idea that 'loving is a transitive verb' might sound like a bit of grammatical nonsense. But it was profoundly meaningful for me. It opened a door in my heart. It tipped something over inside me and when I look back at it, it is at that point where I felt the deepest change. And so it was in my early twenties that I really decided consciously and actively that I wanted to be a Muslim; it was then that I recited, in myself, the *shehada* – the declaration of faith that says: 'There is no God but Allah and Muhammad is His prophet.'

And that was very meaningful for me because it was then that my faith became something I had chosen rather than something I was just brought up with. Most people tend to keep with the faith that they were brought up with. And that is very valid, I would not belittle that. But my conscious decision at this point in my life really changed things for me. And since then I have just been on an exploration of it, and there have been ups and downs and the quality of my relationship with God changes. But ultimately, when my relationship with God is fundamentally centred around love, and the fact that love is the only thing I can give to my creator that is of my own free will, then that becomes something meaningful and something that I become elevated by.

Can you say something about how you see contemporary Islam in this country and the wider world?

I think there are two major trends. The most challenging one is that variety of Islam which offers a very literal interpretation of the faith. There is a trend amongst Muslims to go for a black and white approach to Islam: 'Can I do this? Can I not do that? Give me an answer.' It is an approach which asks very simple questions: 'Should I wear clothes like this or not? Can I talk to this person or not?' And I think there are two reasons for this trend. The first is very specific to Muslims in Britain, who had a sense that their parents' faith was cultural. And so they experienced Islam simply because they grew up in that environment. Now these younger people are starting to ask, 'Is that Islam or is it not?' With the previous confusions about Islam and culture there is an attraction to more categorical answers to their questions. The second reason why the literal interpretation of the faith may be attractive is that in the environment that we live in, in Western Europe, the prevalent liberal attitude, which has many really strong points, can also promote insecurity by offering many distracting lifestyle choices. And so there is a reaction to that. And as religion can be about giving you a framework within which to live your life, and because people tend to veer to the extreme when it is the only place where they can find a little bit of direction or definition for their lives, this can make more literal, black and white versions of any faith seem attractive and solid. I don't think this attraction to literalism as a reaction to the 'anything goes' culture that we seem to live in is restricted to Muslims. I think society as a whole has elements that are drawn to being given black and white answers, to strong direction. And that is this literalist trend.

But there is a counter to that which is a far more spiritual trend and which I find more helpful. This trend encourages us to ask: 'When I am reading this text, or listening to these people, what am I learning from it? How is my heart responding to it? How does this relate to the fundamental principles of humanity?' I'm referring here to those principles of humanity that we talked about at the beginning. And for me, this is the antidote to literalism because it looks at textual specifics in relation to the broader meanings and principles of things.

This approach gives context and framework to some of the specifics which on their own may at first glance seem baffling or even unworthy of Islam. For example, I often receive comments to my writings or on my blog where people write, 'the Qur'an says go and kill the non-believers, they will die and go to hell'. And specifically, yes, that is what it says. But this can only be interpreted within the broader principles of my humanity and faith. The specifics can only be acted on in specific situations and when they become alive in the context of the principles that govern faith. For example, the command to kill those who do not believe is only valid when those people are challenging your faith and self-defence is your only option. The principle that guides the interpretation of killing those who do not believe is self-defence. Those who do not believe will enter hell when God judges them, and it is not permitted for any human being to make that judgement. The principle that guides the interpretation of how to deal with unbelievers is that it is only for God to judge, not human beings.

I personally think religion is about understanding the context and the spirit of the principles, but it also requires action and doing. It is not enough to simply say that you agree with the essence but not engage in the action. In order to be a person of faith you have to believe and do good, and that is the definition in the Qur'an of a person who has faith.

I think what is happening in the UK, Europe and USA is going to be a barometer of what will happen elsewhere. Muslims here have been thrown into a challenging environment and when you get that you see how things might happen faster, you get first-generation people like me saying: 'Well hang on, is that culture or is that faith? How do I reinterpret my faith because I am not in a traditional environment any more?' Whereas I think people who live in more traditional Muslim countries won't feel that in the same way. They will create different dynamics, and interesting things might come out, but when you have faith put in a totally new environment then old ideas are constantly challenged. For example, as a Muslim woman am I really not allowed to work? What are the parameters around that? If you look at the traditional idea that the husband provides and the wife enjoys, well that does not necessarily work in Britain, for example, because both may have to work to afford to live there.

Would you say something about the status of women in Islam?

Do you mean, 'Where are Muslim women today in real terms?' I think it would be a false statement to say that things are rosy in the world of Muslim women. Things currently are in a bad situation. The social reality of Muslim women's lives is that there are a lot of issues like social discrimination, physical and verbal abuse. This is the case in this country where we are supposed to be a bit more liberated. Sadly it also is rife in Muslim countries. The saddest part is that those countries claim Islam came to empower and liberate women – which it did – but the directives of Islam are then not implemented. Muslim societies often feel that agreeing with the theory is enough, and practicality does not require addressing. This is an unjust approach. But the discussion of that reality is fairly well documented and I want to explore some other areas.

First of all we need to get beyond the problem of the Western view of the 'poor oppressed Muslim woman'. This attitude that says 'Isn't it terrible that you have to wear the headscarf; even though you have told me that it is your choice, really you are oppressed because some patriarch somewhere has drummed it into you to make you think it is your choice to wear it but actually it is just a form of control.' I find this view patronizing because it implies that as a Muslim woman I am unable to make a valid autonomous choice. I am being told that if I make a choice that Islam points me to then it's an illusion of free will. However, if I make the choice that the Western view tells me to, then isn't that also an illusion of free will? I assert the right as a Muslim woman to do what I want because my own opinion has its own merit.

I think the best point to start the discussion about women is to use Islamic theology as a blueprint for what the role of women could be. And that comes from the idea that God says in the Qur'an that He created human beings from a single soul and made them into tribes and nations. And so the Islamic view is very different from the prevalent Judeo-Christian view which says that Adam came first and Eve came as a sort of afterthought. And even though this country is, broadly speaking, not a practising Judeo-Christian country, the idea is still prevalent that women are following in the trail of men who set the standard, and that if women want to be successful they have to follow in the footsteps of the men who create the parameters of success, they have to earn half a million a year, or become prime minister or whatever . . . I think this is a false way to view success. And I think these are attitudes that need to be broken through if we are going to level the playing field.

If we go back to the Islamic view we learn that everyone is created from a single soul, and it talks about the fact that we are all created in pairs. When the Qur'an talks about marriage it says that 'God has created you in pairs from amongst yourselves so that you can find peace and tranquillity in each other, and He has put between you deep love and mercy.' This is a very profound statement both about how marriage is designed to create balance and harmony but also about how society can work. You can say 'Well why don't we expand that into a broader understanding of society?' The thing about a Qur'anic text is that you can look at the specific, but you also need to look at the abstract meaning behind it. So you say 'Well, if we use marriage as a description of the way we live, then men and women have to be involved together in a balanced way in order to reach social harmony. And so that means that both of them have to be involved in a way that reaches equilibrium. This allows the discussion to move forward to ask 'Does that mean both men and women have to do the same thing?' which is different from the question of 'Do they both have the same value?' And that is where the confusion is, and the place where the theology of Islam comes into confrontation with Western feminist theory. Just because men and women do different things does not mean that the ultimate value of either is greater or lesser. And that, I think, feminist theory has still to catch up with. That is where I think Islam has a lot to contribute to the society we live in. We need to get away from the idea that men are best and women are second-best and establish the equality of each human creation, which the idea of being created from a single soul allows us to do. Then we need to stop setting the male standard as the golden standard. Finally, Islam values difference – in this case male and female difference – because of the variety of contribution the genders can make. We don't all have to be the same in order to have the same value. This is a false statement, and leads to an imbalanced society. We have the same value but need to do different things to make the whole function successfully.

So we have got to separate the question of 'Where are Muslim women today?' from 'What does Islam say about women' because if we don't then our analysis becomes problematic. But equally, where are non-Muslim women today? They are probably not in a much better state. There is still discrimination, there are still pay issues, there is still abuse at home. So we need to separate those, and then say that value is not dependent on a specific activity, rather it is dependent on this team effort. And I think religion gives you this sense of not having to achieve everything on your own; it tells you that you can do it as a part of a group and that does not diminish your value because everyone has their own contribution to make. And this approach can change your perspective on things. It also gives room for masculinity as well as femininity. One of the great challenges is the question of what role men have nowadays. Could we, instead, just have cucumbers and sperm banks?! If women are now able to do everything up to a 'male standard' and if that is the goal, then what is the function of a man? How do we reintroduce masculinity? There is a dire need for it. And I think when you lose pride in both genders by just focusing on one then we end up at a loss. Women are becoming more masculine – because that is how success is measured – but in doing so they are diminishing the role of men. Both masculinity and femininity are being lost. We need to reclaim pride in these two concepts. If we could go back to this blueprint which shows that there is an equal balance in terms of the value of contribution but a difference in the type of contribution then I think that would be a very simple way to reaffirm both gender roles.

There is a simple way of looking at this described by a woman called Sachiko Murata in her book *The Tao of Islam*. She describes the relationship between men and women in Islam in terms of yin and yang, illustrating that men and women are complementary to each other.

There is an interesting thing that we will see happening in this country, and it has already started – the fact that you are here talking to me bears this out: Muslim women have started to drive the changes. We are challenging everywhere. We are challenging Muslim men who are perhaps used to a more traditional role – and it can be quite hard for a traditional Muslim man in, say, a mosque setting, to argue with practising Muslim women who wear the headscarf and who challenge their views. But equally, a well-spoken British -educated Muslim woman like me can be challenging because we don't fit the stereotype of being oppressed. That is the sharp end of challenging attitudes and creating change, and therefore it is where the biggest changes come from. So a lot of these changes will come from Muslim women and perhaps less so from Muslim men. Though there are men who are doing a lot of the leg work, going round talking to politicians and creating social change, but ultimately women will drive things. But then the challenge comes from women like Ayan Hirsi Ali and Irshad Manji, who are, in a way, reinforcing the ideas that already exist about Muslim women. They argue that if you are talking about reforming Islam, or creating change within the Muslim community, then you have to have rejected it and say that Islam is wrong and oppresses women. But in my reading of both of those women's work, I think they have a very superficial understanding of Islam. They have not actually experienced Islam; they have experienced Muslim society and only a very shallow one at that. Ayan Hirsi Ali talks only about her background in Somalia, and about how things like virginity, marriage and education bind and control women. And yet she was given a choice of who to marry, she was told to go to school but she chose to drop out and then the patriarchs in her community granted her a divorce when she wanted one. So she describes things in a way which is entirely contradictory to her own experience. And I think Irshad Manji is very similar. They are confusing the social reality of Muslims, which I agree needs to be addressed, with the fundamentals of Islam itself.

As I understand it, Ayan Hirsi Ali has completely rejected Islam whereas Irshad Manji still claims to be a Muslim. Is that right?

Ayan Hirsi Ali has an intriguing approach because she has declared she is an atheist which means that in the fundamental doctrine of Islam she is not a Muslim. As long as you declare that you believe in God and that Muhammad is His messenger then you are a Muslim regardless of what you do, even if your actions are completely against the teachings of Islam. But the fact that she says she is an atheist means that she steps immediately out of the Muslim community. However, she does call herself a Muslim; and this is one of these trends that are emerging in Europe. There is a component where people are fundamentally opposed to the theology and the doctrine: they will not practise, will say that they don't believe in God, but will also say that they are Muslim. And this is a real challenge to the Muslim community because if they want to call themselves Muslims then there is nothing I can do about it, but they are not actually Muslim in any technical sense. So does that mean the word 'Muslim' has a new definition? And if so, how do we address that? As for Irshad Manji, she still says that she is Muslim, and is probably closer to the Muslim community – she is at least having a dialogue with us. But there is this sense that says if you want to get a voice in the media and if you want to create new ideas, then you have got to reject Islam. But there will be people like me who are saying 'No, hold on, we can be Muslim, but we have grown up and speak the language here – both verbally and in terms of ideas – and there is a good thing that can come out of this fusion. There are challenges that will force us to address some issues of faith that might otherwise have been left dormant.' So I think there will be a very interesting role for Muslims that will emerge. If you look at television, there was a programme called *She's a Thoroughly Modern Muslim* and it was a very pleasant programme about four Muslim women; one was a councillor, one was a woman like me who wore a headscarf and had kids and was quite well educated and so on. And it is people like that who will create social change. Women do tend to create social change faster than men – speaking in caricatured terms men often create wars, women tend to create love. And so I think the relationship between the Muslim community and the wider world will come through Muslim women. I mean, we saw it with Jack Straw – why pick on the veil? There are only about 5,000 women in this country who wear it. It is really not a big deal; why not focus on social deprivation in East London or Birmingham? Why pick on women who want to participate in the political process, who have come to see you as your constituents, only to hear you say 'No'? I think things like this expose the deep-rooted underlying issues. I think that when Jack Straw said it needed to be talked about, in a way he was right because it showed that actually people are not that comfortable with Muslims.

It brings up an interesting issue with public and private religion in the context of Western secular society.

That is a very interesting point, and I think the headscarf or the veil is a really good demonstration of it. In terms of Western norms, body is considered to be a public thing. When I go out on the street there is a demand that my body is public. People want to see my face and my hair, and actually they would probably prefer it if I wore a shorter skirt – to stereotype. And the fact that I won't share my body with people in that way is problematic. Some men will be upset if I don't shake hands with them, and the fact that if I cover my hair it will be seen to be very inflammatory by some. And I think that Muslims have a bit of a PR issue on their hands because some women have said 'I cover myself because I don't want men to be sexually attracted to me' and that is offensive to men implying that they can't control themselves. And I also think it is misleading to imply that this is the reason for modest dress. It misses the basic idea of reducing sexual tension and injecting ease and harmony into society. Because it is not that I think that men are so lustful that they can't even watch me walk down the street – that is quite disrespectful to men, as most men are basically good people. But the more fundamental point is 'Why should I have to show you my body in order for you to accept me? Why is it insulting to you that I should cover up?' This is the flipside of the argument that says I should expect you to be attracted to me just because we are within a hundred feet of one another. But the argument goes 'Why should it be upsetting to you that I cover up? I am still talking to you.' And so the idea of body being public is a real tension. What is overlaid on it, then, is that Muslims think of faith, religion, and practice as public whereas in wider society it is seen as private, so there is this cross-over. Now I don't see why my faith should be private, because my faith is about everything I do. It is about the way I speak to you, it is about the fact that I give you food and drink when you come to my home, it is about the fact that when I turn up to work I ask how everybody is. And covering is part of that, as is going to pray at lunch time. So I can't make faith private whereas the Western notion is that anything about the self must be private and we take away that personalization of it in the public space, and the *hijab* is where the focus is because we have both of these issues in direct contradiction. So this discussion of 'Can I wear symbols?' for me is a false discussion with relation to modest dress and *hijab*. Because wearing the headscarf for me is not a symbol, it is a practice. It is about being modest. So it becomes public, I can't help it. It is not that I want to rub it in people's faces, it is just who I am. But I think that modern-day Christianity has a very strong sense that faith is private and personal and there is no outward manifestation of it. So I am quite surprised that women of various other faiths don't cover modestly because for me that is part of my understanding of faith in general, that it prescribes modest dress. But because Christianity, for example, is very hidden and is something that we all do in our little castles – which is very British – the faith is restricted to a particular domain. And to be honest, Muslims can be just as guilty of it. They can see religion as being about going to mosque on Friday and then the rest of the week you are free to do as you please. It is like Catholic confession: you confess something and then you are absolved and alright. But for me religion is a more holistic thing; you have got to be in sync with everything around you. And that means that you have got to do it all of the time otherwise you will not be testifying to the truth of who you are, and you will not be the best person that you can be all of the time.

Do you think religion can be dangerous?

I think all thought systems can be dangerous when used for unworthy ends. If you went back and looked at history you might say 'Well, 99 per cent of wars since the Second World War have been instigated by America.' That might be close to the truth, but do you then say 'So let's ban the Bill of Rights and the American Constitution?' No. There is a huge jump of logic between those two statements. So I think that to say religion in its essence is responsible is wrong. Religion is about living a better life and maintaining the fundamentals of humanity that we talked about earlier. The problem of danger comes back to this idea that human beings will use the tools that they have to hand to get what they want. So if you are Richard the Second you will say let's go and defend the Holy Land because it is our religious duty, when in fact it was political, commercial and imperial goals that were the motivation for the wars.

I think the whole point of religion is actually about creating peace and harmony, and is that dangerous? The question is: how do you use something to manipulate others? One of the interesting things in Islam is the discussion of 'What is your responsibility as a follower to your leader?' If your leader says 'You must do x' should you obey or not? And there are two schools of thought in this. One says that it is better to do what an oppressive leader says in order to retain social harmony, than to oppose him. I disagree very strongly with this. The other view, which I believe is supported by Islam's strong sense of justice, is that wherever you see wrong-doing and injustice you must oppose it. For me, being a Muslim is about making sure that everything is as just as it can be. So if your leader says 'We are going to go and start killing innocent civilians' then it is your duty to stand up against that irrespective of the personal cost. And that is one of the things I really love about Islam. It gives you a sense of peacefulness. But when you and society are challenged there is no sense of passivity. We uphold up to a point the concept that is wonderfully brought out by the Christian idea of turning the other cheek because you have to be patient and tolerant – sometimes bravery is to withstand the difficulties and see them through. But there also comes a point where you have to stand up for yourself and society. The problem comes when violence is the first point of recourse and is then taken to an extreme. But the ability to say 'No you are not going to walk all over me; I believe in what I believe and I have assessed the impact of what I believe and it is not your right to do that to me' is vital. And there is a really strong sense in Islam of both rights and responsibilities. And that is really important to me because I have a responsibility to the society I live in, to contribute to it, to point out where I think it needs to be better, and to point out what I think is good about it. But equivalent to that, I have a right to be respected too. Both are equally important, but I think that in our society the onus is very much on rights – 'I expect this, I expect that, this is what I want' – and yet we don't really like responsibility. If we are going to have one we must have the other, and that is where religion is helpful, because it tells you that you have to do certain things whether you like them or not. They may be distasteful to you but you have to do them in order to earn your rights. That idea, as a citizen of this country and as a British, working, Muslim woman, is really important to me in the way that I interact with people around me. So I have a responsibility to you, for example, to explain what I believe and why I wear a headscarf and why I fast and all these other things, and I have a right to expect that you will respect me for that. But I can't expect my rights until I fulfil my obligations to you.

18

Jonathan Sacks

Do you have a working definition of the term religion?

Religion is more than spirituality. It is spirituality translated into the code of a community. Religion begins when a group of people decides to organize its life around a supernatural experience or a series of such experiences. That is religion. 'Spirituality' in the contemporary sense is what happens when religion goes 'bowling alone'. It is an event within the self or the soul. Religion is more than that. It is spirituality turned into the basis of our lives together: our relationships, our families, our communities. The Dean of Westminster, in the first half of the twentieth century, said religion is what people do with their solitude. That is not a Jewish approach. Religion is about what we share.

How do you define faith?

'Faith' is a word that has caused confusion to Western civilization, creating the possibility of a conflict between religion and science. It results from the fact that the two great civilizations on which Western culture is based – ancient Greece and ancient Israel – were brought together in the form of Christianity. Christianity was built on the faith of Israel – Jesus was a Jew. But if you want to understand what is unique about a culture, look at the words it contains that are untranslatable. The first Christian texts – the Gospels, the Pauline letters and so on – were written and published in Greek. So you had the phenomenon of the faith of Israel – dramatically different, even opposed to the culture of Greece – entering European culture in Greek translation.

Though Christianity was predicated upon what Christians call the Old Testament – the Hebrew Bible – Christians knew it as a document in translation. Not until Jerome in the fourth century did anyone study it in the original Hebrew. The key words of the Hebrew Bible are untranslatable into Greek or Latin. They include the words for 'faith', 'knowledge' and 'truth'.

In Western discourse, essentially a Greek discourse, 'faith', 'knowledge' and 'truth' are cognitive attributes. In Hebrew they are not cognitive at all: they are *moral* attributes. So truth does not mean 'corresponding to the facts' or 'What is the case'. Truth means doing what you said you were going to do: keeping a promise. It is less about truthfulness than about honouring your word. In Hebrew, all these terms are related to the keyword of Jewish thought: 'covenant'. Covenant is 'love as loyalty'. You give your word to somebody. Covenant is a bond created by words, a mutual exchange of promises. The most obvious analogy – which all the prophets use, most famously Hosea – is a marriage. So the word *emunah*, which is translated in English as 'faith', actually means 'loyalty'.

Let me illustrate this by way of a story. Isaiah Berlin was a secular Jew. In our first conversation, he said to me: 'Chief Rabbi, don't talk to me about religion. When it comes to God I am tone deaf.' He then said to me: 'What I don't understand is how you, who studied philosophy at Oxford and Cambridge, can believe?' I replied: 'If it helps, think of me as a lapsed heretic!' He said: 'Ah! I quite understand!'

In 1997 I published a book called *The Politics of Hope* in which I argued that we needed to revisit Isaiah Berlin's *Two Concepts of Liberty*. In his day the biggest challenge to free societies was totalitarianism – he had come to Britain from Riga, after the Russian revolution. When I was writing that book, I felt that the danger we faced was the moral breakdown of society. I very much wanted to know his feelings about the argument. So he asked me to send it to him, which I did.

For several months I did not hear anything from him. Finally I phoned him, and his wife answered the phone. She said: 'Ah, Chief Rabbi. We have just been talking about you!' Now I did not imagine that Chief Rabbis were normal subjects of conversation in Headington House, so I asked, 'In what context?' She said, 'Isaiah has just asked you to officiate at his funeral.' I said, they should not talk of such things. Obviously, though, Isaiah knew his death was close. He died four days later, and I officiated at his funeral in Oxford.

His biographer Michael Ignatieff was fascinated by this, because he knew Isaiah was a secular Jew, so he was interested in knowing why he wanted the Chief Rabbi to officiate at his funeral. I said that Isaiah may not have been a believing Jew, but he was a loyal Jew. 'Faith' in Hebrew actually means 'loyalty'. So the nearest equivalent in English is 'faithfulness'.

How does God come into it for Jews?

In three ways: the first, through creation; the second, through revelation; the third, through redemption, history as the working out of the divine plan, which we commemorate in our major festivals. We see God in history. As for creation, we see it as the work of God but not in the sense in which critics like Richard Dawkins supposes. We do not assume that you can prove the existence of God by the evidence of design in nature. It is belief in God that allows us to see the design, not the design that leads us to believe in God.

Could you unpack that a little?

In Judaism we don't try to *prove* the existence of God in creation. We sing it. Several of the Psalms are songs of creation. We say daily the last six psalms from 145 to 150, which culminate in the verse, 'Let everything that has breath, praise the Lord.' Everything that exists, by existing, sings a song of praise to its creator. Or to put it in the way Wittgenstein did: 'It is not *how* the world is that is mystical, but *that* it is.' We do not believe that you can infer the existence of God from nature, as Christian natural theology or Aristotelian physics did. The word for 'universe' in Hebrew comes from the same root as 'to be hidden'. In the world, God is hidden because God is not in nature but beyond it. So we do not try to prove God through science; we try to praise God through song.

People like A. C. Grayling and Richard Dawkins think that religion or belief not founded on provable evidence can be a dangerous thing.

In Judaism we have a religious respect for science. You see this in the Talmud. The rabbis asked, 'Where does the sun go at night?' They cited the Jewish view; then the Greek view; then concluded: 'The Greeks are right.' When it comes to science, Judaism holds, in Maimonides' words, 'Accept the truth, whoever says it.' Judaism respects science. It sees it as part of *chokhmah*, 'wisdom'.

There is even a special blessing, coined some 2,000 years ago, which we say when we are in the presence of a great scientist. I had the privilege of saying it in 1993 when I received an honorary doctorate from Cambridge together with James Watson, co-discoverer of DNA. The sages saw science and secular knowledge generally as part of the universal human heritage implicit in the phrase that we are 'in the image and likeness of God'.

Religion is not science. It is about personal relationships. And in such matters it is an intellectual mistake to think that they can be proved. Can you prove to anyone that love or trust or generosity or altruism, or even a sense of humour, are the right way of relating to your fellow human beings? Philosophers have tried for 2,500 years, and have failed. There are people who live without love or trust or hope, and there is no proof that would persuade them to change. Not everything worth knowing can be proved. Not everything worth believing can be demonstrated scientifically. There is always a leap from 'is' to 'ought'. Science is about the is-ness, religion about the ought-ness of things.

You have written that religion does not do power very well.

Religion was born in the attempt to make structures of power seem inevitable. So Mesopotamian kings of city states and Egyptian pharaohs were not just political leaders but also religious leaders. They were the son of god, or the chief intermediary with the gods. Mesopotamian kings officiated at the annual New Year festival. Ramses the second, the man most likely to have been the pharaoh of the Exodus, had a name very similar to Moses, or *Meses*. *Meses* meant 'child'. Moses was just a child. Ramses was the child of Ra, the Egyptian sun god. So, in its earliest forms, religion was deeply implicated in power.

In the world of myth, the hierarchy of society mirrored the order of the stars and planets. The inequalities of society were seen to be part of the natural order of things. That is part of what Marx meant when he called religion 'the opium of the people'. It spread the aura of inevitability over social differentiation. Religion was a mode of power, and power will always seek to justify itself metaphysically, as it were.

Judaism was and is a protest against this kind of culture that was almost ubiquitous until a few centuries ago. It was a religion of shepherds and ex-slaves, people who did not have power. That is what upset Nietzsche, who saw Judaism and Christianity as the revenge of the disempowered. He called it 'the slave revolt in morality'. When you see God, not in nature but beyond nature, you demythologize the universe. That is what persuaded Max Weber that biblical monotheism was the first step towards science. The universe became, in theory, intelligible instead of being seen as the clash of capricious forces, none of which was particularly interested in humankind.

Biblical monotheism did more than demythologize nature. It also relativized all power structures. Once you take seriously a transcendent God, reality becomes more than the order of the planets and stars. God is beyond the planets and the stars; indeed He did not even create them until the fourth day. That is the politically revolutionary charge in the idea that every human being is in the image of God. That *some* people were in God's image was not new. That is what kings and pharaohs were thought to be. It is when you believe that *everyone* is in God's image that you plant the seed that will one day grow into an egalitarian or democratic society.

How does that relate to the idea that it is the Jews alone who can bring about the kingdom of God on earth?
That is not how I see things. There are certain universal truths you can only learn from living examples. If you want to teach someone about music, you must get them to listen to it. There are no general, abstract rules that would allow you to understand in advance what music is. There are no general rules for leadership; there is no text-book on how to be a leader. All you can do is tell the stories of many kinds of leaders. So there are universal truths that are only learned through particular examples. In Judaism, we see the Jewish people as a living example of universal truths. Many of those universal truths are independent of Judaism, and prior to Judaism.

In Genesis 9, God makes a covenant with Noah, and through him, all humanity. Genesis 9 is our equivalent of, for example, the United Nations Universal Declaration of Human Rights, except that the Bible talks of responsibilities, not rights. Moral universals are too abstract to serve as a detailed set of instructions on which to build a society. They are, rather, a kind of template. The best way to understand what they mean in practice is to look at actual societies and see how they work. Each nation does things differently. In the United States there is separation of church and state; in England there is an established church. These are two different ways of achieving a free and just society.

So God, having set out in Genesis 9 a set of general principles, then turns in Genesis 12 to one particular family, which eventually becomes a nation, and charges them with the mission of creating an exemplary society. Historically, the Jewish example gave rise, in time, to Christianity and Islam, two religions that between them claim the allegiance of more than half the people alive today.

Where was God at Auschwitz?
For me, the question is not, 'Where was God at Auschwitz?' but, 'Where was humanity at Auschwitz?' People knew what was happening. Churchill knew in 1942, the Americans in 1944. The Americans did briefly consider bombing the train lines to Auschwitz but eventually they did not. Today we ask: Where is humanity in Darfur? In Burma? In Zimbabwe?

'Where was God at Auschwitz?' In the words 'Thou shalt not murder'. In the words, 'Do not oppress the stranger'. In the words 'Your brother's blood cries to me from the ground'. If God speaks, and humanity does not listen, there is nothing God can do. Having conferred freedom on us there is nothing He can do because of his self-limiting ordinance without which human freedom would not exist.

An A. C. Grayling would say, 'In that case, sacrifice freedom, because we would have a better world without it.' I would say, 'In that case, the universe would be a place where God has programmed six billion computers to sing His praises daily.' God has no need for approval. He gave us freedom. What we do with it sometimes grieves God to the core, as the Bible says in Genesis 6:6. One American Jewish mother put it well: 'When I became a mother, I found I could understand God much better. Now I know what it is to create something you can't control.'

Could you say a little bit about your journey towards your faith?

I was born into a religious family. But my journey towards faith, my personal search, began in my first year at university in 1967, in the weeks before the Six Day War. During those weeks, when the Arab states were amassing troops and Egypt closed the straits of Tiran and ordered out the UN troops in the Sinai desert, it seemed to me and all of my contemporaries as if, God forbid, a second Holocaust might be about to happen. Nasser was talking about driving Israel into the sea, and Israel was hugely outnumbered. In fact, it didn't happen. But at the time it was deeply traumatic. The impact on my generation was immense.

Until then, I had never thought about the Holocaust. For me, it was the past. I had no desire to revisit it. Those anxious weeks shook me to the core. They led me to explore the Holocaust, and from there to the rest of Jewish history. One thing led to another. I can, though, honestly say that I never had a crisis of faith in God. I knew of Hume's critique of miracles. I knew Kant had disproved the ontological argument. I had read Bertrand Russell's *Why I am Not a Christian*. I had no problem with any of those ideas. But that is how my search began. In Judaism, religion and faith are much more communal, national and historical than metaphysical or quasi-scientific. I was trying to understand: 'Who is this people of which I am a part?'

You are now the head of your faith in the UK. That is quite a specific journey.

I kept going. I am quite tenacious! Since I was a child I wanted to write a book. I started at the age of 20. I failed and kept failing for 20 years. I have a filing cabinet full of unfinished books. Finally, when I was almost 40, I read one of Bernard Shaw's prefaces in which he said, 'If you're going to write a book you'd better write it by the time you are 40.' So I sat down, that year, and wrote my first book. So I'm tenacious. Many people, once they had gone through the 1967 trauma and tension and Israel's eventual victory, got back to life as normal. I kept searching.

Does your role as Chief Rabbi ever bring about a kind of public–private conflict?

Yes, there are certain things you can't say as a public person which you could if you were a private person.

What do you feel your responsibilities to be as Chief Rabbi?

I have many pastoral responsibilities. For instance, at times of tension, like now, when the Jewish community feels that Israel is under attack and Jewish students feel intimidated at British university campuses, I have to do what I can to lift the community's spirits. I have to speak to the fears of the community and try to move beyond.

I was always anti-establishment until I discovered I had become the establishment. But I do not believe that the role of a religious leader is to anaesthetize the intellect or silence serious questions. The word rabbi means 'my teacher', so in the end I see my role as a teacher, finding in the word of God for all time, the word of God for this time.

What is your ambition for religion?

John Stuart Mill called the Conservative Party 'the stupid party'. I never want to hear Judaism called 'the stupid party'. There are many Jews who don't continue studying Judaism after their *Bar Mitzvah*, at the age of 13 (12 for girls). So they carry with them through life a 13-year-old's understanding of religion. The result is that for the past 200 years we have lost most of our greatest minds.

Freud, Durkheim, Lévi-Strauss, Wittgenstein and Karl Marx all came from Jewish families. In some cases they had converted, in others they had assimilated. But none had a mature understanding of Judaism. Jews made up a high proportion of the makers of the modern mind; but they did not carry there Judaism with them. There is little, if anything, Jewish about Marcel Proust or Felix Mendelssohn (whose grandfather was a distinguished rabbi and Jewish thinker). That is what drives me. Jewry in the last two centuries has produced some extraordinarily deep thinkers, but almost all of them were estranged from Judaism. That is what drives me – to try and reconnect these worlds, one secular, one religious, whether by my writings and broadcasts or through public dialogue with figures like Stephen Pinker and Amos Oz.

I believe that religion is answerable to the world – scientifically and morally. It is all too easy to treat religion as a self-enclosed system which nothing can challenge or refute. Religion, for me, must involve a state of openness to discovery. Many scientific discoveries are deeply spiritual, such as the proof that there really was a Big Bang and that at its birth the universe was infinitesimally small, yet almost infinitely potent. What a commentary that is on Genesis 1. To realize that every form of life, biological or botanical or zoological, derives from a single source: that all that lives comes from a single cell. What a way of understanding the miracle of monotheism, that unity in heaven creates diversity on earth.

It is stunning to discover that every human body has a hundred trillion cells; that every cell contains a double copy of the human genome, and the human genome is written in 3.1 billion letters of genetic code. Who would have imagined that the structure of life would be linguistic? But there it is; the genetic code, a form of language. Again there is an echo of the biblical idea that God *spoke* and the world was. Genesis suggests that the universe is linguistic; that life is linguistic. When Bill Clinton said, after the human genome had been decoded, that 'We have finally learnt how to read the book of life', he was using a metaphor all Jews know. We speak on our holiest days about the book of life. So I find the new discoveries of science wondrous in their implications, in the new life they have given to religious metaphor.

Am I right in thinking that Judaism is not an evangelical religion?

That is correct.

How does that set it apart from Islam and Christianity?

We don't believe you have to be Jewish to get to heaven. Many of the heroes of the Bible were not part of the family of Abraham. One of the moral heroines of all time was Pharoah's daughter, who saved Moses when he was a baby. Her father had ordered the killing of all male Israelite children. So she was the daughter of the arch-enemy, yet the Bible describes her as a figure of exemplary courage and humanity.

Consider the most perfect individual in the Bible: Job. Job wasn't Jewish. Job was everyman. So we have never believed that you have to be Jewish to get to heaven. That is why Jews have not actively sought converts, though we admit and accept them.

Is there a notion of an afterlife in Judaism?

Yes. But we don't talk about it very often.

Does the vision of that afterlife differ from that of Islam or Christianity?

The key difference between Judaism, Christianity and Islam, is that although Christianity and Islam borrowed much from Judaism and see themselves literally or metaphorically as continuing the Abrahamic covenant, neither holds that you can reach heaven any other way than their way. *Extra ecclesiam nulla salus* – 'outside the Church none is saved'.

We have never believed that. We are not a proselytizing faith, not an empire-building faith; we do not believe in the conversion or conquest of the world, because we do not believe we have a monopoly on salvation.

Judaism believes in an afterlife, but the emphasis of Judaism is on *this* life. Freud believed that *thanatos*, the death instinct, is one of the two basic human drives. Many religions of the ancient world did, in effect, worship death or the dead. That is what the pyramids are. It is striking that Judaism has no ancestor worship. We do not pray to the souls of the departed. The anthropologist Mary Douglas put this best in her book, *Leviticus as Literature.* She points out that though Leviticus is about purity and sacrifice, there is no worship of dead kings or dead patriarchs in Judaism. In fact, the Bible says very pointedly at the end of the book of Deuteronomy, when Moses goes up the mountain and dies: 'No man knows where Moses is buried.' There might have been Moses worship, but there isn't. Judaism is primarily about life in this world, not the next.

Related to this is the fact that whereas Christianity and Islam each have one central figure, in Judaism there is no equivalent. The question, 'Who is the central figure in the Jewish drama?' has no answer. There was Abraham, founder of the faith. There was Jacob/Israel whose children we are. There was Judah whose name we bear as Jews, Moses who gave us the law, Joshua who conquered the land, King David, Israel's greatest king, Isaiah, most eloquent of the prophets, and so on. Judaism is built on the proposition that there is an ultimate gap between heaven and earth. If we allow God to be God, we can allow human beings to be human beings, no more, no less. Judaism is a kind of democracy of the spirit.

A. C. Grayling sees the three great Abrahamic faiths containing within their manifestos the ambition to dominate the other two. For Giles Fraser, his religion is the best. Archbishop Rowan Williams and Muhammad Al Hussaini say a similar thing about their religion. What is the most hopeful thing you can see for an emerging discussion between what many people see as competing religions?

Stop competing! It is time, if Abraham really is our father, to recognize that we are all part of one family. It is a richly diverse family. And, of course, the best arguments take place within the family. If I have an argument with a friend, I may lose a friend. If I have an argument with my brother, he remains my brother.

God changed Abram's name to Abraham in Genesis 17, saying: 'I will make you the father of many nations.' That is precisely what happened in the post-biblical era. There are today 2.2 billion Christians, 1.3 billion Muslims and a few Jews – not many – 13 million or so. For every Jew there are 100 Muslims and 183 Christians. Taken together, though, more than half the people alive today – 3.5 out of 6 billion – consider themselves to be Abraham's children.

God said that Abraham would become, in time, father of many nations, and his descendants would be as many as the stars in the sky or the sand on the seashore. Something not unlike that has actually happened, in ways no one could have foreseen. Why don't we just accept that – that Abraham has many descendants. Brothers and sisters have to learn not to fight one another. That is the message of Genesis. It tells the story of four sibling rivalries: Cain and Abel, Isaac and Ishmael, Jacob and Esau, Joseph and his brothers.

If you look at the final scene in each of these stories, you will see a progression. The relationship between Cain and Abel ended in fratricide. Isaac and Ishmael stand together at Abraham's grave. Jacob and Esau embrace as friends and go their separate ways. Joseph forgives his brothers and the family lives together in peace. The Bible is telling us that eventually there is peace between brothers, but it takes time. That is where we are and what we are, in our generation, called on to achieve.